The Astors

Virginia Cowles

The Astors

Alfred A. Knopf   New York   1979

For my sister, Mary Holtz

This is a Borzoi book published by Alfred A. Knopf, Inc.

Copyright © 1979 by Virginia Cowles

All rights reserved under International and Pan-American
Copyright Conventions. Published in the United States by
Alfred A. Knopf, Inc., New York, and simultaneously in
Canada by Random House of Canada Limited, Toronto. Distributed
by Random House, Inc., New York. Originally published in
Great Britain by Weidenfeld and Nicolson Ltd, London.
Copyright © 1979 by Virginia Cowles.

Library of Congress Cataloging in Publication Data

Cowles, Virginia Spencer.
  The Astors.
  Bibliography p. 249.
  Includes index.
  1. Astor family. 2. Great Britain – Genealogy. 3. Title.
  CS71.A85 1979 929'.2'0941 79–2219

ISBN: 0–394–41478–0

First American edition

Contents

The Astor family

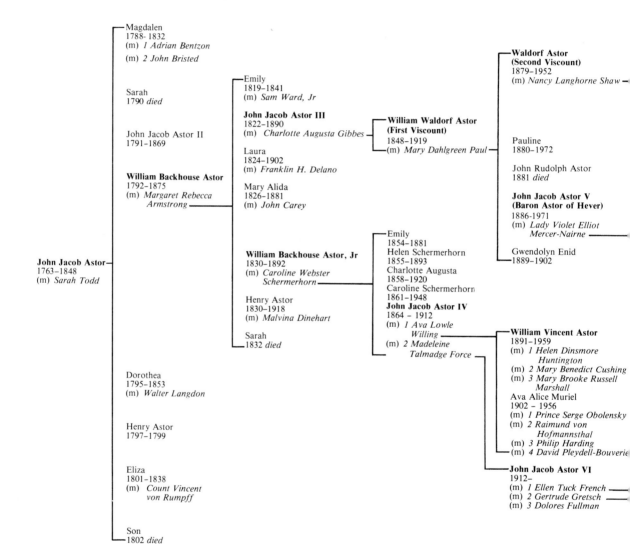

John Jacob Astor
1763–1848
(m) *Sarah Todd*

Magdalen
1788- 1832
(m) *1 Adrian Bentzon*
(m) *2 John Bristed*

Sarah
1790 *died*

John Jacob Astor II
1791–1869

William Backhouse Astor
1792–1875
(m) *Margaret Rebecca
Armstrong*

Dorothea
1795–1853
(m) *Walter Langdon*

Henry Astor
1797–1799

Eliza
1801–1838
(m) *Count Vincent
von Rumpff*

Son
1802 *died*

Emily
1819–1841
(m) *Sam Ward, Jr*

John Jacob Astor III
1822–1890
(m) *Charlotte Augusta Gibbes*

Laura
1824–1902
(m) *Franklin H. Delano*

Mary Alida
1826–1881
(m) *John Carey*

William Backhouse Astor, Jr
1830–1892
(m) *Caroline Webster
Schermerhorn*

Henry Astor
1830–1918
(m) *Malvina Dinehart*

Sarah
1832 *died*

**William Waldorf Astor
(First Viscount)**
1848–1919
(m) *Mary Dahlgreen Paul*

Emily
1854–1881
Helen Schermerhorn
1855–1893
Charlotte Augusta
1858–1920
Caroline Schermerhorn
1861–1948
John Jacob Astor IV
1864 – 1912
(m) *1 Ava Lowle
Willing*
(m) *2 Madeleine
Talmadge Force*

**Waldorf Astor
(Second Viscount)**
1879–1952
(m) *Nancy Langhorne Shaw*

Pauline
1880–1972

John Rudolph Astor
1881 *died*

**John Jacob Astor V
(Baron Astor of Hever)**
1886-1971
(m) *Lady Violet Elliot
Mercer-Nairne*

Gwendolyn Enid
1889–1902

William Vincent Astor
1891–1959
(m) *1 Helen Dinsmore
Huntington*
(m) *2 Mary Benedict Cushing*
(m) *3 Mary Brooke Russell
Marshall*
Ava Alice Muriel
1902 – 1956
(m) *1 Prince Serge Obolensky*
(m) *2 Raimund von
Hofmannsthal*
(m) *3 Philip Harding*
(m) *4 David Pleydell-Bouverie*

John Jacob Astor VI
1912–
(m) *1 Ellen Tuck French*
(m) *2 Gertrude Gretsch*
(m) *3 Dolores Fullman*

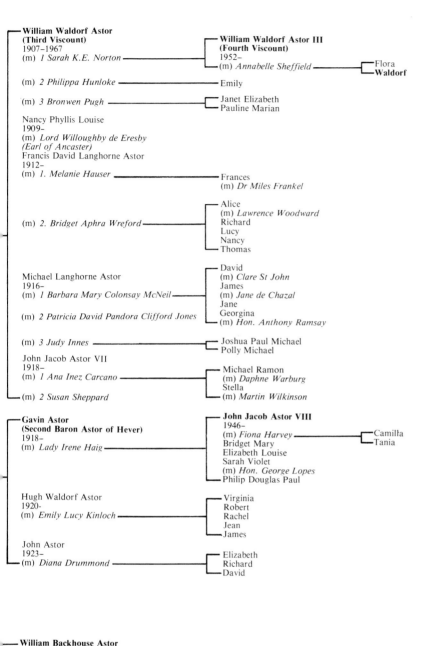

William Waldorf Astor
(Third Viscount)
1907–1967
(m) *1 Sarah K.E. Norton* ——————— **William Waldorf Astor III**
                                    (Fourth Viscount)
                                    1952–
                                    (m) *Annabelle Sheffield* ——— Flora
                                                                  Waldorf

(m) *2 Philippa Hunloke* ——————————— Emily

(m) *3 Bronwen Pugh* ——————— Janet Elizabeth
                             Pauline Marian

Nancy Phyllis Louise
1909–
(m) *Lord Willoughby de Eresby*
(Earl of Ancaster)
Francis David Langhorne Astor
1912–
(m) *1. Melanie Hauser* ——————— Frances
                                (m) *Dr Miles Frankel*

(m) *2. Bridget Aphra Wreford* ——————— Alice
                                       (m) *Lawrence Woodward*
                                       Richard
                                       Lucy
                                       Nancy
                                       Thomas

Michael Langhorne Astor
1916–
(m) *1 Barbara Mary Colonsay McNeil* ——— David
                                         (m) *Clare St John*
                                         James
                                         (m) *Jane de Chazal*
(m) *2 Patricia David Pandora Clifford Jones* Jane
                                         Georgina
                                         (m) *Hon. Anthony Ramsay*

(m) *3 Judy Innes* ——————— Joshua Paul Michael
                           Polly Michael
John Jacob Astor VII
1918–
(m) *1 Ana Inez Carcano* ——————— Michael Ramon
                                 (m) *Daphne Warburg*
                                 Stella
(m) *2 Susan Sheppard*   (m) *Martin Wilkinson*

Gavin Astor
(Second Baron Astor of Hever)
1918–
(m) *Lady Irene Haig* ——————— **John Jacob Astor VIII**
                              1946–
                              (m) *Fiona Harvey* ——————— Camilla
                              Bridget Mary   Tania
                              Elizabeth Louise
                              Sarah Violet
                              (m) *Hon. George Lopes*
                              Philip Douglas Paul

Hugh Waldorf Astor
1920–
(m) *Emily Lucy Kinloch* ——————— Virginia
                                 Robert
                                 Rachel
                                 Jean
                                 James

John Astor
1923–
(m) *Diana Drummond* ——————— Elizabeth
                             Richard
                             David

William Backhouse Astor
1935–
(m) *Charlotte Fisk* ——————— **William Backhouse Astor, Jr**
Mary Jacqueline   1959–
                            Caroline Fisk

This family tree does not list the progeny of female Astors by birth. Male Astors in the direct line of descent who figure prominently in the book are indicated in bold type.

Acknowledgments

The author and publisher have taken all possible care to trace and acknowledge the sources of illustrations used in this book. If by chance we have made an incorrect attribution we will be pleased to correct it in future reprints, provided that we receive notification.

The illustrations in this book appear by kind permission of the following museums, agencies and individuals. References to colour illustrations are printed in *italic*.

Associated Press   199, 222, 225
John Bethell   *165 right, 166–7, 168, 206–7, 208*
The Bettmann Archive Inc.   94
Brown Brothers   Endpapers, 2, 25, 37, 46, 51, 55, 57, 69, 70, 75, 80, 82, 89, 100, 102, 103, 108, 109, 120, 121, 123, 129, 131, 134, 136, 145, 171, 172, 174, 179, 195 left, 215
John Frost Historical Newspaper Service   180
Library of Congress, Washington   128–9
The Mansell Collection   27, 156, 212
Mary Evans Picture Library   9, 44–5, 73
Metropolitan Museum of Art, New York   97
Metropolitan Opera Archives, New York, Gift of R. Thorton Wilson and Orme Wilson, 1949   105
National Trust (John Bethell)   *165 left, 205*
Orbis   *113 above* (I. N. Phelps Stokes Collection, Prints Division, the New York Public Library; Astor, Lenox and Tilden Foundations),   *113 below*
Peter Newark's Western Americana   21, 22, 58, 76–7, 85, 110, *114–15, 116*
Photri, Alexandria   *61, 62–3, 64 above*, 79, 90, 93, 158–9, 228
Popperfoto   219
Press Association   230
Radio Times Hulton Picture Library   13, 14, 17, 30–1, 35, 65, 78, 137, 139, 147, 150, 169, 175, 176, 182, 186, 188, 190, 191, 193, 194, 195 right, 197, 210, 233
Topham Picture Library   81, 226, 227, 236
Valentine Museum, Richmond, Virginia   157
Weidenfeld and Nicolson Archives   *64 below*, 161

No one wept when eighty-four-year-old John Jacob Astor, who had arrived in New York as a penniless German youth to become the richest man in America, died in the spring of 1848. For years people had been commenting on his feeble state of health and predicting that his days were drawing to a close. Indeed, as early as 1844 Philip Hone, a man of fashion and one-time mayor of New York wrote in his diary that 'Mr Astor presents a painful example of the inefficiency of wealth to prolong the life of man'.

Yet three years later the old man was still clinging to his worldly possessions. In the summer of 1847 he moved from his four-storey brownstone house on lower Broadway to his country residence which was situated on the East River at a spot that is now intersected by 88th Street. In the evening he was carried down the steps to his summer-house to watch the boats passing to the Sound through Hellgate, or 'Hurlgate' as the more genteel would have it. The vessels reminded him of his own ships that had once criss-crossed the Seven Seas carrying Astor trade goods – goods that gave him the profits to buy the farm lands of upper Manhattan.

Now the old man was so feeble and debilitated it was plain that the end could not be far away. He was wheeled from room to room in his bath chair, while every morning, on doctors' orders, two male nurses tossed him about in a blanket to get his circulation going. 'It is time for me to take my leave of the world,' he observed dejectedly to his son and heir, fifty-five-year-old William Backhouse Astor. Yet his mind was still sharp and his love of money as obsessive as ever. He spent his mornings poring over his real estate accounts, and his land agent called daily to discuss the business of his massive rent roll, of which no item was too small to escape Astor's attention. On one occasion the agent arrived while Astor was undergoing his blanket exercise. Between bounces the old man cried out, 'Has old Mrs — paid the rent yet?'

'No,' replied the agent.

'Well, she must pay it,' said the poor old man.

'Mr Astor, she can't pay it now; she has had misfortune and we must give her time.'

'No, no,' said Mr Astor, 'I tell you she can pay it and she will pay it. You don't go the right way to work with her.'

When the unhappy employee reported the conversation to Astor's son, the latter counted out the requisite sum and told the agent to give it to the old man as if he had received it from the tenant.

'There,' exclaimed Mr Astor when he received the money, 'I told you that she would pay it if you went the right way to work with her.'

This story, related by Astor's first biographer, James Parton, may be apocryphal, yet it perfectly reflects the octogenarian's character. 'So, to the last breath, squeezing arrears out of his tenants; his mind focused upon those sordid methods which had long since become a religion to him; contemplating the long list of his possessions with a radiant exultation; so Astor passed away.'

Every major American newspaper devoted columns to the event, comparing the departed tycoon to such eminent Europeans as Nathaniel

Rothschild, the Duke of Devonshire, even Louis Philippe, King of France, and accurately assessing his fortune at $20,000,000. Almost all the comments were laudatory, for the New World was beginning to judge a man's worth by the success with which he multiplied his dollars. Indeed the growing adulation for millionaires was emphasized a few years later when Walter Houghton published a book on the careers of successful magnates, *Kings of Fortune*, subtitled 'Or the Triumphs and Achievements of Noble, Self-Made Men – whose brilliant careers have honoured their calling, blessed humanity and whose lives furnish instructions for the young, entertainment for the old and valuable lessons for the aspirants of fortune.'

The twenty million dollars that Astor had accumulated was a sum of money so enormous for the times that one newspaper declared it 'as incomprehensible as infinity'. It represented one-fifteenth of all the money in the United States invested in such industries as 'cotton and wool, leather, flax and iron, glass, sugar, furniture, hats, silks, ships, paper, soap, candles, wagons – in every kind of goods that the demands of civilization made indispensable'. Even run-of-the-mill millionaires such as Peter Goelet with his two million dollars, Cornelius Vanderbilt with his one and a half million, and Moses Taylor with his one million, felt quite naked when they contemplated the fortune of the modern Croesus.

What were the qualities that enabled this German immigrant to reach such spectacular heights? Was it luck or ingenuity, or both? The Victorians liked to believe that sterling worth reaped the greatest rewards; yet Astor had grown into a singularly unattractive being, a man without a scrap of generosity, whose only aim seemed to be to extract the last ounce of flesh that was his due. There was only one chink in his armour: a sense of obligation to those tied to him by blood or marriage. And in fulfilling this responsibility he was so successful that even today Astors of the fifth and sixth generation live comfortably on the bounty of this unmourned, unloved but not unsung Founder.

John Jacob Astor's devotion to family ties stemmed far less from warm-heartedness than vanity. As he had raised the Astor name to pre-eminence, he wanted the world to continue to honour it. No doubt this desire sprang from the bleakness of his childhood. His father, Jacob Ashdour – or Ashtor – or Aoster – was descended from a French Huguenot family which had fled to Germany in the sixteenth century to escape persecution, and settled in the country village of Walldorf, not far from the famous university town of Heidelberg. Ashdour was the community butcher, sometimes described as 'the worthy and profound bailiff of Waldorf', sometimes as 'a convivial person who spent more time in the tavern than in the shop'. In 1750 he married a local girl, Maria Vorster, who produced two daughters and four sons of whom John Jacob was the youngest. Three years after his birth, she died, and Ashdour took another wife who produced a second batch of six children. Thus John Jacob grew up under the hand of a stepmother too preoccupied to give him much care, dependent on his elder brothers for affection.

Although Walldorf and its flat wooded plain seemed cut off from the world, life was not altogether parochial. Germany was composed of three hundred independent states governed by absolute rulers, ranging from imperial knights to sovereign abbots, from landgraves to dukes, electors to princes and kings. These feudal states were part of a sophisticated European pattern – a voluntary confederation presided over by the Habsburgs and still known as the Holy Roman Empire. The organization was so patently on its last legs that Voltaire had recently pointed out that it was difficult to see 'in what sense it was either Holy or Roman or an Empire'; nevertheless it proved virile enough to plunge the whole of Europe into the Seven Years' War. This occurred in 1756 when Frederick the Great of Prussia appropriated Silesia which the Habsburgh Empress, Maria Theresa, claimed was part of her inheritance. Russia, Sweden and France lined up behind Austria, while Britain, who always ranged herself against France, supported Frederick and his only ally, the Duke of Brunswick. Britain did not send her own soldiers to fight but hired mercenaries from the Landgrave of Hesse-Cassel, who was married to a daughter of George II.

Many foot-soldiers were recruited by the Landgrave's son in Frankfurt, only a day's drive from Heidelberg; so the Astor boys often saw Hessian infantry trudging along the dusty roads and probably even French regiments sailing down the Rhine to their battle points. The children had an exceptionally good schoolmaster, Valentine Jeune, who supplied them with maps and opened their minds to the great world outside Germany. The Landgrave's allegiances rubbed off on the Astors and gave them a liking for Britain; when the war between France and England spread to North America they studied the campaigns and in 1762 heard with satisfaction that the French had been defeated and evicted from their Canadian possessions.

Under these circumstances it was not surprising that as the boys reached manhood they began to seek their fortunes abroad. The eldest, George, went to London where he joined his uncle who was employed by Shudi and Broadwood, a firm that made musical instruments. The second boy, Henry, was attracted to the New World. When the Revolutionary War broke out in 1776 and once again Britain began hiring Hessian mercenaries to fight her battles, he was quick to see the chance of a free passage.

We do not know whether he joined up in Frankfurt or enlisted in England; but before long he was riding through the streets of New York as a sutler to the British Army. However, when his unit moved from Manhattan he deserted and stayed behind to open a butcher's stall in Fulton Market. He overcame the shortage of meat by creeping into the countryside at night and stealing cattle from the farms.

Despite Henry's enthusiastic letters, the third brother, Melchior, clung to Europe and became a tenant farmer on the estate of the Prince of Neuwied who lived near Heidelberg. This left only John Jacob, who helped his father in the butcher's shop for two years; then in 1779, at the age of sixteen, he joined his brother in London. He stayed there four years, working in the tiny music factory that George had just set up.

During this period John Jacob saw life as a very serious affair, believing implicitly that God had selected him for great events. He was awakened every morning by the sound of Bow Bells, and he later told a friend that he always read either the Bible or the Lutheran Prayer Book until it was time to go to work. This religious phase was short-lived for as he grew older he tended to rely less on the Almighty and rather more on himself.

In 1783, Britain made peace with victorious, independent America and Henry wrote from New York predicting that unlimited opportunities awaited men with the courage to cross the Atlantic and gamble on the future. He emphasized that humble birth was no handicap. This was enough to convince John Jacob, but as he had a strong streak of caution, he decided to enter a trade that he knew something about. He would open a shop in New York and sell George's musical instruments. Brimming with enthusiasm the twenty-year-old youth, who spoke only guttural, ungrammatical English, travelled to Bristol and paid £5 for a steerage passage to Baltimore on the good ship *North Carolina*. He had with him a parcel of musical instruments – seven flutes and one or two clarinets – and £5 in cash.

The Tontine Coffee House, on the north-west corner of Wall and Water Streets. Erected in 1792, it was a meeting place for politicians and business men – and here young John Jacob met many of the men who later proved useful to him as he expanded his fur business.

The journey was a memorable experience as the weather was appalling. Sometimes the wind died and the vessel floundered to a near stop, its sails flapping disconsolately; other times the sky darkened and the ocean was swept by a howling gale with such high waves that the passengers feared their end was approaching. On one such occasion John Jacob suddenly appeared in his Sunday suit. On being asked why he had attired himself thus, he replied that if the ship was wrecked and he was drowned it would not matter; and if the ship was wrecked and he was saved at least he would have his best suit.

Bad luck pursued the vessel all the way, for when it was within a day's sail of Baltimore the temperature fell and the passengers awoke to find themselves trapped in the solid ice of Chesapeake Bay. It was a strange sight for half a dozen ships were caught like flies in a huge spider's web. Everyone waited for the weather to change and, in order to while away the time, passengers from other vessels began walking over the ice to call on one another. In this way, John Jacob met a fellow German, a youth not much older than himself, who told him that he was trading in furs in upper New York and had just been to Europe to secure new markets. The advantage of the business, he said, was that no capital was necessary as it was possible to buy furs from the Indians for a pittance and sell them at great profit. John Jacob listened politely but confided that he was planning to open a music shop.

After a melancholy week frozen in the ice, some of the passengers were so restless that they set off across the Bay on foot. At first John Jacob refused to adopt this method of escape as the Captain was obliged to feed and lodge him until the ship reached harbour, and Astor calculated that he would save money in transport if he remained aboard. But after a second week he could bear the inactivity no longer and departed across the ice. He wrote later to his friend, Washington Irving:

I remember the day that I arrived in Baltimore. I took a walk to see the town, getting up Market Street while standing and looking about, a little fat man came out of his shop. This was Nicholas Tuschdy he addressed me saying – young man I believe you are a stranger, to which I replied yes, – where did you come from – from London – but you are not an Englishman – no a German. Then he says we are near countrymen I am a Swiss – we are glad to see people coming to this country from Europe. On this he asked me into his home and offered me a glass of wine and introduced me to his wife as a countryman.... When I stated that I had some articles of merchandise to dispose of, chiefly musical instruments, he observed that if I could put some in his store that he would sell them free of any commission or expense....

Astor remained in Baltimore for three weeks while Tuschdy disposed of his flutes and with a pocket full of money he proceeded to New York by boat and coach. He had no difficulty in finding Henry who had prospered greatly as a butcher and now had a horse and cart. Even more important he had a pretty wife, Dorothy Pessenger, a German immigrant like himself, whom he introduced to John as 'de pink of de Powery'. The couple were living on First and Fisher Streets but their quarters were so small that they sent John Jacob to board with a German-American baker, George Dietrich. The latter promptly offered John

A view of the city of New York from the south. In the late eighteenth century Upper Manhattan was still open countryside and farmland.

Jacob free bed and board in return for peddling his bread and cakes around the streets. Although Astor only kept the job three weeks, in later life he was deeply ashamed of this interlude for he soon learned that youthful peddlers were despised as 'wastrels and blackguards'. Indeed while he was so engaged a local newspaper declared that the 'great number of idle boys who infest our streets and markets with baskets of cookies and other articles are a glaring reproach to the city'.

Nevertheless the hours that John Jacob spent hawking his wares introduced him to his new surroundings, and it did not take him long to see that New York was more important as a seaport than as a town. Upper Manhattan was still open country and farmland. The urban development was in Lower Broadway, Pearl and Cherry and Wall Streets; but even this area was in sad repair. The retreating British army had burned the public buildings and the unpaved streets ran with mud and garbage. The population had declined to 23,000 and there were few amenities. Small boys sold fresh water at a penny a pail, while West Indian slaves, imported from the south, cleaned the public carriages and groomed the horses. But there was no such thing as a sanitary department, or even an organization to collect rubbish.

Astor sold most of his bread and cakes at the port which was crowded with schooners from all parts of the globe. Ships were being loaded and unloaded as quickly as possible to make way for new arrivals; and on the quay hundreds of sailmakers plied their trade while sailors of every nationality wandered about looking for diversion. In February 1784 the *Empress of China*, America's newest vessel, left the harbour on an epic-making voyage to Canton.

The sight of so many ships stacked with valuable cargoes began to fire John Jacob's imagination. He would start his shop as soon as he could get more musical instruments from London, but he would also trade in furs and perhaps other commodities as well. A number of Indian trappers were wandering about the harbour selling their skins for such trifles as cooking pans and pocket knives, and Astor made his first timid purchase. But he was not a man who liked to gamble in goods about which he knew nothing so he got a job with Robert Browne, a local furrier, to beat pelts at two dollars a week, the accepted method of keeping furs free of moth. Only by handling hundreds of skins so that his fingers could gauge the quality, only by sorting and packaging could he hope to become an expert. It did not take him long to realize how much there was to learn. Although mink and otter commanded the highest prices, beaver was in the greatest demand as it was the most fashionable commodity for gentlemen's top hats. These furs could be bought from the Indians for a few shillings and sold at profits ranging from six hundred to nine hundred per cent. His mind reeled at the thought of such enormous gains but of course the high prices only applied to the best furs. Summer skins were never as valuable as winter pelts while those classified as *castor gras* fetched the most money. This meant that they had been worn next to a human skin for several months until the body oil rendered them soft and downy, a service the Indians were glad to perform in return for a monetary consideration.

John Jacob was fascinated by the talk he heard, but nevertheless he still hankered for his music shop. He did not come to a final decision about his future until he met William Backhouse, the most eminent fur merchant in America. No one knows how the young German emigrant with the guttural accent made the acquaintance of the elderly Englishman who had come to New York thirty years earlier and whose brother, Thomas Backhouse, ran a successful fur business in London. Yet the meeting was a turning point in Astor's life. Although John Jacob has come down in history as an unsmiling man obsessed by business, he must have had plenty of charm as a youth for he always succeeded in making an impression on people who would be useful to him. The truth was that Astor invariably appealed to serious-minded men as he had a penetrating mind and pondered deeply on the events and pressures of the day. He never made a foolish remark and his well-founded opinions were often original and provocative.

William Backhouse took a great fancy to Astor, entertaining him in his large house on lower Broadway and talking to him like a Dutch uncle. Certainly, he said, John Jacob could make a comfortable living selling musical instruments imported from England; but the fur trade was an entirely different matter. Half the North American continent consisted of forests inhabited by millions and millions of fur animals: and furs were in world-wide demand for the simple reason that people liked to keep warm. Musical instruments spelled a life of security and ease; the fur trade was rough and demanding, yet Backhouse was sure that the way was wide open for a young American with imagination and organizing ability. Although the United States had become an independent nation, the only serious fur companies were Canadian, and sooner or later America must enter the field. Backhouse spoke eloquently, conjuring up a vast empire of trading posts and ships and foreign markets crowned by fame and fortune. His persuasive tongue stirred his guest so deeply that then and there Astor made up his mind to become the greatest fur merchant that America had ever produced.

John Jacob wasted no time in embarking upon his new career. But first, as a natural precaution, he persuaded Robert Browne to send him into Indian territory so that he could try his hand at bargaining with the natives. As a result, in April 1785, only thirteen months after his arrival in Manhattan, he took a boat to Albany, the chief trading centre in New York state, seven days by sloop up the Hudson River. Here Indians, Frenchmen, Englishmen and Americans padded over the rough cobblestones in their moccasins and bartered their skins to the highest bidder. John Jacob watched the sales and listened to what was said but he did not try to bid as he was sure that he could do better by buying pelts in the interior.

The large tracts of land in upper New York running north to the Canadian frontier and west to the Great Lakes were still Indian territory.

A Mohawk village in Central New York around 1780. Large tracts of land in upper New York and along the Canadian frontier were still Indian territory, and the Indians were glad to trade their furs for the white man's baubles and hardware.

Here the Iriquois, descendants of the once supreme Five Nations, had villages and hunting grounds and were glad to welcome white traders who brought them fascinating gadgets in exchange for furs. As they traded regularly with Europeans there were always one or two members of a tribe who could speak a few words of English while the rest had developed a fairly graphic sign language. Dressed in rough, thick clothes, a fur hat and strong boots, John Jacob began to walk along the trails to the Iriquois settlements. He had a heavy pack on his back containing the trinkets with which he hoped to barter. He carried a rifle, a bullet pouch and powder horn were slung over his shoulders and a skinning knife was at his belt. He also carried a flute as a means of amusing himself when the sun went down and it was too early to sleep. However, he soon discovered that the Indians liked the plaintive, piping sounds and before long he was treating his prospective buyers to a repertoire of German folk songs. When he returned to Manhattan he brought with him two canoes full of pelts. Robert Browne was so pleased that he raised the young man's wages, but Astor was now planning to branch out on his own.

The year 1785 was not only eventful because of business. In September John Jacob took a second momentous step by marrying Sarah, the daughter of Adam Todd, a gentleman of Scottish descent who had died fifteen years earlier leaving his widow almost penniless. Consequently Mrs Todd ran a boarding house at 81 Queen Street, helped by her daughters. John Jacob met Sarah when he was selling cakes for Mr Dietrich and she was washing her doorstep. She smiled and he stopped to talk. When John Jacob confided that he knew no one in New York except his brother Henry she invited him to call and soon he was a regular visitor. The Todds had a piano in the sitting room and Astor frequently entertained them by playing the songs of his childhood and singing in German. Although the Todds were poor they were proud and well-connected for Sarah's father had married twice and the children of her step-sisters – all much older than herself – had made good matches. One niece was the wife of Henry Brevoort, whose family had considerable social standing, while a nephew, James Whetton, was a ship's officer who one day would captain vessels carrying valuable cargoes to China.

John Jacob was greatly attracted to Sarah, and Mrs Todd encouraged the courtship. The German was conscientious and hard-working while many young Americans, particularly those who had served in the army, tended to be wild and undisciplined. Although Sarah's face was too thin for beauty Astor loved her shy smile and her large, dark eyes. Half-a-century later, when one of his grandchildren asked him why he had married Sarah, he thought for a moment and said: 'Because she was so pretty.' However, good looks were not all that she brought her husband for she had a dowry of $300, and her mother gave her two rooms in the boarding house which they could call home.

Sarah was an astute and eager business woman who threw herself into her husband's affairs and did all she could to promote his interests. She encouraged him to strike out on his own, and within a few weeks of their marriage waved him goodbye as he departed once again for the rough regions of upper New York. A few months later, when a consignment of musical instruments arrived from Astor's brother, she turned one of her two rooms into a shop and put an advertisement in the New York *Packet* of May 1786. It announced that John Astor 'had just imported from London an elegant assortment of Musical Instruments, such as piano fortes, spinnets, piano-forte guitars, the best of violins, Herman Flutes, clarinets, hautboys, fifes, the best Roman violin strings, and all other kinds of strings, music books and paper, and every other article in the musical line, which he will dispose of on very low terms for cash'.

Meanwhile John Astor was in the wilds learning his trade. With his thick boots and hunter's cap, a rifle over his shoulder and a pack on his back, he looked as though he had been born and bred in the Indian country. Although he was powerfully built – five foot nine inches tall with broad shoulders and sturdy legs – he had never taken physical exercise which in any way fitted him to lead the life on which he was now embarking. Yet he not only survived but drove himself forward relentlessly. For the next two and a half years he spent only a few months at a time with Sarah. His world was one of interminable journeys, tramping through the rough Catskills, the forests of New Jersey, the swamps of Long Island, the mountains of Pennsylvania and the far reaches of the Adirondacks, often spending the night before an open camp fire or under a lean-to hastily constructed to break the bitter winds.

Astor met dozens of independent trappers and traders and agents who were doing the same thing as himself, but although he made a point of getting on good terms with them they had very little in common. Basically they were rough, out-of-door men who had taken up fur trading because it allowed them the independence to run their own lives. They found danger exhilarating and loved their months of freedom when they gambled and got drunk and caroused with women. Astor concealed his distate for these feckless souls whose improvident ways offered a sharp contrast to his own sober outlook. He loathed the great open spaces and derived no excitement from hardships which he regarded as exasperating inconveniences.

However, he had the good sense to keep his opinions to himself and made a point of never complaining. He had come to the wilds to trade with the Indians and to make large profits, both of which he was doing with remarkable success. Indeed, he became a well-known figure trudging stolidly along the trails, or arguing over prices in Cornelius Persen's store, which had become a popular meeting place. 'Astor came with the earliest sloop up the Hudson,' wrote a contemporary, 'and trappers and hunters from the Catskills and beyond the mountains resorted to this store to meet him. At times the old storehouse was filled with them and Astor carried the overflow into the kitchen against the indignant protests of the mistress of the house.' Astor never talked anything but shop. He liked to exchange notes on prices to make sure he was exacting the best possible bargains. Beaver skins were being sold for about $7 each, and they commanded the following prices:

1 gun	10 beaver skins
1 thick blanket	8 beaver skins
1 axe	3 ,, ,,
$\frac{1}{2}$ pt gunpowder	1 ,, ,,
1 small twist of black tobacco	1 ,, ,,
$\frac{1}{2}$ pt rum	2 ,, ,,
1 lb glass beads	2 ,, ,,
1 cloth coat	6 ,, ,,
1 petticoat	5 ,, ,,
1 lb snuff	1 ,, ,,

John Jacob had many dangerous moments. Once in western New York he lost his way and nearly perished. 'John Jacob Astor,' wrote another contemporary, 'with a pack of Indian goods upon his back (to barter with) got lost in the low ground at the foot of Seneca Lake in an inclement night, wandered amid the howl and rustling of wild beasts, until almost morning, when he was attracted by the light of an Indian cabin and...obtained shelter and warmth.' Another friend, James Wadsworth, told how he once met Astor in the woods of western New York in a sad plight. 'His wagon had broken down in the midst of a swamp. In the mêlée all his gold had rolled away through the bottom of the vehicle and was irrevocably lost; and Astor was seen emerging from the swamp covered with mud and carrying on his shoulder an axe – the sole relic of his property.'

Sometimes Astor auctioned his skins at the market in Albany; sometimes he sent them to Sarah who put them in the room with the musical instruments and tried to persuade piano players and violinists to buy them; sometimes he shipped them abroad. But whatever he did, the preparation was long and laborious; much of the hard work took place at the house of Peter Smith, a youth three years older than himself who had become a close friend. Smith had started up on his own with a shop in New York which sold books, bees-wax, canes and snuff boxes. Smith was just as precocious financially as Astor and for a short time the two men joined hands. On two occasions they tramped through the interior of New York together on foot from Schenectady to Old Fort Schuyler and back again.

At Smith's house, there was the long process of preparing and grading. 'Many times have I seen John Jacob Astor with his coat off,' wrote an anonymous gentleman from Schenectady, 'unpacking in a vacant yard near my residence with a lot of furs he had bought dog-cheap off the Indians and beating them out, cleaning and unpacking them in more elegant and saleable form to be transported to England and Germany, where they would yield him one thousand per cent on the original cost.' Although the friendship survived until Smith's death, the partnership did not last long for Smith's wife, Elizabeth Livingston, persuaded her husband to give up travelling and settle down with her at Utica. Astor did not demur as once again fate was beckoning him forward.

Opposite John Jacob must have closely resembled this Canadian fur trapper, wrapped up against the elements and armed with axe, knife, rifle and powder horn as he walked the trails to the Iroquois settlements. Drawing by P.R. Skelton.

An old proverb says that luck often comes 'in threes', and as far as Astor was concerned the adage proved true. At some time during 1786 or 87 chance came his way in the robust shape of a famous Montreal trapper, Alexander Henry, whom he met in Schenectady. Astor became lively and informative the moment he realized whom he was talking to and he captivated Henry just as he had charmed William Backhouse and fascinated Sarah. Indeed, Astor impressed Henry as a very uncommon young man who had more of a grasp of the fur business than any youth he had ever met. Indeed Astor asked so many questions that Henry impulsively invited him to visit him in Montreal. Not only would he introduce him to the leading fur men but he would arrange to send him down the river with one of the early spring brigades so that he could see how the North West Company organized its affairs.

Astor was thrilled. Until 1780 the Hudson Bay Company, the greatest fur company in the world, had enjoyed a monopoly in Canada. But this organization operated in the northern part of the country around the great basin that drained into the Arctic. South of this region, all the way from Saskatchewan to the Ohio River, competition between small competitors and individual traders raged uncontrolled. Most of the traders and trappers and *voyageurs* were Indian half-breeds and they had all the treachery of primitive people. The French-Indian *voyageurs* who blazed the trails through the forests and took the canoes over the rapids were 'as full of latent tricks and vice as a horse'; while traders and trappers

A fur trader negotiating payment for furs in an Indian council lodge, by Frederic Remington.

often 'fought to the death for a pack of beaver skins, for the trade of a tribe, or to hold their own in a certain area'. By 1780 the violence and murder had reached such proportions that the leading fur dealers of Montreal – mainly Scottish-born Canadians – decided to form a new company to establish order throughout the territory. Thus the North West Company sprang into being, with sixteen famous Canadians holding the equity, of whom Alexander Henry was one; and within five years the group not only had established some order but were making high profits as well in the lawless regions.

The company was organized as a hierarchy. Every year the manager-owners travelled to Fort William, a village on the banks of Lake Superior, to meet the agents and trappers from the company's 117 trading posts. Outsiders were rarely allowed to attend this council, but Alexander Henry arranged for John Jacob Astor to be present. The highly-placed directors arrived in great state as befitted the subjects of a great empire. To the American writer, Washington Irving, they seemed 'like sovereigns making a progress; or rather like Highland chiefs navigating their subject lakes. They were wrapped in rich furs, their huge canoes freighted with every convenience and luxury, and manned by Canadian *voyageurs*, as obedient as Highland clansmen. They carried up with them cooks and bakers together with delicacies of every kind, and abundance of choice wines for the banquets which attended this great convocation.'

Astor's journey was not so comfortable. He travelled up the St Lawrence and Ottawa rivers in a forty-foot-long cargo canoe, constructed of birch bark, and paddled by ten men, but it was so light it could be carried on ten shoulders. The cargo weighed four thousand pounds and consisted of goods for the company's white agents and all kinds of flashy objects for payment to the Indian trappers. The boat was unloaded at the little town of Mattawa and carried to Georgian Bay. It then began to wend its way through a maze of islands into the North Channel, travelling past St Joseph's island, and up St Mary's river. Another portage took them across St Mary's Falls and at last they were on the cold, steely waters of Lake Superior.

Fort William lay on the western shore. Here, in an immense wooden building was the grand council hall decorated with Indian arms and accoutrements and the trophies of the fur trade. The tables of the banqueting hall, wrote Irving, groaned with the weight of game of all kind; of venison from the woods and fish from the sea. 'There was no stint of generous wines for it was a hard drinking period, a time of loyal toasts and bacchanalian songs, and brimming beekers.'

Even more interesting than the visit to Fort William was Astor's journey that same year, 1788, to the North West Company's largest trading post, Michilimackinac, situated on an island at the head of Lake Michigan. Although the Peace Treaty between Britain and America, signed in 1783, had defined the United States' boundaries which included both Detroit and Michilimackinac, the Canadian companies still retained their posts.

On this particular trip John Jacob saw the effect of alcohol on the Indian tribes. Although the British government forbade the use of spirits in the Indian territories, the North West agents announced airily that as His Majesty's writ was no longer valid in the United States they would conduct their business in the most advantageous way. Their canoes were laden with hundreds of gallons of cheap West Indian rum made from molasses; and John Jacob was left in no doubt that spirits were far more effective as a means of barter than glass beads or knives. The Indians fought to get their hands on the forbidden dynamite and for days after they had won the battles, whole families, from grandmothers to grand-children, staggered around the villages quarrelsome and drunk.

Astor returned to New York, his head brimming with ideas. He was impressed by the huge scale on which the Canadian companies operated, dealing not with thousands but hundreds of thousands of furs a year. The sheer weight of numbers allowed them to keep their prices low and still make a handsome profit. John Jacob took the lesson to heart and decided then and there that he would no longer go tramping through upper New York trying to do his own trading. He would buy his furs in Montreal and concentrate on the markets rather than the primary sources. Furthermore, he too would try to deal in bulk.

However, the precarious position of the Canadian companies had not escaped John Jacob's sharp eyes. A great deal of the wild unexplored area in which the North West Company operated belonged to the United States (eventually it formed part of Illinois and Michigan); and one day the American government would be bound to curtail the activi-ties of Canadian agents in favour of its own nationals. And when that day arrived, Astor would be ready.

In 1788 the golden moment of American self-assertion seemed a long way off. The thirteen states were still operating under the Articles of Confederation and the first government was still a year in the offing. Not until April 1789 did George Washington walk onto the balcony of Federal Hall in New York to be inaugurated as the first President of the United States. Although a few weeks later the French Revolution broke out and on 14 July the people of Paris stormed the Bastille, Ameri-cans took little interest in European affairs, and continued to argue hotly about what title their new head of state should have. Apparently Washington himself liked the idea of 'High Mightiness' as used by the Stadholder of Holland, but General Mullenberry laughed the matter out of court by asking what would happen if a little man was elected president? Committees were appointed by both houses of Congress and finally settled in favour of plain 'Mr President' – according to Cleveland Amory this was 'a title so bare that on one occasion Washington was refused lodging at a village inn upon the assumption that he was the President of Rhode Island College'.

However, none of these events – even the fact that all over France chateaux were beginning to burn – succeeded in arousing the interest of John Jacob who was wholly absorbed by the fur trade. Although he no longer threaded his way through the forests of upper New York battling against the elements, he now spent over six months a year in Montreal buying and selling. As an independent trader he had saved over

On 30 April 1789, George Washington walked onto the balcony of Federal Hall in New York to be inaugurated as First President of the United States. In 1795, Washington proposed the setting-up of government fur-trading posts – a development which John Jacob did not welcome.

$10,000, enabling him to guarantee large orders; and for some specific deals he went into partnership with Alexander Henry, buying furs a year in advance for an agreed sum and selling at a price arranged equally far ahead. Today this would be called gambling in 'futures', a precarious business which Astor did not follow for long. Nevertheless he continued to develop his European markets. One of his best customers was William Backhouse's brother, Thomas, who was a leading London furrier. By the end of 1790 casks of furs bearing Astor's mark J-JA were being shipped both ways across the Atlantic.

Although Astor was now a man of affluence he was not eager to move out of his two rooms in his mother-in-law's boarding house, even though Sarah had turned one of the rooms into a store crowded with musical instruments and frequently with ill-smelling skins. She gave birth to a baby daughter, Magdalen, in 1788 and two years later lost a second child. When she was pregnant again in 1791 she begged her husband to provide a house for them and before the year was out he had bought a new store with living quarters on the upper floors at 40 Little Dock Street. He paid $850 for it, and Sarah was thrilled to have three bedrooms.

However, when Astor wanted something enough he did not quarrel about the price. In 1794 he commissioned Gilbert Stuart, the celebrated American artist who had just painted George Washington, to do a likeness of himself. Apparently he did not like the painting and, determined to get his money's worth, refused to pay until Stuart had done a second portrait. The picture shows a young man of elegance, with a long, rather aristocratic face and a large nose. But the eyes are hard and fixed and there is not a trace of gaiety or even sympathy in the appearance; only the concentrated look of a man determined to make a good bargain out of everything that came his way.

At the time of the portrait Astor was reputed to be worth over $50,000 and was considered such an expert in furs that he was frequently asked by government and custom officials to appraise their wares and put a value on them. Despite John Jacob's success in the Canadian market he was very critical of the North West Company and its new subsidiary, the Michilimackinac. Not only did it seem ridiculous that a Canadian company should collect furs from the United States territory without cost, but quite ironical that under these peculiar circumstances the British government should maintain its rigorous restrictions on colonial trade. All Canadian furs had to be shipped to England before they could be reshipped to the purchaser. This meant that if Astor bought furs in Montreal for delivery in New York he had to wait while the consignment went on a leisurely voyage to London, underwent a leisurely delay, then made a leisurely trip back across the Atlantic again. Astor complained loudly that if he had a faster turnover he could double and triple his profits.

In 1795 the wind started to blow his way. Trouble broke out in the north between American and Canadian trappers and President Washington sent Chief Justice John Jay to London to negotiate a new treaty. By this time the United States had lost any interest it had in radical France, so Jay swapped the Franco-American alliance for British concessions. The latter agreed to vacate all forts and settlements in America's north-west territory by 1796, and, even more beneficial to Astor, to allow free trade between Canada and the United States, which meant that furs would no longer be shipped to England. 'Now,' exulted John Astor, 'I will make a fortune in the fur trade!'

However, for a while it looked as though President Washington might be a major obstacle in the achievement of this goal, as he suddenly seemed eager to abandon the profit system for the loss system. Or so it seemed

Opposite The portrait John Jacob commissioned of himself, by Gilbert Stuart.

to Astor. Washington proposed to Congress that the government set up its own trading posts and supply the Indians with goods marked up no more than thirty-three per cent over the trade price. Government agents would not be allowed to trade in spirits, nor to visit the villages to 'drum up trade'. The President was aware that these restrictions would not attract private enterprise. 'Individuals will not pursue such a traffic, unless they be allured by the hope of profit,' he wrote, 'but it will be enough for the United States to be reimbursed only.'

Astor was outraged by these ideas. How could any private trader hope to compete with such idealistic nonsense? However, his alarm subsided when he saw at what a snail's pace the bureaucracy moved. It took Congress five years to establish two posts and both were in the south; and as private operators flaunted the law and enticed the Indians with liquor, the government attracted less than ten per cent of the trade. Another interesting development was the fact that although the Canadians relinquished their forts at Detroit and Niagara and Michilimackinac, they were not prohibited from carrying on their business and as the North West Company had so much expertise it continued to dominate the fur market. Although John Jacob sent a number of his own agents into the territory to gain experience, he continued to buy the bulk of his skins in Montreal as he had always done. But just as he had foreseen, his profits increased as he now could ship his furs directly to his purchasers, which saved him both time and money. By the turn of the century he was rumoured to be worth $250,000; but no one knew the exact figure, and years later Astor confided to a friend that he was a millionaire long before anyone suspected it. He had always been reserved and secretive; but now this latter trait was so pronounced that the richer he grew the more loudly he complained of poverty.

His wife Sarah was the only person who knew the true facts and in 1801 she presents a picture of serenity. By that time she had borne her husband eight children, three of whom had died soon after birth. Although he was devoted to his family he worked so hard he had little time for them. At that time his eldest daughter, Magdalen, was fifteen; his two eldest sons, John Jacob and William Backhouse (the latter named after the New York furrier who had helped him get his start), were ten and nine years old, and his two younger daughters, Dorothea and Eliza, five years old and a babe in arms. Sometimes days would pass without Astor catching even a glimpse of the children, for when a ship was in port he often worked sixteen hours a day clambering over the holds to inspect cargoes and checking the goods in his warehouses. On top of this, he had the arduous journey to Montreal every year, and frequently a long and uncomfortable voyage to Europe. Occasionally when he came home exhausted he would sit down at the piano and play an old German melody, or pick up his flute and trill out a mournful tune. The children would gather around and try to join the fun, then suddenly it would come to an end and their mother would hurry them off to bed.

Despite Sarah's household duties she always supervised the sale of her husband's pianofortes and flutes and clarinets. Every few years she moved the shop to larger premises, but in 1802 Astor decided that the profit no longer was worth the effort and sold the business to the Piaff brothers. That same year he purchased a large house at 223 Broadway above Vesey Street, for $27,000. It was the home of Rufus King, the first United States senator from New York. It was large and spacious with enough rooms for all the children and a series of drawing rooms that opened into one another. But as Sarah felt that the children should have 'country air' he also bought a house at Hellgate, near what is now 88th Street. It was a wonderful house with a green lawn that swept to the water's edge, facing the little strait of Hurlgate where schooners at half sail moved toward the harbour. Apart from this fascinating spectacle which never failed to interest John Jacob, he had the satisfaction of knowing that he was surrounded by such important neighbours as the Crugers, the Gracies, the Schermerhorns and the Rhinelanders.

Sarah was delighted as she had always insisted that her husband 'know the right people'. For years she had made him go to church every Sunday to be seen by respectable lawyers and bankers. And she encouraged him to become a Mason because of the company he would keep – among others, George Clinton, a future Vice-President of the United States, his brother, Dewitt Clinton, who would soon be Governor of New York and Henry Livingston, an influential merchant. Even more important, she often took him to Mrs Keese's boarding house, which stood on the corner of Broadway and Wall Streets, where he could engage in conversation with more young men destined for fame and fortune: John Armstrong, a future Secretary of War in Madison's government, General Stephen van Rensselaer, the Squire of Albany, and a dapper, vivacious, United States senator, Aaron Burr.

Everything seemed to go well for the Astors save for one tragic exception. Their eldest son, John Jacob Astor II, was born an imbecile. He usually existed in a state of mental torpor, but occasionally he was almost normal. Sometimes he even wrote poetry; then he would sink back into his lethargy and stare at the world with unseeing eyes for months at a time. His mother prayed constantly for his recovery and his father professed to believe that it was perfectly possible for a miracle to occur. The boy lived in luxurious surroundings, attended by people who were well paid for their services.

As the new century made its debut John Jacob began to develop a wonderfully profitable market at the other end of the world. Napoleon's shadow had fallen across Europe and Astor knew that if the cocky little Corsican plunged the continent into war, his own fur trade would be badly hit, so he turned his gaze to China.

He had plenty of people to advise him as his wife's brother, Adam, and his wife's nephew, James Whetton, were sea captains who knew the Far East; and there was a niece, Margaret Whetton, married to yet another ship's officer on the Pacific run.

As a result, John Astor formed a syndicate in 1800 and chartered the ship *Severn* which sailed for Canton carrying 30,573 seal skins, 1023 beaver skins, 321 fox skins, 103 otter skins and 132 piculs of ginseng,

Overleaf In 1802 John Jacob purchased the third building from the corner of Vesey Street, 223 Broadway (on the left). From a painting by Baron Axel Klinickowstrom, engraved by Akrell.

a root-plant grown on the North American Atlantic coast and greatly in demand in China as an aphrodisiac. The trip from New York to Canton around the Cape and back took anywhere from thirteen to eighteen months, but the profits were enormously high: not only did the ship's cargo fetch a large sum in China but she carried a return cargo laden with Chinese silks – 'black and coloured sattins', 'yellow and white nankeens', shawls, fans, china ware and thousands of pounds of the choicest teas, all of which sold at a premium in the New World.

Furthermore the United States government was eager to help American shippers to compete with the British and allowed them eighteen months' grace before demanding the duties payable on imported goods. This meant that merchants were allowed to operate on what amounted to a government free loan. They could send a second ship to China and back on money due to the treasury at no cost to themselves. Although Astor always paid his duties when they came due, apparently many shippers defaulted. According to a contemporary, Joseph Scoville, one firm which went bankrupt 'owed the United States millions and not a cent has been paid'. Altogether the nation lost $250,000,000 while this scheme was in operation.

Nevertheless Astor's profits were so large that his brother, Henry, urged him to buy Manhattan real estate. Henry had sold John Jacob several small plots in 1789 on Bowery Road and Elizabeth Street for 'Forty-Seven Pounds Current Money in New York'. But John Jacob did not continue these speculations as he preferred to plough the money back into his business. Henry, on the other hand, put every penny he could scrape together into real estate and was now worth nearly $100,000. Plenty of people cautioned John Jacob against following Henry's example. If a depression came, the property market might crash and remain in the doldrums for years. Businessmen needed liquid funds, not money locked up in bricks and mortar.

But John Jacob took his brother's advice, for New York clearly was a growing centre. Had not the 23,000 inhabitants of 1784 become 50,000 in 1800? And had not the city advanced a mile up the island in the nineteen years since his arrival? In 1803 he invested over $184,000 in land, and in 1804 and 1805 $80,000 each year. He bought from many illustrious people: a house in Richmonds Hill and a large parcel of land from Aaron Burr, Vice-President of the United States, for which he paid $62,000. The following year Burr challenged his political opponent, Alexander Hamilton, to a duel and killed him. Desperate for money with which to start a new life, he appealed to Astor who bought another lease from him for $8000.

Astor had always made a point of cultivating Vice-Presidents and he now turned his attention to George Clinton, a friend of many years. Clinton found politics an expensive diversion so he was glad to sell Astor a half-interest in his Manhattan property for $75,000. The land lay in Greenwich Village and ran from 9th Avenue and Hudson Street to the Hudson River. An even more profitable investment was the purchase of the Eden Farm which sloped from Broadway to the Hudson River just north of 42nd Street. Astor paid $12,500 for a half interest in the seventy acres. Less than a century later the 'great White Way' cut a swathe through the property.

However, the legend repeated in almost every account of Astor's life, declaring that what he bought he never sold, holding on to his investments as security for his descendants, is totally false. During the first twenty years of the century Astor traded in land just as he traded in furs, always selling when he could get a good profit. For instance, there are records to show that in February 1803 he sold for $4500 a water-lot which he had bought twelve years earlier for $200. That same year he sold for $2500 a small part of the land and buildings that he had bought for $3000 a few months earlier; in 1805 some of George Clinton's Greenwich Village lots bought at $300 fetched $1000 each; and in 1806 a slice of land bought three years earlier gave him a return of $9000.

Yet Astor's real estate transactions were only a hobby. His true interests lay in the China trade. Indeed he worked so hard that by 1805, when he was forty-one years old, his appearance no longer suggested an energetic man who could beat furs and walk through the woods, but a tycoon who spent his time bending over his account books. The lean body had gone to fat and the thin face was as flabby and over-ripe as a melon. Indeed, now that he was a rich man, he looked like a butcher's boy.

However, his looks belied his character for he should have been good-natured and jolly, whereas he was reserved, he never told anyone his plans and whenever possible he took great pleasure in misleading people as to his real intentions. As for money, he was so niggardly it was almost pathological. The more he accumulated the more he complained about his expenditure, and the more he complained the more he tried to cut down on the wages of his employees. He never rewarded long and faithful service and even failed to honour promises which would not have cost him more than a few dollars. Astor's biographer, Kenneth Porter, declares that on one occasion when one of the merchant's ships arrived from China and had to be dispatched immediately to Amsterdam, Astor was greatly concerned about two pipes of precious Madeira wine which were lying under a mountain of tea chests.

'Can you get out that wine,' he asked the captain, 'without discharging the tea?'

The captain thought he could.

'Well then,' said Mr Astor, 'you get it out, and I'll give you a demijohn of it. You'll say it's the best wine you ever tasted.'

It required the whole labour of the ship's crew for two days to get out the two pipes of wine. They were sent to the house of Mr Astor. A year passed. The captain had been to Amsterdam and back, but he had received no tidings of his demijohn of Madeira. One day when Mr Astor was on board the ship, the captain ventured to remind the great man, in a jocular manner, that he had not received the wine.

'Ah,' said Astor, 'don't you know the reason? It isn't fine yet. Wait till it is fine and you'll say you never tasted such Madeira.' The captain never heard of that wine again. It was therefore literally true that he 'never tasted such Madeira'.

Astor would spend money to make money but that was all. For instance in 1803 he built a fast and lovely ship, the *Beaver*, purely for the China run. She had two decks and three masts and was 111 feet long and 29½ feet wide. Cutting through the water under tall white sails she completed her first trip to Canton and back in the remarkably short time of nine months – that meant more money in Astor's pocket. Indeed, he was so delighted with her that he built a companion ship which he named after his daughter, *Magdalen*. As captain of the new vessel he appointed John Cowman, a master mariner who had sailed on many voyages for him and to whom he often referred as 'the King of Captains'.

One day Cowman told Astor that the insurance company insisted that he install a chronometer on the ship, at a cost of $500. Astor insisted that the instrument was not the owner's responsibility but the captain's. Cowman was adamant and Astor finally capitulated; but when the bill came Astor once again refused to pay. In disgust Cowman walked off the ship.

It took Astor a week to find another captain, and Cowman a month to find another vessel. Although Cowman sailed for China six weeks after the *Magdalen* he was such an experienced navigator he arrived back in New York with a hold full of tea only seven days after Astor's ship. Astor had not yet unloaded the vessel as he hoped the tea price would rise. Cowman on the other hand hurried his goods to auction. This caused a tea glut and compelled Astor to wait another month, by which time more ships had arrived from China with cargoes of tea. The result was that Astor lost $70,000. However, he seemed to value a man who could score off him, for when he ran into Cowman walking along Broadway one day, he said: 'You were right. I had better pay for that chronometer.' And he re-hired the old captain on the spot.

Astor found his trade with China particularly profitable when he sailed to the north-west coast of America and loaded his vessels with the skins of sea otters trapped by the Indians. This animal had been discovered by Captain Cook in 1778. Its skin was soft and smooth, glossy black and sprinkled with silver. The Chinese sometimes secured sea otters in small numbers from North Asiatic seas. However, when American merchants took their skins to China and found that they would get $120 apiece for them, they felt that they had discovered a new gold coast. Unfortunately these beautiful animals were almost exterminated by hunters; the few that remain today are rigorously protected.

However, as the new century progressed the struggle between Britain and France began to have far-reaching repercussions. Each power was trying to starve the other out by destroying its commerce. The British issued Orders in Council forbidding neutral ships to trade with ports on the continent under Napoleon's control; Napoleon issued an Imperial decree authorizing the seizure of ships which traded with the British Isles. This enmity even extended all the way to the Orient, for in 1806 the British Navy's China Squadron cast menacing glances at the Yankee clippers, and began to search them for British deserters from the Merchant Navy, above all to make sure that the American vessels were not carrying cargoes to France. Astor hoped that he could induce the United

The Beaver, *the steam and sailing ship that Astor built in 1803 for trade with China. It was the first vessel owned by Astor to cross the Pacific.*

States government to send a naval escort with his ships, and in July 1807 wrote a letter to Secretary of State James Madison asking whether under present circumstances it would be advisable to let his ship 'the *Beaver* being coppered and...carrying 12 guns...sail for Canton in China?'

Unfortunately the letter had the opposite effect from that which Astor had hoped. President Jefferson was greatly agitated by the attack of a British warship on the American warship *Chesapeake*, on her way to the Mediterranean. When the *Chesapeake* refused to stop on orders from the *Leopard*, the latter poured a broadside of shot into her and her captain struck his colours. As President Jefferson was aware that the defence of America's coast was impossible against the mighty British fleet, he restrained his anger and adopted a new policy of coercion. In 1807 American exports were worth over $100,000,000; therefore he decided to gamble on the fact that neither Britain nor France could afford to do without American goods, and ordered an embargo prohibiting American vessels from travelling to foreign ports.

This drastic remedy provoked a howl of anger from shippers and merchants. Cutting off one's nose to spite one's face seemed a poor way for a government to do business. Astor racked his brain to find an answer to the dilemma; and before long cunning and ingenuity sprang to his rescue. He approached Senator Mitchell of New York (whom the Mayor of New York, Philip Hone, later described as strangely deficient in that useful commodity called common sense) and in mid-July 1808 Jefferson received a letter from Mitchell which said 'Punqua Wingchong, a Chinese merchant, will be the bearer of this note of introduction. He came to New York about nine months ago on business

... and he is desirous of returning to Canton where the affairs of his family and particularly the funeral obsequies of his grandfather require his solemn attention ... the chief object of his visit to Washington is to solicit the means of departure ... to China. ...'

President Jefferson was in Monticello when Wingchong arrived in the capital but the latter sent an urgent appeal 'praying permission to depart for his own country with his property in a vessel to be engaged by himself.'

By this time word had spread that Wingchong was a distinguished and powerful Mandarin. Secretary of State James Madison (who was in debt financially to Astor) was told of the matter and also wrote to the President pressing the Chinese request. Jefferson approved it and advised his Secretary of the Treasury, Albert Gallatin, a brilliant Swiss-born financier who was a personal friend of Astor, to support it. 'I consider it,' he wrote to Gallatin, 'a case of national comity. ... The departure of this individual with good dispositions may be the means of making our nation known advantageously at the source of power in China to which it is otherwise difficult to convey information. ... I think therefore he should be permitted to engage a vessel ... and for this purpose send you a blank passport for the vessel etc. etc. ...'

When Gallatin learned that the ship which Wingchong had engaged was the *Beaver* he was badly shaken; and his unease was increased when he received an indignant letter from eleven Philadelphia merchants declaring that the government had been deceived and the alleged 'Mandarin' was an imposter. These merchants emphasized that many of them had been resident in Canton several years where they had acquired sufficient knowledge of Chinese customs to make the fraudulent character of the 'Mandarin' quite positive. 'To some of us,' they added, 'he is known only as a petty shopkeeper in Canton. ...' Despite this disquieting information Gallatin carried out the President's affirmative instructions without passing on the information he had received. Was he desirous of maintaining Astor's friendship because of political ambitions? Whatever the reason he gave the vessel permission to sail, armed against Malay pirates and carrying Wingchong and his retinue and their personal effects consisting of furs worth $45,000.

When the New York *Commercial Advertiser* announced briefly that 'yesterday the ship *Beaver*, under Captain Galloway, sailed for Canton' a howl of fury arose from the American shippers, and the press referred to the 'Mandarin' as 'a Chinese picked up in the park', 'a common Chinese deck loafer' and 'an Indian dressed in Astor's silks and coached to play his part'.

Jefferson suspected that he had been hoodwinked but as the *Beaver* had departed there was nothing to be done. A year later the ship came back from Canton with 500,000 pounds of tea and a large quantity of silks and china ware. Because of Jefferson's embargo all these goods fetched top prices and Astor made a profit of $200,000 on this one journey alone. At Canton, Wingchong vanished and was never seen again.

2 The richest American

Previous page *Port Astoria, founded by John Jacob Astor in 1811 on the Columbia River as a centre for Pacific trade.*

In 1808 John Jacob Astor took his daughter, Magdalen, to Montreal on one of his annual trips. An English merchant, Samuel Bridge, recorded in his diary that at dinner he sat next to 'a Miss Astor from New York – her father who is at present here is said to be worth £200,000 – report says he will give this daughter £25,000'. Apparently Miss Astor was entertained in a way befitting an heiress for Bridge goes on to talk of a party given by Alexander Henry at which 'the sprightly dance was kept up till past twelve – chiefly country dancing but some reels and one cotillion in compliment to Miss Astor, as they scarcely dance anything else at New York'.

Napoleon Bonaparte's ascendancy in Europe and President Jefferson's shipping embargo deflected Astor's gaze from the sea, and once again he turned his attention to the vast, unexplored American territories along the Canadian border. Always at the back of his mind was the grandiose conception of monopolizing the North American fur trade all the way from the Atlantic to the Pacific. First, of course, he would have to bring about the downfall of the Canadian companies with whom he had worked for the past twenty years but this prospect did not trouble Astor who did not believe that sentiment should interfere with business.

The idea was to build a line of trading posts up the Missouri and across the Rockies, then along the Columbia River which wound its way through territory now known as Oregon and emptied into the Pacific. The new trading centre would be named Astoria and established not far from the mouth of the Columbia, perhaps a hundred miles from the coast. It would be supplied by vessels from New York sailing around Cape Horn and Astoria's furs would be taken to China and exchanged for goods suited to the American market: '...a smooth, glittering, golden round,' wrote the historian H.H. Bancroft, 'furs from Astoria to Canton, teas, silks and rich Asiatic merchandise then to New York, then back again to Columbia with beads and silks and bells and blankets, knives, tobacco and rum.'

John Jacob Astor was cunning enough to outline his plan in patriotic colours to President Jefferson. His aim, he said, was to wrest away the fur monopoly from the two Canadian giants, the North West Company and the Michilimackinac Company. He talked about 'extending the American domain' and 'adding new states to the Union'. He even talked about protecting the Indians. If the government would grant him an exclusive charter to operate in this region he would be in a position 'to prevent irresponsible fly-by-night traders whose only interest was in quick killings from gaining a foothold'. He went on to emphasize that 'only a permanent organization would find it advantageous to treat the Indians fairly and secure their allegiance'.

The President was deeply impressed and referred to Astor as 'a most excellent man'. Unfortunately, he did not understand the project at all. He believed that several American companies would engage in the trade, whereas Astor's idea was to establish a monopoly controlled by himself, or, as he explained to a friend, 'to take the whole'. As for cosseting the Indians, Astor's only aim was to trade advantageously enough to make a handsome profit. With joyful innocence, the President gave his approval and on 6 April 1808, the New York state legislature granted a charter to the American Fur Company.

However, Astor's dream could only be accomplished by slow stages. His primary goal was to establish 'Astoria' on the Columbia River. For this feat he needed half a dozen sagacious councillors in the form of partners, as well as the most experienced *voyageurs* and trappers in the business, all of whom were Canadian. As a preliminary move he formed the Pacific Fur Company and persuaded fifteen or twenty employees of the North West Company of Montreal to join. Once the whole operation had proved a success, his secret intention was to merge his own controlling interests into the American Fur Company and to buy out his Canadian partners explaining sorrowfully that the United States government would not allow foreigners to own shares in the American monopoly.

He decided to dispatch two expeditions to the Pacific Coast – one by ship carrying supplies necessary for the settlement, including goods for barter with the Indians, the second to travel overland along the route recently pioneered by Lewis and Clark.

But everything went wrong. First of all, Astor made a cardinal mistake in choosing a naval captain, Jonathan Thorn, to take charge of his vessel, the *Tonquin*. Thorn had a reputation for being a martinet which pleased Astor but the truth was that this man was quite mad, a cross between a sadist and a psychopath. Although half the people on board were passengers, he tyrannized them all, drawing his revolver if anyone even argued with him. The company consisted of four of Astor's newly-acquired partners, Canadians of Scottish extraction; eleven sophisticated young men from good English families who had travelled to Canada to serve apprenticeships as clerks; thirteen French-Canadian *voyageurs*; and five mechanics.

The first quarrel began when the captain ordered all lights out at eight o'clock. The partners protested and he threatened to clap them in irons. Next he made the young clerks share the sailors' quarters in the forecastle and their hours of rising and retiring, and announced that he would blow out the brains of the first man to oppose the regime. He stopped at the Falkland Islands, and when three of the partners were ten minutes late in reporting back on ship, he sailed off without them. They rowed after him frantically but only caught up with him when the big vessel was becalmed. The vessel finally reached the Hawaiian islands and many of the crew tried to desert; but he had them rounded up, flogged and thrown into irons.

The passengers rejoiced in March 1811 when they sighted the mouth of the Columbia River in territory which has since become part of the state of Oregon. Mercifully the hazards that lay in wait for them were still hidden. This stretch of the Pacific coast was wild and rough, and the mouth of the river was almost blocked by a sand-bar. A north-west gale sent the sea crashing against the bar and, despite the protests of the crew, Captain Thorn ordered the first mate to take four men and do a reconnaissance in the small whaling vessel. Two boats and eight men were lost before the *Tonquin* started up the treacherous river.

Two weeks later the senior partner aboard the ship, Mr MacDougall, selected a piece of land above Baker's Bay for the new settlement. It was known as George's Point and had a bay capable of providing a fine harbour. He renamed it, and at last Astoria was born. While the *Tonquin* was unloading materials and supplies for the men who would stay behind and build the settlement, the local Indians swarmed over the site or paddled up to the ship asking to come aboard. Captain Thorn was annoyed to find that they had very few skins to sell and were only prompted by curiosity; he referred contemptuously to them as 'Indian ragamuffins' and refused to have anything more to do with them.

As soon as the vessel was unloaded, Thorn had orders to journey northwards, up the Pacific coast, trading wherever he could. When he sailed away from Astoria he had twenty-three men with him, including one of the company partners, Mr McKay, and the ship's clerk, Mr Lewis. The first port at which the *Tonquin* dropped anchor was Neweetee, a harbour in Vancouver (now Victoria) Island. Mr McKay went ashore to pay his respects to the local Indian chief, and while he was away the incredible Captain Thorn, who knew nothing about Indian customs or barter or furs, decided to start trading himself.

He spread blankets and beads and cooking utensils on the decks and allowed the Indians, who had surrounded the boat by canoes, to come aboard. One of the visitors was the son of the chief to whom Mr McKay had already paid his respects while the other, old Nookamis, was chief of a neighbouring area. Nookamis knew all about the skill with which the white men cheated the redskin. He took charge of the negotiations, refused the goods that Thorn was offering, then began to jeer at him for his niggardly 'bargains'. Thorn lost his temper, grabbed the furs and flung them in the chief's face. Then he ordered the Indians off his ship.

The crew sensed trouble and begged Thorn to set sail without delay, but he reminded them of the rifles and ammunition in the hold for defensive purposes and refused to move. Next morning, several canoes again came alongside the *Tonquin*. The Indians laughed and pointed to their furs saying they had changed their minds and were ready to do business. As they were unarmed the ship's officer allowed them aboard, and within an hour two hundred were on deck. They agreed to exchange their beautiful sea otter skins for knives which Thorn, amazingly enough, allowed to be distributed to them.

He was suddenly gripped by apprehension and ordered the crew to weigh anchor and set sail with no further delay. But it was too late. The Indian smiles turned to war cries. The redskins fell on the crew and killed all of them save for Mr Lewis, who was badly wounded but still alive, and four men who had been at the top of the rigging. All night the sails flapped as the wind blew mournfully through the darkened ship. The next day Indian canoes again approached. The badly-wounded Mr Lewis had decided on a plan of action. He staggered onto the deck and motioned to them to come aboard. He went below and waited until several hundred were swarming over the deck, eying the booty they meant to take, then set fire to the powder magazine. According to Washington Irving in *Astoria*: 'Arms, legs and mutilated bodies were blown into the air and dreadful havoc was made in the surrounding canoes.... The ship had disappeared but the bay was covered with fragments of the wreck, with shattered canoes, and Indians swimming for their lives or struggling in the agonies of death, while those who had escaped the danger remained aghast and stupified, or made with frantic panic for the shore.'

Meanwhile the land expedition was still struggling toward Astoria ignorant of the tragedy. They did not reach the settlement until early in 1812, seven months after the loss of the *Tonquin*. They staggered into Astoria sick and half-starved, out of touch with every important happening, chief of which was the outbreak of war between the United States and Britain.

America completely failed to understand the life and death struggle taking place between England and France. In order to crush Napoleon, Britain was determined to prevent neutral vessels from carrying goods to French ports, and announced that any vessel that did not touch at a British port and pay duty would be subject to seizure. This enraged the Americans and a few months later they declared war. The conflict spread to Canada and sometime during 1814 a detachment from the Canadian North West Company appeared with the alarming news that a British frigate would soon sail into the Columbia River and train its guns on Astoria.

These emissaries proposed that Astor's partners – all of them British subjects and former members of the North West Company – should capitulate and sell out, lock, stock and barrel rather than lose everything in unavoidable defeat. After much agitated thought, the partners agreed and sold Astoria's stores and guns and furs for the best price they could get – forty cents in the dollar. More than $200,000 worth of furs were relinquished for less than $80,000. When John Jacob Astor learned about the massacre on board the *Tonquin* he refused to cancel his theatre engagement. 'What would you have me do?' he asked a friend who expressed amazement at his coolness. 'Would you have me stay at home and weep for what I cannot help?' However, when he heard how much money he had lost at Astoria, his wrath knew no bounds. 'While I have breath and so long as I have a dollar to spend I'll pursue a course to have our injuries repaired,' he fumed.

Nevertheless, before the end of 1814 he had made back every penny he had lost ten times over, by forming the first bond syndicate in American history to help pay for the war. Astor put up two million dollars – a great deal of which he borrowed from the banks on the strength of his property – and bought six per cent bonds at eighty-eight cents guaranteed to be worth a dollar on maturity.

Astor also managed to get a ship through the British blockade, which netted him another huge profit. Despite the war he was still buying furs from Canada although it involved a certain amount of subterfuge. One shipment alone consisted of 20,000 martin, 46 bear, 18,000 muskrat, 526 fisher, 6021 otter, 3389 mink, 2048 fox, 271 cat and 6 wolf skins. But how was he to get them to Europe?

This time he stumbled upon a *bona fide* French General who was living quietly in New Jersey. General Moreau was a pro-royalist, anti-Napo-leonic man, but he had no great desire to get mixed up in the current madness and only wanted to be left alone. However, Astor persuaded the General to offer his services to the British and persuaded the British to allow one of Astor's ships, the *Hannibal* to carry the General to Europe – along with a great many furs. A few months later Moreau was mortally wounded in the Battle of Leipzig, but Astor had sold his furs at a stunning profit. For once he did not grumble. 'I have done very well on the voyage,' he wrote to a friend.

By 1815 – the year that Britain beat Napoleon at Waterloo and made peace with the United States – fifty-one-year-old John Jacob Astor was known in three continents as a millionaire merchant. Yet he was still dreaming of ways to increase his fame and fortune. He knew the advan-tage of influential connections and began to look around for an associate who would advertise the business in a gentlemanly way – a task which in modern parlance would come under the heading 'public relations'. His eye fell on Albert Gallatin, the brilliant Swiss-born financier whom he had first known as President Jefferson's Secretary of the Treasury, and whose wife had entertained seventeen-year-old Dorothea Astor in Washington.

Throughout most of 1815 Gallatin had been in Europe serving as United States peace commissioner, and in October Astor wrote to him outlining his proposal. Astor had about $800,000 engaged in trade and reckoned on an annual profit of anywhere from $50,000 to $100,000. He would give Gallatin a twenty per cent interest if he would become his partner.

Gallatin's snobbish and foolish son, James, felt that he understood his father 'perfectly' when the latter declined Astor's offer. 'I am not sur-prised,' he wrote in his diary, 'as Astor was a butcher's son at Waldorf – came as an emigrant to this country with a pack on his back. He peddled furs, was very clever, and is, I believe, one of the kings of the fur trade. He dined here,' he added, 'and ate his ice-cream and peas with a knife.'

The accuracy of this observation seems unlikely as the ability to eat peas or ice cream with a knife would have been a talent deserving great praise. Nevertheless, a few years later James Gallatin again referred to Astor's table manners. 'Really Mr Astor is dreadful,' he wrote. 'He came to *déjeuner* today: we were simply *en famille* he sitting next to Frances [James' sister]. He actually wiped his fingers on the sleeve of her fresh white spencer. Mama in discreet tones said: "Oh Mr Astor, I must apolo-gise: they have forgotten to give you a serviette." I think he felt foolish.'

It is improbable that Astor's lapses compelled Gallatin to give up an income of $20,000 a year. As the financier had been taken in by 'the Mandarin incident' Gallatin probably took a poor view of Astor's busi-ness ethics and did not want to become involved in any more sharp prac-tices.

Astor was not a man to brood over arrangements that did not material-ize. Besides he was too rich to let incidentals bother him. When the war ended he was the owner of nine ships which he had picked up at bargain

Overleaf *New York Bay in 1800. John Jacob was one of the first to recognize the potential of New York as a seaport, and the city rapidly became one of the foremost trading ports in the world.*

prices during the embargo. His vessels travelled from New York to Europe and sometimes to the Middle East; and from New York to the West Coast and China. He traded in anything and everything that made a profit. His Mediterranean ships picked up opium in Smyrna and smuggled it, under cover of darkness, to the Cantonese sampans in the Pearl River. His Pacific ships sailed from Oregan to China groaning under the weight of sea otter skins. Sometimes the cargoes carried sandalwood picked up from the Hawaiian Islands, in those days known as 'the Sandwich Islands'. King Kamehameha cooperated vigorously, sending his whole population to hack down the trees as he was delighted to exchange the lovely, scented wood which the Chinese treasured, for firearms and cloth. Astor's captains became his favoured protégés, but when the sandalwood was gone, John Jacob's interest waned and the islands were left to the missionaries.

When Gallatin refused to participate in his business, Astor decided to take his second son and heir, twenty-three-year-old William Backhouse Astor, as his junior partner. William had been educated at a private school in Connecticut until he was sixteen, after that at Heidelberg University where he remained for two years. In 1810, after returning to New York for a brief stay, he transferred to Gottingen University where he was given a tutor who was only a year older than himself. This was Baron von Bunsen, who later became famous as Prussian Ambassador to the Court of St James. 'I am now,' Bunsen wrote to his sister, '... residing with the son of an American merchant named Astor, boarded and lodged in the very best manner, and am to receive between this time and Easter 30 louis d'or for which I give him instruction in German and other things.... I have occasion to improve my English and such a mode of life is in more than one respect useful to me....'

The four years that William spent at Gottingen was the most interesting period of his life. One of Bunsen's friends who frequently visited their flat with a poodle on a leash was Arthur Schopenhauer, a moody fellow who smiled even less than William and eventually became a world-famous philosopher. In the summer of 1811 William toured the German States with Bunsen and two friends, and the following year went on a trip to the Great Lakes. In 1813 when Napoleon Bonaparte launched one battle after another John Jacob Astor became convinced that William had been caught up in the fighting. 'William is no more,' he wailed to anyone who would listen; but his fears proved false and he managed to get his son back to New York in 1814 on the ship the *Hannibal* that had taken poor General Moreau to Europe. William remained in America only a few months and in 1815 hurried back to his amusing friends in Germany. He was a scholarly man who would have liked to spend his life studying and travelling and visiting the great museums. But John Jacob decided that William was necessary to him – particularly as Gallatin had declined to form a partnership – and summoned him home in 1816.

In 1814 the British raided Washington and burnt down the White House – the final touch in a series of disasters for the American government. John Jacob was quick to profit from these events and persuaded Secretary of State James Munroe to get a bill passed prohibiting foreigners – mainly the British – from trading with the Indians east of the Rockies.

William arrived in New York to find his father's mind consumed with the idea of 'revenging himself on the Canadian North West Company which had robbed him of Astoria and thousands of dollars worth of furs'. For a while John Jacob talked of re-establishing Astoria, but he was unwilling to embark on a second adventure unless his ship was escorted by an American naval vessel, and President Monroe preferred to compromise. Shortly after Astor's partners had capitulated to the enemy and relinquished Astoria's valuable furs for a pittance, a British sloop-of-war had appeared, commanded by a jaunty little officer, Captain Black. Black viewed the primitive settlement with a mixture of amusement and exasperation, boasting that he could have battered the whole establishment to the ground in two hours with a single four-pounder. He was disappointed that he had not arrived earlier to claim the furs as 'prize money', but carried out his task by changing the name of Astoria to Fort George, then raised the Union Jack and sailed away. Apparently this act enabled the American government to argue after the peace treaty that Astoria had not been 'sold' but captured as an act of war. The US therefore took back the fort and hoisted the Stars and Stripes, and in 1817 the two governments agreed to occupy the territory jointly, which they did until 1846. In the end they divided it on the 49th Parallel from the Rockies to the Pacific, which suited both countries and of course made Astoria part of the United States.

Although Astor's interest in Astoria faded during the long period of joint occupation, he was still determined to launch the American Fur Company which had existed on paper since 1808 but had always lain dormant. He would expand the company into the monopoly he had dreamed about for so many years and drive his Canadian rivals out of the field. And thus he would create the empire that William Backhouse had talked about so thrillingly thirty years earlier.

First he would have to persuade the government to ban Canadian traders from doing business on United States soil. He had always had strong opinions on this subject and as American feelings were still furiously ruffled by the recent war he felt that at last he had a good chance of success. The Americans had rushed into the conflict convinced that the British would put up a poor show just as they had in the Revolution, and boasted exuberantly of the large slices of Canada they would confiscate. Instead, the British had whipped them in half a dozen encounters, capturing the whole of Maine, not to mention Detroit and Niagara and Michilimackinac, and finally committing the crowning insult of raiding the capital and burning down the White House.

In this atmosphere it was not difficult for Astor to pour oil on troubled waters. He told his friend, Secretary of State James Monroe, that the Canadians were inflaming the Indians against the Americans. Monroe always listened patiently to Astor as he was in debt to him for $5000. (Incidentally Astor did not press Monroe for repayment until after he had served as President of the United States and retired from politics. Monroe then wrote gloomily to a friend that he had been obliged to sell his slaves to raise the necessary cash.)

In 1816 Monroe was successful in getting a bill passed 'prohibiting all foreigners from trading with the Indians on American soil except that land west of the Rockies unless by express direction of the President of the United States'. Astor wrote to Monroe expressing his approval of the Act 'which ought to have been...passed some years ago', then coolly asked for further help. Without Canadian traders experienced in the Indian country, he said, it would be impossible to supply the natives, particularly those in the interior; and as this would cause 'great distress among the Indians' (not to mention financial loss to Astor) he requested Monroe to ask the President for six to nine blank licences for Astor's use. President Madison did not grant this request but empowered Governor Cass of Michigan to issue whatever licences he deemed fit.

This suited Astor as Cass soon became putty in his hands. Years later no one was surprised when a faded ledger revealed that Cass had received $35,000 from Astor's company for unspecified services. The agent at Michilimackinac naturally was not aware of this arrangement and warned Cass against Astor. 'I wish to God the President knew this man Astor as well as he is known here. Licences would not be placed at his discretion to be distributed among British subjects....'

The way thus prepared, the American Fur Company, with a million dollars of Astor money behind it, became operational in 1817 and remained a potent, if malign force, for seventeen years. It occupied many of the posts along the Canadian frontier that had been vacated by British traders and turned its gaze toward the Rockies. The most serious stumbling block in Astor's path were the United States government trading posts, or 'factories' as they were called, which had been introduced by Presidents Washington and Jefferson to protect the Indians. These stores sold their goods only a fraction above cost prices, rigorously banned alcohol and gave the Indians fair returns for their furs. Indeed, many altruistic people believed that relations between the Indians and Americans would be transformed if only the factories were given a chance.

However, the very mention of factories sent Astor into a rage. He argued that they would bring about the ruination of all private business, a view supported by his agents in the field who informed him 'that unless the government factories are abolished it will, in our opinion, be imprudent in you to continue interested in the trade'.

Once the gloves were off no holds were barred. The employees of the Fur Company not only were encouraged to spread scurrilous stories about the government workers, their restrictions on credit, even their refusal to sell alcohol, but when the occasion warranted, they were empowered to cut their prices dramatically, even though it resulted in heavy losses. Their most effective weapon, however, was the use of alcohol. Spirits had a disastrous effect on Indians, sometimes turning them into homicidal maniacs ready to stab and scalp their neighbours, sometimes into pitiful sots willing to trade their guns and last blankets for a single swallow. Alcohol not only left in its wake inter-tribal wars, wrote Kenneth Porter, but 'hostility between the natives and the border settlements, disease, poverty, starvation and death. But it also left, here and there, fur traders with weighty packs of furs and well-filled pocket books, the fruits of the ruin which their greed and their kegs of rum had brought upon the natives. It was inevitable that government officials inspired ... by a desire for the safety of the frontier should endeavour to prevent liquor from reaching the Indians.'

Astor, however, was determined to bring about the demise of government officials and government posts alike, and to this end threw in all his money, experience and political influence. In 1818 Governor Cass wrote to the Secretary of War criticizing the factories and urging their abolition. He cited the fact that one by one the posts were faltering and declining in trade. In 1822 the victory was won. 'You deserve the unqualified thanks of the Community,' crowed Astor's manager, in a letter of thanks to Senator Benton of Missouri who had led the congressional campaign, 'for destroying the pious monster. The country is indebted for its deliverance.' Benton was not only a senator, and a leading light in the Democratic party, but Astor's legal representative in the West, and worth every penny of the fee he was paid, and better still, Governor Cass had acquired the exalted position of Secretary of State for War.

During the last phase of this battle – 1819–22 – John Jacob Astor spent most of his time abroad. He called on relations in England and Germany, visited Rome and Naples, spent a number of months in Geneva and finally settled down in Paris where he took a keen interest in the European political situation. His old acquaintance, Albert Gallatin, was the American Minister to France, and he had a letter of introduction from President Monroe to General Lafayette. Some people say that he met Metternich and Guizot and Louis Philippe, the future King of France. However, he formed a dim opinion of European stability, writing to Monroe 'that all Europe is threatened with revolution', and that 'those in power are trembling'. His prophecy was only partially fulfilled by an unexpected uprising in Naples and a minor revolution in Portugal.

Needless to say, Astor was not altogether out of touch with his business. Before he left New York he drew up a memorandum containing detailed instructions for the fur trade, dictating how particular skins should be sold and stating that all orders for goods from Europe and all furs shipped to Europe should be referred to him personally. He could not have planned his long sojourn abroad if it had not been for his son, William, in whom he had the greatest confidence, and who was now acting as president of the American Fur Company. William was not only painstaking, cautious and dependable, but he had greatly pleased his father by marrying the right girl, Margaret Armstrong. The bride was the daughter of General John Armstrong, who had been an acquaintance of Astor for many years. Armstrong's wife was a member of the famous Livingstone family, and although the General was not in the least clever, he had profited from his wife's connections to make friends with James Madison, James Monroe, Albert Gallatin, the Clinton brothers and a host of other important men. As a result Armstrong was appointed American Minister to Paris in 1804, and although he remained there until 1810 he never succeeded in getting on with Napoleon who described him as 'a morose man with whom one cannot treat'.

This pronouncement resulted in Armstrong's recall, but in 1813 President Madison made him Secretary of State for War which proved even more disastrous. Although the British were raiding America's Atlantic coast, due to their massive sea power, Armstrong flatly refused to provide Washington with any defences, insisting that the enemy would strike at Baltimore, a major sea port, and not at the capital. When Britain's Major General Ross landed on the Patuxent, fought an easy battle at Bladensburg and marched the seven miles to Washington, pandemonium broke out. President Madison fled in the night, gathering such valuables as he could, while the marauding force burnt the White House, the Capitol, and other public buildings.

No one was surprised when Armstrong was again relieved of his post. This time he retired to Rhinebeck in upper New York State and built himself a small manor house on the Hudson. He named it Rokeby, and it is still standing today. As he had very little money he welcomed the marriage of his daughter to the fabulously rich Astor heir in 1818. After the wedding John Jacob made his son a junior partner in John Jacob Astor & Sons, and when he went to Europe left him in charge of the American Fur Company. As William was placid and conscientious he became more of an assistant than a partner which was exactly what the old man wanted.

Astor followed the lives of his children with keen interest. Although he disapproved of divorce, he made an exception in the case of his eldest daughter, Magdalen, who was very different in character from her unperturbable brother. Magdalen was a high-handed, imperious maiden, noted more for her money than her beauty and, as such, was a natural target for ambitious suitors. In 1807 she married a Dane, Adrian Bentzon, who was Governor of the Danish West Indies. They had two children, a boy who was drowned at the age of ten, and a girl who died in infancy. Some people claimed that these tragedies soured her nature, but the truth was that Magdalen was hopelessly spoiled, and when she saw how sycophantic people became in the presence of the rich, she grew increasingly arrogant.

Like Shakespeare's shrew, she should have been beaten every day by her husband, but of course never was. Although Bentzon was ousted from his job by the British, eventually he was reinstated but Magdalen refused to accompany him to Santa Cruz and remained in New York. In 1819 she created a scandal by divorcing him. Her father stood by her for Bentzon cheerfully admitted adultery, and John Jacob did not see why his daughter should suffer the humiliation of neglect. The following year Magdalen married an Englishman, John Bristed, who had emigrated to New York, and who dabbled as a writer, lecturer and magazine editor. However, the marriage was a failure and the following year Bristed returned to London finding it 'impossible', as Sarah's nephew, Henry Brevoort, wrote, 'to bear the matrimonial yoke any longer with that Lamb of Bellzebub, my well-beloved Cousen the late Mrs Bentzon . . . she certainly is a maniac.' However, she had a son by him, Charles Bristed, born in 1820, who in later life became Astor's favourite grandchild.

Although Magdalen always succeeded in enlisting her father's support, Dorothea, the second daughter, who was seven years younger than Magdalen, was not so lucky. Astor was more concerned about the marriages of his children than any other single thing. He hoped they would make brilliant matches but, failing that, at least seek his approval. Dorothea did neither. In 1812 Albert Gallatin's wife invited the seventeen-year-old girl to visit her in Washington. Here she met Colonel Walter Langdon of Portsmouth New Hampshire, a member of the Governor's staff. Whereas Dorothea was sometimes alluded to as 'the fat German, Dolly Astor', Langdon was five years her senior and considered 'very handsome and fascinating'. He was quick to seize his chance and made a rapid courtship.

Gallatin was alarmed and wrote to Astor that 'he had better send for his daughter to return home since Col. Langdon had every recommendation except wealth, being one of a very large family'. However, Dolly was so infatuated that when she saw trouble brewing she eloped with Langdon. The couple settled in New York, but it was many years before Astor forgave them. Apparently sometime around 1818 he went to a children's party and spotted an attractive little girl who stared at him with large blue eyes. He asked her name and she said 'Sarah Sherbourne Langdon'. Astor laughed and replied: 'For your sake I shall have to forgive your father and mother.' The reconciliation was complete, and when the old man died he left all the Langdons handsome legacies.

Astor's favourite daughter was his youngest child, Eliza, born in 1801. She was a slim, attractive girl who was interested in literature and who liked to write stories. She was said to have inherited her mother's 'benevolence and piety', and when she grew up became a companion to her father, frequently accompanying him on trips. In 1820, when Astor had returned to New York for a brief stay, one of the physicians attending Astor's demented son, John Jacob II, ventured the opinon that the boy might recover his wits if his mind was stimulated by travel. Without more ado Astor took Eliza, his son and a trained nurse to Paris in the winter of 1821. Washington Irving met Eliza there and described her as 'a clever agreeable girl'. Apparently she remained in Paris for well over a year and during this period fell in love with Count Vincent Rumpff, a Swiss gentleman who was acting Minister for the Hanseatic Free Cities to Paris. Perhaps this was the reason why Astor paid $50,000 in 1824 for a charming villa, *Genthod*, on Lake Geneva. During the next two years he spent a good deal of his time here accompanied by Eliza, disproving the critics who claimed that he had no interests apart from making money. He revelled in concerts and theatres and delighted in literary and political talk of which he had no shortage, as writers and statesmen were only too pleased to make the acquaintance of a modern Croesus. Eliza was happy as well for she succeeded in capturing her Count, and was blissfully content. Sadly, she died eight years later to the grief of husband and father.

Astor's second son, the demented John Jacob Astor II, who was so carefully tended that he lived to the age of seventy-eight.

The trip to Paris did not help Astor's unfortunate son, who was sent back to New York within six months of leaving the city. 'He ... is in very bad health,' wrote Washington Irving from France, 'and seems in a state of mental stupor. His situation causes great anxiety and stress to his father and sister, and there appears little prospect of his recovery.'

Astor placed the young man in an institution at Cambridgeport, Massachusetts, where he was cared for by a Mr Chaplin and his wife, Hannah, at a cost of $2000 a year, a huge sum at the time. However, when Mrs Chaplin died in 1828, John Jacob II, now thirty-seven years old, was brought to New York and installed in a large house under the care of Dr O'Donnel. In 1838 Astor gave him even more luxurious quarters, building a house for him at 9th Avenue and 14th Street, surrounded by a garden with a high wall so that he could exercise and not be seen by passers-by. The poor demented man was tended so carefully that he lived to the age of seventy-eight.

When Astor returned from his long sojourn abroad he took up the cudgels of business with renewed vigour. His unpretentious brownstone house at 223 Broadway opened on to a yard leading to a building where both his firms, John Jacob Astor & Sons and the American Fur Company had their offices. The building had an open piazza, supported by pillars and arches, where Astor frequently sat after lunch playing checkers and drinking a glass of beer. After an early lunch he would mount his horse and ride about the island keeping a sharp look-out for property investments. Sometimes he went to the theatre, sometimes he engaged a professional pianist to come to his house and play waltzes to him. His family always gathered round and often his grand-daughter, Emily, sang his favourite song 'Am Rhine Am Rhein' (Which Gives Our Vines Life) and he would join in with his own version of it: 'Which Gives the Sweetest Life'.

The American Fur Company was expanding rapidly. It had invaded the region of the Great Lakes, fought its way across the Rockies and established a powerful monopoly on the Mississippi and Missouri Rivers. Yet Astor's ruthless outlook created a pyramid of scoundrels who not only spread misery and destitution throughout the Indian territories but managed to bring about the ruination of many of the company's own employees.

It is difficult to cite any other company of the period with such a deplorable record of human unhappiness as the American Fur Company. It was the policy of this organization not only to make profits from furs, but from the goods sold to the trader for barter with the Indians. The traders were compelled to pay such enormously high prices that they could scarcely make ends meet, and were forced to practice deceit and fraud on the Indians to stay alive. 'And to cheat them more completely,' wrote William Johnson, the son of a fur trader, 'he brings to his aid ardent Spirit... which has sent more to the grave... than all the wars they have waged with the whites, or among themselves, even sickness and disease added to it.'

Liquor had of course, been freely employed in the past by the British companies in Canada as well as by hundreds of individual traders, but by 1825 the United States was doing its best to stop the use of spirits, and government agents were reporting regularly to Washington. 'He who has the most whiskey generally carries off the most furs,' Colonel Snelling, the commander of the US garrison at Detroit, wrote to the Secretary of War. 'The neighbourhood of the trading houses where whiskey is sold presents a disgusting scene of drunkenness; it is the fruitful source of all our difficulties and of nearly all the murders committed in the Indian country.' 'The traders that occupy the largest and most important space in the Indian country are the agents and *engagés* of the American Fur Trade Company,' reported Andrew Hughes from St Louis. 'They entertain, as I know to be the fact, no sort of respect for our citizens, agents, officers of the Government or its laws or general policy... a clear gain of more than $50,000 has been made this year on the sale of whiskey to the Indians on the River Missouri; the prices are from $25 to $50 a gallon....' This type of complaint was frequently made to the Secretary of State for War; but as the Secretary of State for War was Lewis Cass, the criticisms were ignored.

More often than not, American Fur Company traders who defrauded the Indians stood on the brink of ruin themselves. Frequently they became so indebted to the company for the highly priced goods they were forced to buy that they had no alternative but to mortgage whatever land they owned, and often lost it through foreclosure. Astor was well aware of the traders' plight and states accurately, if not regretfully, that 'all our traders... with very few exceptions have been losing time and money in the trade.' 'You may well ask the question,' wrote one trader, 'why do you continue since you find it a losing business? I will say I do not know what to do else as I am not capable of doing or following any other kind of business.'

Higher up the scale, but scarcely better off than the Indians, were the

French-Canadians who worked as *engagés* doing all the manual work. 'The men who manage the boats,' wrote Johnson, 'are obliged to perform all that is required of them ... to carry the baggage on their backs across the portages ... their labour is very hard for in a few years they are completely broken down, they have to work more like beasts of burden than men. ...' Although the *engagés* were paid only $100 a year, the Fur Company managers refused to allow them any prerequisites except a portion of Indian corn; and they cut their wages from $300 to $250 for three year stints. 'The American Fur Company,' wrote the historian, Hiram Chittenden, 'was thoroughly hated, even by its own servants. Throughout its career it was an object of popular execration as all grasping monopolies are. Many are the stories, largely exaggerated, no doubt, that have come down to us of its hard and cruel ways. Small traders stood no show whatever and most desperate measures were resorted to, to get them out of the way. Many an employee it is said, who had finished his term of service and had started for St Louis with a letter of credit for his pay fell by the way and was reported killed by the Indians. ...'

Nevertheless the company managers were always eager to please their owner and decided to copy the Canadians in distributing medals; but whereas the British decorations portrayed the King, the American Fur Company struck its own medals bearing the head of John Jacob Astor. As for John Jacob Astor in the flesh, he was continuously complaining that his company was in 'a decaying state of poverty', and even petitioned the government for a tax on foreign furs. At the same time, November 1831, his son William Backhouse Astor was writing to the Secretary of War that the company had a capital of $1,000,000 and an annual return of something in the neighbourhood of $500,000. This was a huge turnover and his official biographer reckons that his profits during his seventeen years as head of the company must have been close to two million dollars. Unfortunately the profitability of the company did not make it any more appealing. 'Take the American Fur Company in the aggregate,' wrote Zachary Taylor, an independent trader, 'and they are the greatest scoundrels the world has ever seen.'

Fortunately, the days of this unhappy group of people were numbered. In the summer of 1832 John Jacob Astor again went to Europe, this time to consult his doctors. He remained abroad for over a year and a half complaining of 'bad nerves', and celebrating his seventieth birthday in Paris. When he finally sailed for home his ship ran into a storm in the English Channel which threatened the complete collapse of his nervous system. He offered the captain – a man named De Peyster who had taken one of Astor's ships to China – ten thousand dollars to put him ashore. He guaranteed the payment in writing but it was so illegible no one could read it, and as De Peyster was aware of Astor's sharp practices he refused to budge, and the old man continued to wail the whole way across the Atlantic.

No doubt it was the constant weight of disapproval that finally decided Astor to rid himself of the American Fur Company. The reasons he gave were that beaver was going out of fashion for men's hats, and that sales were falling in Europe due to a widespread belief that furs carried the disease of cholera which was then raging. Whatever the true explanation, in 1834 he sold the American Fur Company and turned his full attention to real estate.

Astor's alarm and despondency on the trip across the Atlantic may have been prophetic. He arrived home to learn that his wife Sarah had just been buried, and that his favourite brother Henry, and his eldest daughter Magdalen, had died a few weeks earlier. 'I called to see Mr Astor yesterday,' wrote Philip Hone in his diary. '... The hand of death has laid heavily on the family during his absence and his spirits are much depressed....' However, as Hone also recorded, the old man had arrived home 'in time to witness the pulling down of the block of houses next to that on which I live – the whole front Barclay to Vesey Street on Broadway – where he is going to erect a New York *palais* [an hotel] which will cost him five or six hundred thousand dollars.... The dust and rubbish,' he complained, 'will be intolerable but the establishment will be ... an ornament to the city and an ornament to its wealthy proprietor.' However, a few days later Hone was wondering if Astor would ever see his fabulous hotel. 'He appears sickly and feeble, and I have some doubt if he will live to see the completion of his splendid edifice.'

Hone underestimated Astor's vitality. The merchant took a keen interest in creating a *de luxe* establishment, mainly because he believed that it would be immensely profitable. When it was finished Astor House consisted of six stories and was described as 'the marvel of the age'. It boasted three hundred rooms and seventeen bathrooms, and was furnished throughout in black walnut, a striking change from the usual mahogany. Every room had its own door key and was equipped with a pitcher and bowl and free soap. Its corridors were carpeted and the walls hung with pictures 'every whit as elegantly furnished as the rooms'. Attendants were always on duty in the lobby to take hats and coats and to brush shoes. When Davy Crocket stayed there he was amazed to hear how much Astor had spent on the hotel. 'Lord help the poor bears and beavers!' he exclaimed, then added philosophically, 'but they must be used to being skun by now.'

The hotel served such exotic dishes as stewed kidneys in champagne sauce, and boasted a superb cellar dominated by sixteen different sherries and twenty different madeiras. British visitors were loud in their praise of American luxury – all except Charles Dickens who was horrified when he walked out of the main entrance to see pigs gobbling up the garbage. The cost of a room was two dollars a day which was thought to be exorbitant. Indeed, the editors of the *New York Herald* decided that people who could afford such prices were worth writing about and inaugurated America's first gossip column, reporting the comings and goings of the Astor House clientele.

The column was an instant success for the guest list included such celebrities as Jenny Lind, William Makepeace Thackeray, the Prince of Wales, Edgar Allan Poe, Abraham Lincoln, Jefferson Davis and Henry Clay. The amount of money people spent there was also a subject of

Opposite Astor House. Built in 1834, it was the most luxurious hotel of its day, and boasted such famous visitors as Jenny Lind, the Prince of Wales, Abraham Lincoln, Edgar Allan Poe and Charles Dickens.

avid curiosity, for Americans were notoriously money-conscious. Indeed, when the sharp-eyed Mrs Trollope, mother of the famous novelist, Anthony, published her book in 1832, *Domestic Manners of the Americans*, she dwelt on this consuming preoccupation. 'I heard an Englishman who had been resident in America, declare that in meeting or in overtaking, in the street or on the road or in the field, at the theatre, the coffee-house or in the house, he had never heard Americans conversing without the word DOLLAR being pronounced among them. Such unity of purpose, such sympathy of feeling can, I believe be found nowhere else except perhaps in an ants' nest.'

However, none of the ants was as successful as John Jacob Astor. Now that his mind was concentrated wholly on real estate he used the last fourteen years of his life to multiply his fortune many times over. During the financial panic of 1837 he was in an impregnable position. He had no debts, plenty of ready cash, and was the owner of a great many mortgages on urban land. 'Here in the city of New York,' wrote Philip Hone, 'trade is stagnant. Local stocks are lower than ever; real estate is unsaleable at any price. The pressure is severe enough upon the owners of houses and stores who are out of debt but if the property is mortgaged and the seven per cent interest must be regularly paid, God help the owners!' During this period Astor gained control of seventy pieces of property by foreclosure.

There was nothing new, of course, about his interest in real estate. From 1800 to 1819 he had invested $700,000 in Manhattan property, and from 1826 to 1834 yet another $400,000. His two most spectacular buys had been the Eden Farm in 1803 that lay between Broadway and the Hudson River in what became the 42nd Street area, and the Cosine Farm in 1809 also running from Broadway to the River near today's 55th Street. But in 1830 his policy underwent a change. Although he continued to buy farmland on the outskirts of the city and wait for the development to catch up, he no longer put the emphasis on trading. In the past he had always advised his son: 'Buy in acres and sell in lots.' Now, instead of *selling* in lots he began to *rent* in lots. During the last fourteen years of his life – from 1834 to 1848 he invested over $800,000 in Manhattan property and during the last eight years – 1840 to 1848 – he took over $1,250,000 in rentals alone.

Later, when people asked him what he considered his best real estate buy, he would chuckle and talk about the Morris estate, which, according to many people, was not a transaction but straight extortion. During the Revolution of 1776 a British major, Roger Morris, fled to England with his wife, Mary. The State confiscated their land in Putnam County and sold it to the farmers who worked on the estate. Apparently Aaron Burr told Astor that Mrs Morris held only a life interest in the land and that when she died the property would become the legal possession of her three children. Astor had no difficulty in persuading the heirs to sell him their rights in the confiscated farm for $100,000: he then waited for Mrs Morris to die, which she declined to do until 1826 when she was ninety-six. Astor marked her demise by sending eviction notices to the seven hundred farmers who, believing that they owned the land, had built their own cottages and barns. When the case was fought in court Daniel Webster and Martin van Beuren pleaded for the State, but Astor won on the grounds that Mary Morris' children were the true owners of the property and had never been dispossessed; indeed they had sold their interests to Astor. However, John Jacob gracefully relinquished his rights when the State offered him compensation in the form of $520,000 in five per cent stock, assuring him of a yearly revenue, *ad infinitum*, of $26,000.

There was no doubt that John Jacob Astor was on to a good thing when he turned his full attention to real estate. Yet in the panic of 1837 many people believed that the market would never recover, and regarded the old man as quite mad to go on plunging his capital into a 'bottomless pit'. 'Could I begin my life again,' he was fond of saying, 'and had I the money to invest, I would buy every foot of land on the Island of Manhattan.'

Washington Irving was installed by John Jacob Astor in his country house at Hellgate so that he could write about the founding of Astoria. This dramatic and horrific story, published in 1836, was an instant 'best-seller'.

In his seventies Astor was famous as America's richest man – no one knew how rich as real estate values were always rising making it impossible to gauge their worth year by year. The notoriety weighed on Astor's mind, and he began to wonder how posterity would judge him. When the well-known American writer, Washington Irving, creator of the immortal Rip Van Winkle and author of tales about the Alhambra, the Moorish palace in Spain, returned to New York, Astor persuaded him to write a history of the ill-starred but splendidly romantic attempt to found Astoria. Astor had known Irving in Paris, and he now installed him at Hellgate, assigned him a suite of rooms, and paid for his assistants. 'Astor,' wrote Irving, 'is doing everything in his power to render our residence with him agreeable, he takes the true way, by leaving us completely masters of ourselves and our time.' *Astoria* was published in 1836 and became a great literary success. More important, John Jacob Astor was depicted as a hero. 'The remarkable form of John Jacob Astor stands out like a statue of granite,' wrote Henry Wadsworth Longfellow: 'a sublime enterprise.' Even in the field of public relations Astor had triumphed, but the picture was not yet complete. He wished to be seen against a family background, simple but appealing. He therefore rid his mind of the picture of his father in a butcher's apron stained with blood, and depicted him in the market, pipe in mouth, basket in hand, selling pretty little woodcocks. His stepmother, rosy-cheeked and smiling stood beside her husband daintily proffering golden eggs. The portraits hung at Hellgate, but after Astor's death his daughter Dorothea was believed to have removed them and they were never seen again.

In his last years Astor craved intellectual companionship and when Irving departed he persuaded the poet, Fitz Green Halleck, and the man of *belles lettres*, Joseph Cogswell, to come and live with him. They both found the millionaire an astonishing character, still counting every penny, yet astute and imaginative and with a sense of humour that suddenly put things right. Once when Astor refused to subscribe to a charitable fund on the grounds that he had no money Halleck said coolly:

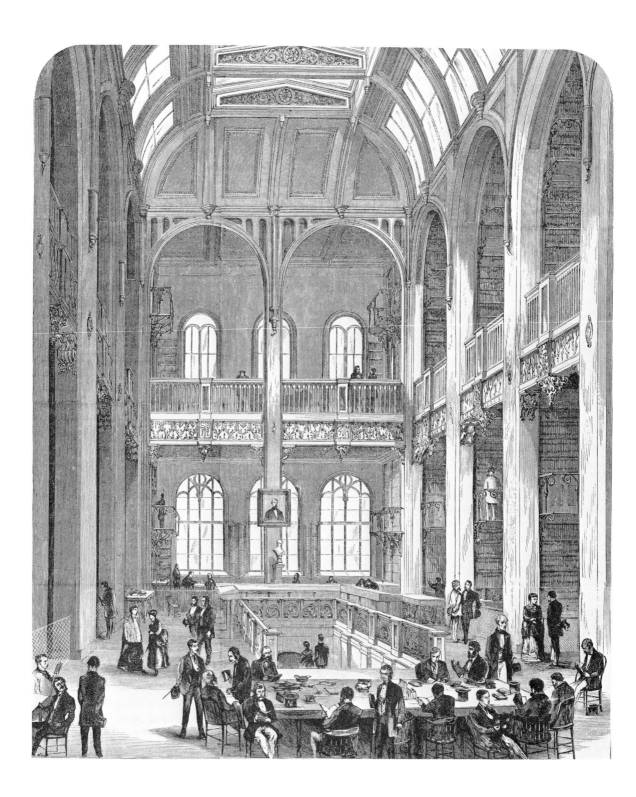

The Astor library, New York's first free public library, which was partly built with the $400,000 bequest from John Jacob's will. It was completed in 1854. From Harper's Weekly, 2 October 1875.

'Mr Astor, if you're out of money, I'll endorse your note for a few hundred dollars'; the old man burst out laughing and signed a cheque.

Cogswell was much closer to Astor than anyone else and genuinely enjoyed his company. 'He is not a mere accumulator of dollars as I thought,' he wrote to a friend the night he met the millionaire, 'He talks well on many subjects and shows a great interest in the arts and literature.' Astor often took excursions with Cogswell by carriage or boat. Once, according to Kenneth Porter, when they stopped at a hotel on the Hudson for a cup of tea Astor pointed to the proprietor and said: 'That man will never succeed?'

'Why not?' asked Cogswell.

'Don't you see,' said Astor in disgust, 'what large lumps of sugar he puts in the sugar bowl?'

Cogswell was passionately eager for Astor to create a public library in New York and did everything in his power to persuade him. At long last he felt he had won the day and happily spent several weeks with an architect drawing up plans for the building. But he had failed to take Astor's full measure for when the old man asked how much the outlay would be in the first year and Cogswell replied, 'About $65,000', Astor pursed his lips and said, 'That will do'. He then took the plans and locked them away in a trunk where they remained until his death.

Astor ordered only one book for the unbuilt Astor Library – Audubon's *Birds of America*, containing over four hundred plates of superb coloured aquatints, one of the great books of the century. The subscription price was $1000, but whenever Audubon asked to be paid Astor fobbed him off with an excuse: 'Ah, M. Audubon, you have come at a bad time; money is very scarce: I have nothing in the bank; I have invested all my funds.' At length, for the sixth time Audubon called upon Astor.... As he was ushered into the presence he found William B. Astor, the son, conversing with his father. No sooner did the rich man see the man of art than he began '... Hard times, M. Audubon – money scarce!' But then, catching an inquiring look from his son he changed his tone.

'However, M. Audubon I suppose we must contrive to let you have some of your money if possible. William,' he added calling to his son who had walked into an adjoining parlour, 'Have we any money at all in the bank?' 'Yes, father,' answered the son, supposing that he was being asked an earnest question, '... we have $220,000 in the Bank of New York, $70,000 in the City Bank, $90,000 in the Merchants, $98,400 in the Mechanics, $83,000....' 'That'll do, that'll do... it seems that William can give you a check for your money.'

In 1844 when Astor was eighty, people used to wait outside his house to catch sight of America's richest citizen. The old man could not resist playing to the gallery and began to attire himself like some medieval prince. The poet, Walt Whitman, remembered seeing him as a child: '... a bent feeble but stoutly built old man, bearded, swathed in rich furs, with a great ermine cap on his head, led and assisted, almost carried down the steps of the high front stoop (a dozen friends and servants, emulous, carefully holding and guiding him) and then lifted and tucked in a gorgeous sleigh, envelop'd in other furs, for a ride. The sleigh was drawn by as fine a team of horses as I ever saw. . . . I remember the spirited champing horses, the driver with his whip, and a fellow driver by his side, for extra prudence. The old man, the subject of so much attention I can almost see now. It was John Jacob Astor.'

The old man clung to life with remarkable tenacity, in the last days of his life even taking his nourishment from a wet nurse. He was finally defeated on 29 March 1848. On that morning a servant opened the door of his house and hung a wreath upon it. The journalists waiting outside pressed forward, and a doctor came out and announced that Mr Astor was dead. Soon the magical invention known as a 'magnetic telegraph' was clicking out the news to Boston, Washington and Chicago. The obituaries appeared on the front page of all American newspapers, in many cases in larger type than that used to describe the flight of Louis Philippe from the throne of France.

Astor's only unexpected bequest was $50,000 to his ancestral town, Walldorf, Germany, for a home for the poor. He kept faith with Joseph Cogswell by leaving $400,000 for an Astor library which became the forerunner of the New York Public Library. But the bulk of his fortune went to his son and heir, William Backhouse Astor. He did not overlook a single member of his large family from daughters to granddaughters, cousins and nephews to half-sisters and even in-laws. Like all true Lutherans he believed in the welfare of his family. 'If any provide not for his own, especially for those of his own home, he has denied the faith and is worse than an infidel.' Although John Jacob had destroyed the Indians, bled the traders white, exacted the last penny from his tenants, he required no prompting when it came to those connected to him by blood, even by marriage.

Not every voice was complimentary. The *New York Herald* cried out that of Astor's fortune, 'ten millions at least belong to the people of the city of New York', arguing that it had accrued to Astor not by his own exertions but 'by the industry of the community'. Horace Mann of Boston, however, objected to the Will, not the fortune, and was even more savage in his denunciation, describing the departed millionaire as 'the most notorious, the most wealthy, and, considering his vast means, the most miserly of his class in the country'. 'Nothing,' he continued, 'but absolute insanity can be pleaded in paliation of the conduct of a man who was worth nearly or quite twenty million of dollars but gave only some half million . . . of it for any public object. If men of such vast means will not benefit the world by their *example* while they live we have a right to . . . use them as a *warning* after they are dead.'

3   *The obedient heir*

BUSINESS OFFICE OF THE LATE WILLIAM B. ASTOR, NO. 85
PRINCE STREET, BETWEEN BROADWAY AND MERCER STREET.

Previous page *The imposing Astor Estate Office which in fact had only two rooms – one in which William Backhouse sat; the other for his oldest son John Jacob.*

'William will never make money,' John Jacob Astor said of his son and heir, 'but he will never lose any either.' There was little reason for William Backhouse Astor to enlarge the family fortune, for when he was fifty-six years old he stepped into his father's shoes as America's richest man. He had been extremely well-off for many years since his Uncle Henry had left William a cool million in cash.

The recipient of all this bounty was singularly unattractive with 'a decided German look, a countenance blank, eyes small and contracted, a nose much too large' and a frame that was both awkward and top-heavy. And as he had not a spark of vivacity he produced a mournful effect. 'He was sombre and solitary,' continued his contemporary, Matthew Smith, '... mixed little with general society, gave little and abhorred beggars.'

John Jacob was very fond of this dutiful son who counted his money and never made trouble. William was justly famous for the frugality which had been instilled in him since childhood and although he was not a man of imagination he grasped the understanding that profits could be made from reducing expenditure. As a result he always went about brandishing a pruning knife, particularly when he studied the company accounts or checked the company bills. Indeed, soon after John Jacob's death he decided to review the household expenditure for which he himself was responsible, and was dismayed to find what large sums were being spent on his imbecile elder brother, John Jacob II, now fifty-seven years old.

The latter was living in the spacious house which his father had built especially for him, with a fully qualified physician as a companion receiving a salary of $5000 a year. William thought this sum so large that he encouraged the doctor to hand in his notice, confident that his vacant-eyed brother would not notice his absence. But when John Jacob went about the house calling for his companion and receiving no answer, he guessed what had happened. He went into a rage, smashing mirrors and throwing furniture out of the window. Then he flung himself on his bed sobbing. William went after the doctor and begged him to return, but the latter refused. 'I'm not coming back,' he said, 'I'm a free man for the first time in years.' In the end William persuaded him to change his mind, but he was forced to raise his salary to $10,000 a year. As John Jacob II lived to the age of seventy-eight, the doctor's retirement, when at last it came, was extremely comfortable.

William and his blue-blooded wife, Margaret, lived in a house at Lafayette Place, about half a mile below the juncture of Broadway and the Bowery. William had built the house in 1824 when many of the surrounding streets were unpaved, and people drove there to take country walks through bowered lanes, and to sip lemonade at an open air café. Lafayette Place was a wide, tree-shaded cul-de-sac opening onto Art Street, later renamed Astor Place in his father's honour. On the west side was a superb row of colonnaded residences. On the east side William erected a splendid red-brick residence with stables facing the Bowery. Despite his parsimony, William understood *noblesse oblige* and, encouraged by his wife, spared no expense to maintain the family status.

Indeed, when his sister, Dorothea Langdon, built a mock Florentine house faced in granite next to her brother's, the two mansions were so imposing that people said it took a thousand candles to light them. On Sunday afternoons crowds of sightseers made expeditions to Lafayette Place to marvel at the grandeur of America's millionaire families.

Apart from the size of his house, William indulged in few luxuries. He loathed social gatherings and at night preferred to stay at home reading by the fire. Margaret was dutiful and uninteresting. Although as a girl she had pretty curls and a good complexion which inspired William to call her 'Peachy', by middle age the hair had lost its colour and the skin its bloom, leaving nothing to distract attention from the thin mouth and long nose. However, she almost always got her way. She had a staff of five or six servants, and insisted that they wear livery as it was 'cleaner and neater than anything else'. She even engaged a valet for William Backhouse but the servant was deeply frustrated by his failure to improve his master's appearance and finally left to take a job at the White House with President van Beuren.

Margaret also persuaded William to look for a house in the country where the children could spend weekends and holidays. The place she wanted was the house her father had built on the Hudson, near Rhinebeck, about eighty miles from Manhattan. General Armstrong was finding it difficult to make ends meet yet could not bear to part with his estate. He had named the farm *La Bergerie* because Napoleon Bonaparte, hoping to make an impression on Armstrong when he was Minister in Paris, had urged him to raise sheep there, and had even sent him a flock of merinos. William stepped forward and solved the General's problems. Although he bought the property and paid the bills he insisted that Armstrong continue to make it his home. Margaret renamed the house Rokeby after a poem by Sir Walter Scott; but as her family grew, the house became too small, and William added a wing with a tower overlooking the Hudson.

The Astor family consisted of six children, three of whom were boys. William's eldest son, John Jacob Astor III, pleased his parents by marrying Charlotte Augusta Gibbes of South Carolina. Although the bride's family was not rich, she had the right connections. Her father, Thomas Gibbes, was one of the founders of the Union Club. The wedding took place in 1847 and Philip Hone, that man about town, described the ceremony as 'a good wedding . . . attended by all the fashionable people of the city'.

Six years later, in 1853, the second son, William Backhouse Jr, made an even more impressive match by marrying Caroline Schermerhorn, whose Dutch ancestors had come to America in the early-seventeenth century. In many ways it was an unlikely liaison as Caroline loved the bright lights of the city and the social round that went with them, while William was only happy in the country. The ball that Caroline's sister-in-law, Mrs Schermerhorn, gave in 1854 probably strengthened William's resolve never to have anything to do with fashionable society.

Mrs William Schermerhorn lived next door to the Astors in Lafayette Place. She sent out six hundred invitations to a fancy dress party,

ordering her guests to appear in French court costume of the period of
Louis xv. Apparently this decree spread panic among the gentlemen as
beards and whiskers were then in high fashion, yet it was well known that
in Louis xv's day all facial hair was forbidden. What to do? A deputation called on Mrs Schermerhorn to find out how literally her decree
was to be followed, and returned with the dispiriting news that gentlemen could retain either beards or moustaches but not both. Luckily, when
the despondency was at its most acute, someone came forward with the
happy news that the King's musketeers had been allowed to wear as
much hair on their face as they deemed necessary to frighten the enemy.

Needless to say, most of the gentlemen, including William B. Jr,
appeared that night as musketeers. The ladies, however, outdid themselves in magnificent costumes, some of which were rumoured to cost
$30,000. Although the evening was a great social occasion, it was far
from exhilarating, and poor William stood first on one leg then on the
other wondering how to escape. The boredom was accentuated because
Mrs Schermerhorn, not satisfied with reproducing the court clothes of
Louis xv, suddenly decided to reproduce the court dances of Napoleon iii.
As this Emperor and his lovely consort, Eugénie, had recently forbidden
the lively polka because it smacked of the immoral 'can-can', Mrs
Schermerhorn followed the imperial lead and announced a German
cotillion. Unfortunately this dance took two hours to perform and was
exquisitely dull to watch; and young William vowed then and there that
New York would not see him for many a day. Soon after this, he bought
1200 acres of farm land near Rhinebeck where he spent most of the year.

No one talked much about old William B.'s third son, Henry.
Although the famly did not like to admit it, Henry bordered on lunacy.
'He was not insane,' a relation insisted, 'just a little queer.' William Sr
built him a little home at Rokeby, but in 1871 when Henry suddenly
married the gardener's daughter, Malvina Dinehart, a handsome, pink-
cheeked maiden of twenty-seven, the Astors were indignant. 'Nothing
but a peasant,' said William B., who seemed to have forgotten his father's
origins. He cut Henry's inheritance to a paltry $30,000, but Henry did
not appear to mind. 'Money counts for little in this world,' he said,
'compared with love and life.' Apparently this remark alone convinced
the family that he was more deficient than they had imagined.

However, Henry was far from destitute. His grandfather had left him
a quarter share of the Eden farm, that nicely-placed land between 40th
and 42nd Streets running from Broadway to the Hudson, and the
annual rentals were mounting dramatically. He therefore was well able
to buy a 200-acre farm at Copake, in the Berkshires, where he and his
wife settled in a rambling Victorian house. Here he built his own private
race track, and impulsively paved one of the rooms in his manor in silver
dollars.

Henry had a wild red beard and drank heavily; and as he was six feet
tall and very powerful, people moved out of his way when he flew into
one of is very frequent rages. Sometimes, when he was drunk, he would
put on a surplice and preach a sermon in an empty room, striking a bell
with a crowbar to emphasize a point. On one occasion he lost control

of himself and struck the four-year-old daughter of his sister-in-law, Mrs Ash. Despite the family connection, the Ashes sued for $20,000. The jury found in favour of Mrs Ash and William B. paid the bill. Not unsurprisingly, the latter then gave control of Henry's property to John Jacob, who managed the estate so well that when Henry died at the age of eighty-eight, unmourned and unsung, his property was sold at auction for $5,000,000.

Of the three boys, John Jacob was the only one on whom old William B. could rely. He had a business relationship with this son patterned after his own understanding with his father. But now he was the general and John Jacob III the chief of staff. Every day William left his house at Lafayette Place promptly at 9.30 a.m. and walked to the Astor Estate Office at 85 Prince Street. Despite the imposing name, the premises consisted of only two rooms: one where John Jacob worked flanked by three clerks; the other a large, sparsely furnished expanse where William sat in solitary splendour behind a long desk. Although there was no secretary

William Backhouse Astor inherited money both from his father and his uncle, and at the age of fifty-six became America's richest man. Although he was noted for his meanness, his wife insisted on his employing a valet, something which most Americans regarded as 'European nonsense'.

to ward off unwanted callers, William himself was so cold and taciturn that most people preferred to communicate with him by letter. 'I would walk into his office and he would look up without speaking,' wrote a businessman. 'He would look at me but ask no questions. It was up to me to tell him what I was there for.' Once Astor had a visitor who was not prepared to make the running. He was a poor parson, a former classmate of William Astor, who simply called on him for old time's sake. Apparently William did not recognize him, looked coolly across his desk and asked: 'Can I do anything for you?' The parson stared back thoughtfully. 'No sir,' he said, picking up his umbrella and bowing himself out of the room.

The exact part played by the first John Jacob Astor and William Backhouse in the development of the family real estate policy will never be known because each generation burnt the private papers of his predecessor. All Astors had such a fear of newspaper publicity they could not bear to preserve anything in writing. When Astor *père* died in 1848 William B. destroyed fifteen packing cases filled with old documents and when William B. died in 1875 John Jacob III himself confined his father's letters to a bonfire. The first John Jacob's real estate policy underwent a drastic change in the 1820s. Did William B. play a part in influencing him? Or had the old man, who returned from a long trip to Europe in 1826, studied the English leasehold system and taken a leaf out of the Duke of Westminster's book? Whatever the answer, at that time the family founder no longer treated urban property as a commodity to be bought or sold, no longer even granted leases of forty or fifty years. By the end of the 1820s a twenty-one-year lease had become standard Astor policy.

Most of these leases, of course, did not mature until after old John Jacob's death, when William B. was in charge of the company. All tenants erected their own houses and were responsible for their own repairs and their own taxes. Occasionally the agreement stipulated that when the lease expired the building would be valued by an impartial body and the landlord would give compensation. More often the fine print read that compensation would take the form of an extension of the lease at a reasonable rent, perhaps for a further ten years. But sometimes it specified that the tenant had the right to 'remove' his building if he did so within ten days of the expiration of the lease. One wonders if the suggestion was in the least feasible as the work of pulling down a building and carting away bricks and mortar must have cost nearly as much as selling the debris for scrap. However, the majority of tenants were not confronted by these problems, for three quarters of the leases offered no terminal advantage. The building lots were cheap to rent but at the end of the twenty-one years the houses erected on Astor land became Astor property.

Under such favourable conditions it is not surprising that William B. loved the Astor Estate Office and spent hours brooding over projected maps of Manhattan. Throughout the 1850s men were working feverishly, building and paving new streets to meet the demands of a fast-growing population that was already over half a million. The rumble of omnibuses and the clatter of hackney carriages echoed through all the big avenues, but Broadway still remained the showpiece of the city. The gaping holes about which travellers had complained thirty years earlier had been filled in to accommodate the traffic, and private houses were surrendering every day to the demand of shops and hotels. 'The mania for converting Broadway into a street of shops,' wrote Philip Hone in 1850, 'is greater than ever. There is scarcely a block in the whole extent of this fine street of which some part is not in a state of transmutation.' Indeed the relentless floodtide of people and vehicles made Broadway so difficult to cross that a fashionable hatter petitioned the city for the right to build an iron footbridge over the avenue to protect his customers.

William B. viewed the growth of Broadway with deep satisfaction as the Astor Estate owned a great deal of property on the thoroughfare, including the famous Astor House Hotel which stretched from one cross-street to another. But Broadway was not the only avenue that was growing. Everywhere in Manhattan there was bustle and movement and expansion, as the city moved up the island. Indeed, William's most sensational purchase – a buy that equalled his father's acquisition of the Eden farm – was the $25,000 he paid for the Thompson farm, then on the outskirts of Manhattan, but now between 32nd and 34th Streets. He presented his daughter-in-law, Caroline Astor, with a piece of this land and in 1859 she moved from Lafayette Place to a new house at 5th Avenue and 34th Street, a neighbourhood where the rich were edging out the poor, but which still abounded in shanties and rubbish-filled lots. William's other daughter-in-law, Charlotte Augusta Astor, thought it such a daring move that she followed suit, and soon the John Jacob IIIs and the William B. Jrs were installed in large, ornate, red-brick mansions, side by side with a garden between, covering the whole block from 33rd to 34th Street.

Old William B. had no desire for a fine house. He hated spending money and although he allowed his wife to cover the dining-room sideboard with gold plate and dress the servants in livery, he refused all luxuries for himself. Most rich men delighted in carriages and fine horses but William walked everywhere, never wasted money on wine, and scanned and revised the smallest items of expenditure. In the office he spent hours studying his rent rolls and jotting down in the margin higher assessments to keep pace with rising values. 'He knew every inch of real estate that stood in his name,' wrote a contemporary, 'every bond, contract and lease. He knew what was due when the leases expired and attended personally to the matter.' He also knew how to exact high rentals for choice positions. For instance, he often allowed his corner plots to lie derelict until the centre of the block was developed. Matthew Smith wrote: 'In the upper part of New York, hundreds of lots can be seen enclosed by dissipated fences, disfigured by rocks and waste material or occupied as truck gardens.... They are eligibly located, many of them surrounded by fashionable population as [Astor] knows that no parties can improve the centre of a block without benefiting the corners.'

At his desk, William B. carefully perused city plans and pondered the effect that changes would have on his possessions. Every street was divided into hundreds of neat little building plots like a mosaic fresco of ancient times. This parcelling out of urban land, inch by inch, was not an Astor conception. In 1811 the Street Commissioners of New York City had plotted Manhattan all the way from Greenwich Village to Harlem, still open country, into a gridiron of streets and avenues. The avenues numbered about a dozen and ran from south to north, intersected by several hundred narrow streets numbered chronologically and running from river to river. The streets were so close together that they produced long thin blocks which, in turn, were divided into long thin building plots measuring twenty-five feet by one hundred.

These strips of land were in great demand in the 1850s for the building of tenement houses. The population explosion began in 1848 with the potato famine in Ireland which sent a first wave of 300,000 immigrants across the seas to New York, almost swamping the local population of 500,000. In the 1850s immigrants from Central Europe began to pour into the metropolis – Germans from Bohemia, Jews from Prague and Warsaw. The best sort of building that could be erected on one of these narrow building lots went back no more than fifty feet, allowing another fifty feet for a garden that gave light and air. Yet as the population grew and costs mounted there was no room for gardens – or so the speculators said – and bricks and mortar spread over every inch of space. The only windows were front and back. The long interiors shared common walls with next-door houses and were plunged into permanent

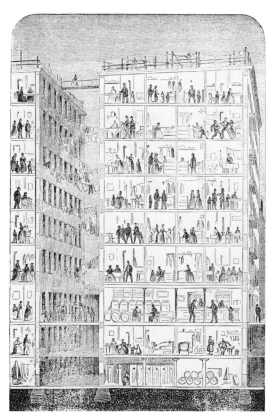

In the 1850s the population explosion in New York led to the construction of tenement houses, and these multiplied rapidly up and down the lower part of the city. Dark, airless and overcrowded, they – and landlords such as William Backhouse – were heavily criticized.

darkness save for an occasional dim light from an overshadowed skylight.

Tenement houses were highly profitable for the entrepreneur despite the fact that he had to pay to erect his building, and the whole property reverted to the owner at the end of twenty-one years. The mathematics were simple: a thousand families housed in a block at a rental of $10 a family per annum came to $10,000 a year – twice as much as a hundred families paying $50 a year. And as the building only cost seven or eight thousand dollars to construct and the landowners only charged a ground rent of a few hundreds a year, it was possible for the entrepreneur to get his money back in the first twelve months.

Unfortunately the sub-landlord often saw the project as an opportunity to amass life savings and, as a current report pointed out, was absolutely ruthless in his 'inflictions and exhortations'. Nevertheless tenement houses began to multiply rapidly up and down the lower stretches of the city below 14th Street. No laws regulated their height or depth or darkness. They were fire traps and their lack of sanitation sent hundreds into city hospitals. The State Legislature appointed an investigation committee which attacked 'landlordism as the wickedest exploiter of the poor'. 'The halls and doorways of tenement houses usually are filthy and dark, and the walls and bannisters foul and damp, while the floors are not infrequently used as toilets for lack of other provisions. The dwelling rooms are usually very inadequate ... and many of the sleeping rooms are simply closets, without light or ventilation save the means of a single door,' runs the 'Report of the Metropolitan Board of Health for 1866'. At the same time the *New York Times* pointed out that 'the tenement houses on Second and Third Avenue owned by the Astors are estimated to pay 50 per cent annually'. It went on to lament that 'the man of wealth lives on the poison of the poor', and reflected on the proposition that the owners did not know how their properties were being used. 'The agents let and underlet and hand the proceeds to the landlords. Still with a humane man even ignorance is no excuse. He should know.'

William B. did not choose to know. He had no intention of involving himself in New York's social problems. He was a business man, not a reformer, and that is what he intended to remain. The city was not so much hundreds of thousands of people as tens of thousands of lets, all neatly laid out in his plot book, each with an appraised value, a rental, a tax rating. Good tenants paid their rents promptly; bad tenants broke his windows, fouled his premises, and sometimes walked out in the dead of night and disappeared. He did not believe that the slums created derelict citizens, but that derelict citizens created the slums. If John Jacob Astor, an immigrant, could triumph in America, so could the German and Irish immigrants now flooding into the country.

William B. was not in the least naive. Just as his father had done before him, he knew the importance of remaining on close terms with the politicians who ran Manhattan. That was far more important than wasting time in arguments with radical critics. William, therefore took infinite pains in making friends with the Democratic mayor, Fernando

A photograph of the Democratic mayor, Fernando Wood, in later life. Wood was careful to exact support and money for favours rendered from landlords such as Astor, Roosevelt and Vanderbilt.

Wood. This handsome, debonair man with the sweeping black moustache had grasped control of that tight little band of thieving officials known as 'Tammany Hall'. Fernando was always careful to play both sides of a game, and not only joined hands with bankers and landlords but excited the crowds by his golden oratory which consisted of passionate denunciations of the intolerable conditions of the poor.

Fernando Wood always rewarded those who supported him, and in 1850 he gave Astor the block between 12th and 13th Streets that was under water, for a mere pittance. It was a gift that eventually came to be worth millions. At that time Manhattan Island was marked by ponds, streams and marshes; and when an individual received a 'water grant' it meant land under water, which he had the right to fill in and make solid land. The city's excuse for selling these rights for next to nothing was that the authorities were short of cash and it was advantageous to have private landlords spending their own money in adding to the mainland. Wood, of course, had not invented this particular form of bribery. The first Astor had received valuable water grants in 1806 and 1810. But Wood eclipsed his predecessors by scattering his largesse, until it included half a dozen lesser landlords such as Goelet and Rhinelander, Roosevelt and Vanderbilt.

Wood quite naturally exacted tribute for his bounty. In fact he took thousands of dollars from Astor by property settlements which never appeared on the books. 'Year after year,' wrote an early biographer, James Parton, 'Astor saw a gang of thieves in the City Hall stealing his revenues under the name of taxes and assessments but he never led the assault upon them nor gave the aid he ought to those who did.'

It is no mystery why William B. remained aloof from the struggle. In 1855 he did not lift a finger to aid the Republicans who were doing their best to remove Wood on grounds of corruption. No doubt he felt he had chosen the right side as Fernando was too clever for his opponents. He held a large, open-air meeting at which, to the astonishment of the belligerents, a whole galaxy of eminent men walked on to his platform led by William Backhouse Astor. This impressive backing was so effective in silencing his critics that when the same reformers lifted their heads again the following year, and tried to beat him in the primaries, he adopted the same trick. This time he drew up a document asserting that he, Fernando Wood, was a man of rare executive ability and unquestionable honesty; and he persuaded a dozen distinguished citizens to put their signatures to it. All were men who relied on city patronage: merchants who sold goods to the municipality; bankers who held city funds in their vaults; landlords whose ground taxes were fixed by City Hall. Once again the signatories were headed by William Backhouse Astor and once again Fernando Wood triumphed. Indeed, Wood eventually went to Washington as a duly elected member of Congress.

Overleaf At the ball given for the Prince of Wales at the Academy of Music, the ladies' costumes were 'recklessly magnificent'. Only diamonds were permitted to be worn and these were in such profusion that the 'floor and the galleries sparkled like dew-laden banks of flowers in bright sunlight'. This picture from Harper's Weekly *of 20 October 1860 shows the Prince, in the centre, opening the ball by dancing with the wife of the Governor of New York.*

No matter how close to the wind William Backhouse sailed, no criticism assailed the name of his eldest son and heir, John Jacob Astor III. John was too rich and too well born, the very personification of the American dream. From his mother he inherited the blue blood of Livingstones

John Jacob Astor III, William Backhouse's eldest son and heir. He opposed his father's Democratic ideas by supporting the Republican candidate of 1860, Abraham Lincoln.

and Armstrongs, from his father the promise of millions beyond the dreams of ordinary man. He was snobbish and conceited, and at times incredibly pompous. Whenever he had to fill out a form that asked for 'occupation', he always wrote, in a flowing script, 'Gentleman'.

When the Prince of Wales, the future Edward VII, visited America in October 1860, accompanied by the Duke of Newcastle, young Astor with his haughty stare and superior smile was one of a committee of five who arranged a ball in his honour. At first the elderly gentlemen of New York decided to give his Royal Highness a banquet, but the nineteen-year-old Prince was so disappointed at being denied an opportunity to meet girls of his own age that the plan was quickly changed to suit him. When a deputation arrived at his hotel to escort him to the Academy of Music where the ball was taking place, they found 'Bertie' trying to squeeze his large hand into a white kid glove. 'These gloves,' he whispered to one of his hosts, 'were given to me by a lady in this house with the request that I wear them tonight. I don't

A photograph of the Prince of Wales taken when he visited New York in 1860. The young John Jacob Astor was one of the committee of five who arranged the ball in his honour at the Academy of Music.

know where or who she is. They are much too small for me but I intend to work my hand into them if I can.'

Later the poet, Edward Stedman, wrote:

> It was even said that his great delight
> Established etiquette scorning
> But – once escaped from Newcastle's sight –
> To go home with the girls in the morning.

The Prince did not go home with the girls in the morning, but there was a rumour that before his visit came to an end he managed to escape Newcastle's vigilant eye and to disport himself at New York's most famous brothel.

However, while 100,000 people lined Broadway to cheer the Prince of Wales, crowds gathered in other cities for a very different reason. A momentous election campaign was drawing to a close which looked as though it might settle the fate of the Union. Fundamentally the struggle lay between the cotton-growing South whose shipments to Britain accounted for nearly half of America's exports, and the industrial ambitions of the North; between a land-holding, slave-owning aristocracy favouring unrestricted trade with Europe and a free-labour capitalist society crying for protective tariffs to prevent cheap foreign goods from undercutting their manufactures. As the verbal battle developed, other issues such as state rights, constitutionalism and the introduction of slavery into territories not yet states, became subjects of increasing, and eventually frenzied, importance.

For once, John Jacob Astor III opposed his father and supported the Republican candidate, Abraham Lincoln. Old William B. clung to the Democrats – and Mayor Fernando Wood, who favoured slavery – arguing that if the South broke away, the rich merchants of the North would not be able to ship cotton to Europe, New York would be plunged into a depression and property values would fall. Wood made the startling suggestion that Manhattan should strike out on its own and declare independence. William did not commit himself to this novel idea but backed the senator from Kentucky who, in May 1860, proposed writing slavery into the constitution as the only way to avoid a conflict. 'I firmly believe that the slave-holding South is now the controlling power,' declared Senator Hammond of South Carolina. '... Cotton, rice, tobacco and naval stores command the world ... the North without us would be a motherless calf, bleating about and die of mange and starvation.' Apparently Astor agreed with these contentions for he gave thousands of dollars to the anti-Republican candidates.

When Abraham Lincoln won the election, however, old William became a staunch supporter of the Union. Almost at once the eleven Southern states declared their independence and formed a Confederacy. In April 1861 the Southern troops demanded the surrender of Fort Sumpter in the harbour of Charleston and when the commander refused, fired upon it. The Civil War had begun. Forty-year-old John Jacob Astor III bought himself a uniform and hurried to Washington where he reported to army headquarters and was immediately given the rank

Right *When the Civil War broke out, John Jacob rushed to enlist and was assigned to the staff of Major-General George McClellan. Here McClellan is pictured discussing tactics with Abraham Lincoln on the field of battle.*

Left *Abraham Lincoln's first inauguration at the White House on 4 March 1860. After the election William Backhouse Astor changed his allegiance and became a staunch supporter of Lincoln and the Union.*

of colonel. At the same time, his wife Augusta defied her South Carolina background and began raising a regiment of coloured troops to fight for the North.

John Jacob was assigned to the staff of Major General George McClellan, commander of the army of the Potomac, along with two illustrious foreigners, the Comte de Paris and the Duc de Chartres. Every ship, ferryboat, schooner, barge and tugboat was being requisitioned to carry McClellan's army down the Potomac; the General, therefore, appointed Astor his aide-de-camp and put him in charge of transport. 'So that I always know,' he explained, 'the exact condition of the transports and their locality.' It never crossed Astor's mind, or anyone else's for that matter, that he would be expected to live at army headquarters when there was a luxurious alternative at hand. So he rented a house in Washington equipped with chef, steward and valet and waited for orders. At last the great day came when McClellan and his army moved down the Potomac to a debarkation point between the James and York rivers.

Everyone had high hopes of McClellan – 'Little Mac, the young Napoleon'. After achieving a spectacular initial success in western Virginia, he had been summoned back to Washington to try and instill some discipline into the mob that had fled at Bull Run. His instructions were 'to turn out a force capable of defeating General Lee's army in Virginia'. This should not have been a difficult assignment as the eleven states of the Confederacy with its six million white citizens faced twenty-three Union states with a population nearly four times as large.

McClellan decided to attack at Yorktown, then move on to Richmond. Unfortunately he was too slow in mounting his offensive and the enemy withdrew in the night. When Mac approached Richmond he again delayed too long, allowing General Lee to launch an offensive which resulted in a bloody retreat for the army of the Potomac. McClellan was recalled to Washington with a shattered reputation and relieved of his command. John Jacob followed suit and handed in his own resignation in July 1862 after only eight months service. Later, he looked back nostalgically to his days in a colonel's uniform. 'These,' he declared mournfully, 'have been the only exciting days of my life.' Although Astor saw very little warfare, once when he made a tour of inspection he unexpectedly came under fire. A fellow officer was deeply impressed by his cool nerve. 'I am only a poor soldier with nothing but my sword,' he said, 'but if I had been the heir to the Astor fortune and estate, I would have run away, if I had been hanged for it.'

It soon became apparent that many more people, with or without fortune, also felt like opting out. When the Draft Act was introduced in 1863 there were riots in New York that brought the city to the brink of civil war – this time not for secession or slavery but the straightforward issue of poor versus rich. The trouble arose because only the poor were compelled to fight as it was perfectly legal for the well-to-do to buy their way out of the draft for $300.

This gave the socialist agitators a splendid opportunity to make trouble. In *Incredible New York* Lloyd Morris describes the New York slum-dwellers as 'packed 290,000 to the square mile in a density more choking than Bombay or Canton and they listened eagerly to flaming tribunes ... who cried that if they must fight let them fight against their oppressors, the capitalists'. The mob obeyed the agitators and for three days held off the police while they set fire to draft offices, gutted newspaper premises and lynched negroes simply because the colour of their skins was symbolic of the hated war. Armed with paving blocks and stolen rifles they fought against hastily mobilized volunteers and killed hundreds of them. Only when seasoned federal troops arrived was order at last restored. Hundreds of thousands of dollars worth of damage had been done, and although no one knew exactly the number of casualties, it was said that a thousand people had perished.

William Backhouse Jr, the second son of William Backhouse, preferred his yacht and the farm at Rhinebeck to real estate and New York.

William B. was known as 'a mole-capitalist', a man who, according to Harvey O'Connell, 'burrowed his way undramatically through land to more wealth without benefit of newspaper headlines, showy splendour or outward political pomp. He never went near Wall Street or Newport; his name was connected with no great or novel enterprise; he refused to pontificate for the press.... It was said of him that he sat in his office as though it were a house of detention to which his father had condemned him for life.'

Although William cared nothing for friendship he was a kind if uncommunicative man as far as his large family was concerned. The children grew up during the 1820s and 1830s when old John Jacob was still alive. Apart from his three sons – John Jacob III his trusted lieutenant, William Jr who preferred his yacht to the real estate office, and Henry 'the queer one' – William had four daughters, the youngest of whom died in infancy. Alida married a dull Englishman, John Carey, who came to America in search of a fortune and found it in his Astor bride, while Laura married Franklin Delano of Massachusetts and achieved fame as the aunt of Sarah Delano who became the wife of a Roosevelt and the mother of a United States president.

William's favourite daughter, however, was the eldest, Emily, the gayest shoot of the Astor tree and a favourite of old John Jacob I who loved to sing *Am Rhein* with her. They lived the subdued sort of family life that their father favoured, and Emily pleased her parents by marrying young Sam Ward, the son of a banker, who had travelled and studied in Europe and had a taste for literature and the arts. Although this young blade was the antithesis of William B., the latter presented them with a fine house on Bond Street and the groom's sister wrote that the wedding was 'the most cheerful I ever saw'.

Emily died in 1841 when her daughter, Margaret, was only two. Sam, however, was not a man to mourn for long and eventually married a fascinating lady, Medora Grymes. The Astors – the Founder and obedient William B. – exploded with wrath, for Sam had done the unpardonable: he had given the house which they had settled on Emily to his new wife. 'An untoward event had just happened in the family which has stirred his ire,' wrote a cousin, Henry Brevoort. 'Master Sam W. has married Miss Medora Grymes and settled upon her *his* house in Bond Street, which house has been purchased, and previously given or settled upon his first wife, but by our laws became his after her decease. The affair sticks deep into the old gentleman's gizzard. He views it as a sort of outwitting and overreaching in the art of bargaining ... and resentment of the As is, I think, carried beyond all bounds.' Indeed Sam Ward's sister was visiting the William B.'s at Rokeby when word of Sam's engagement to Medora broke upon the Astors. And William, his face black with rage, commanded the butler: 'Order the carriage for Miss Ward at once!'

Apart from this dramatic incident William B.'s life was amazingly uneventful. His only trip to Europe, once his university days came to a close, was in 1857 when he was forty years old. He wrote to his Gottingen teacher, the now famous Baron von Bunsen, who was thrilled to think that America's richest man would soon be calling upon him. 'I have for many years wished for a renewal of our old acquaintance. I had bestowed such love upon him, and he had considered and acknowledged me as his guide. He now writes with real friendship. I shall answer him as soon as I am again at Heidelberg – using "*du*" as of old.' Yet the meeting was disappointing as Bunsen had hoped for an 'interchange of thought and opinion' and there was nothing but a rather stiff exchange of pleasantries, after which William pointed out that since he was touring with his wife he would have to be on his way.

As the 1860s drew to a close, old William B. retired to his country estate at Rokeby and left the management of the Astor property to John Jacob. But before this happened he had several tiresome matters to settle. In 1865, when the Civil War ended, William was outraged to receive an income tax demand. As he had the largest income in the country, said to be in the region of $1,300,000, he received the nation's largest assessment. This was not what angered Astor. He was incensed that although peace had been established the war-imposed emergency tax was retained. He put the matter in the hands of his lawyer, Charles Southmayd, a crusty old gentleman who had no wife, no family, no sport, no amusement, in fact no other interest apart from the law. He was precise and unsmiling, old beyond his years, 'the most conservative man I ever knew', as someone described him, but he had a sixth sense – the sense of property – which was invaluable to Astor. Southmayd wrote a brilliant brief that finally went to the Supreme Court; the Astor Estate won the case on the grounds that the income tax was unconstitutional. This gave the family another forty-eight years of untrammelled money-piling for it was not until 1913 that direct taxation became a legal method by which the government could raise funds.

John Jacob III had his hands full when his father retired in 1866 since by this time there were very few neighbourhoods in Manhattan entirely devoid of Astor-owned houses. In 1871 he moved his office from Princes Street to West 26th Street, a stone's throw from Madison Square and only a few blocks from his 5th Avenue mansion. Behind a simple bronze plaque saying 'Astor Estate' were quiet dignified rooms where agents in round-cut jackets and derby hats slipped in and out, while a small group of clerks, chosen for their neat, flowing handwriting, filled in reports and accounts.

Here, in these ledgers and plot books, was the record of the largest real estate operation in the New World. The Estate owned every sort of building from tenements to warehouses, from offices and hotels to brownstone dwellings. Astor property could be found on Avenue A (renamed York Avenue) and all the Avenues from 1st to 11th; on the numbered streets, east and west, from 3rd Street through 20th; from 25th to 30th; from 32nd to 39th; 40th to 56th; from 74th to 79th; from 90th to 96th; 107th, 117th, 125th, 129th, 130th, 150th, 185th. And on forty-six named streets and avenues from Amsterdam and Barclay and Barrow to Elizabeth, Greene and Hudson, from King and Liberty and Madison to Park, Pearl, Wall and Washington.

The Estate was involved in many new ventures, including the launching of large office buildings. John Jacob III completed some of these plans during the years 1870 to 1890, others were carried out later by his son Waldorf and his nephew, another John Jacob. They included the Astor Building at Pine and Wall; the Schermerhorn Building at Broadway, Pine and Wall; Exchange Court at Broadway; New and Exchange Place; the Guarantee and Indemnity; Oriole Building and the Rogers Peet Building at Prince and Broadway. North of Broadway and 42nd Street the Astors had created one thousand brownstone houses, while the 'radish patch' which the Founder had bought for only $20,000 on the lower East Side, was solid with six-story tenements built by the Estate itself. 'So from the tenements of the poor, the brownstones of the middle class, the palaces of the rich, the buildings for finance and trade and the Old Astor House poured revenues that would have flattered any half-dozen English dukes,' wrote Harvey O'Connell. 'By the 1880s probably as much as $5,000,000 a year was being taken in at the Astor Estate office, more than half to the account of John Jacob III, a third or so to negligent William and the rest to nourish the collateral branches.'

Opposite Over half of the $5m dollar income of the Astor Estate came from slum property. The conditions in which most of the tenants lived prompted the State Legislature in 1867 to pass the first tenement law in New York's history.

A Boarder's Cellar.

Interior of the Court.

The Home of Five Men.

Children of the Neighborhood.

Entrance of the Alley.

And of the five million dollars, over half came from slum property. Tenements were cheap to build and cheap to run; and as only a small capital investment was required, an important factor in assessing profitability in a world with no income tax, they were a tempting investment. They were built with four apartments on each floor, but the only rooms with direct light were on the street, and the only ventilation came from the stairway passage, which stank of cooking smells.

In 1867 the State Legislature decided that American citizens were entitled to God's sun and air and passed the first tenement law in New York's history. No one could erect a building more than sixty feet long on a hundred foot lot. Contractors' and landlords' lobbies descended on the city authorities in a fury. It was not fair to the working man, they argued, to deprive him of a place to live. Land prices were soaring, immigration mounting, the city simply could not afford to leave forty per cent of every building lot vacant. In the end the Legislature lamely agreed to allow the Board of Health discretionary powers to modify the dictum; and as the Board of Health was amenable to financial pressure, the new law was more or less void. The *New York Times* singled out John Jacob III for attack. 'He loses no opportunity of raising rents, never repairs a street if he can help himself and takes good care to do less for his tenants than any Landlord in the city.' 'An ideal landlord,' countered the *New York Herald*. 'His tenants believe that there was never a more just or reasonably liberal owner, with such well kept properties.'

The Astor lawyers worked all the year round to protect the Estate against rapacious contractors and politicians, not to mention the ruinous threat of new-fangled inventions. There was endless talk about rapid transit. An influential group put forward the idea of the Arcade Railway, an underground street twenty feet below the surface of Broadway with side walks and gas lamps and fine shops, and of course, railway tracks for a steam engine. However, when it neared the shovel stage, Astor's legal injunctions stopped the digging. Charles Southmayd insisted that the franchise was 'unconstitutional' as it clearly was impossible to run a railway 'without smoke, gas or cylinders'. The Croton Water Board joined the opposition on the grounds that it would interfere with the city's water mains. So in the end rapid ransit went skyward, and elevated railways were built. They started at the Battery, ran along 6th Avenue to Central Park, and along 3rd and 9th Avenues. Astor's injunction had put an end to subway talk for the rest of the century.

The Astors could not always rely on the law courts to protect them, and John Jacob III, like his father and grandfather before him, was astute enough to see the advantage of keeping in well with Tammany Hall. The truth was that he did not object to corruption when he was the beneficiary – although the word corruption was not a term that New York landlords ever applied to themselves.

Despite this immaculate approach, at the end of the 1860s John Jacob was on good terms with the most notoriously crooked politician of the century, Boss Tweed, who had risen from the slums to wrest control of the city from Mayor Fernando Wood. As soon as Tweed was undisputed master, the landowners applied for water grants. In December 1865 William Rhinelander was presented with under-water rights from 91st to 94th Street, East River, and in 1867 Peter Goelet received East River land between 81st and 82nd Streets. That same year Mrs Laura Delano, William B.'s daughter, was given a grant from 55th to 57th Streets, Hudson River, at $200 a running foot, while John Jacob Astor was granted under-water land between 49th and 51st Street, Hudson River, for the trivial sum of $75 a running foot. However, the storm of public criticism that arose over these grants (which critics called straight bribery) so frightened the city officials who were up to their necks in huge thefts that many of the grants – including those of the Astors – were never issued.

Tweed had set up his own 'ring' consisting of Peter Sweeney who served as his chief of staff, Mayor Oakley, Governor Hoffman and, most important of all, Richard (Slippery Dick) Connolly, Controller of the City Treasury. The plundering began in 1868 and was done on such a scale that the *New York Times* was stung into a long, running battle. The County Court House, which should have cost $250,000 to build, was finally completed after an expenditure of $12,000,000. It was the most costly public building in the United States though far less ostentatious than the Capitol at Washington. The ring told contractors precisely what they must charge and how much money must be returned as a 'kick-back'. A plumber received $5000 to install three basins, an electrician $8000 for wiring a single room, while the simplest chairs averaged $450 each. When the newspapers complained indignantly, the Burglar, as Tweed was called, merely smiled and began building himself a mansion on 5th Avenue as grand as the Astor houses. The public liked the affable Tweed. Forty-seven years old, heavily-bearded and a man of enormous bulk, Lloyd Morris describes how 'his eyes glittered as coldly as the huge diamond adorning his shirt front, but his ruddy face wore a jovial expression'.

However, as the election of 1870 approached, Tweed decided to answer the newspaper attack by taking a leaf out of Fernando Wood's book. He invited John Jacob Astor III to head a committee of six to examine Controller Connolly's accounts. It was astonishing that Astor should agree to lend his name to this 'cover-up' operation. No doubt he weighed the pros and cons and came to the conclusion that it would not be wise to run foul of Tweed. And, like his father before him, John Jacob reported that everything was in order. 'We have come to the conclusion and certify that the financial affairs of this city under the charge of the Controller are administered on a correct and faithful account.' The statement was signed by Astor and all five of the committee members.

The *New York Times* was furious. Yet the editor had no proof of corruption and could only declare: 'These gentlemen are large owners of property. They wish to stand well with the city. It is important, or they think it is, that their assessments should be as low as possible.... They have made themselves parties to a great fraud and if we are not mistaken they will live long enough to regret it.'

The words proved prophetic. In the summer of 1871 a disgruntled member of Boss Tweed's ring stole Controller Connolly's books and deposited them with the *Times*. Triumphantly the newspaper made revelations, one more shocking than another, over a period of several weeks. For instance, it published in facsimile details showing that, on one day alone, the ring had stolen $14,000,000. A member of Astor's committee, Marshall Roberts, broke down and admitted that the certificate he had signed 'was used as a cover and a shield for those who were robbing the city' and blamed himself for having 'fallen into the trap'. However, it was not until 1877 that Mr Taintor, the auditor employed to examine Connolly's books, estimated the theft at $50,000,000. Connolly fled abroad with $6,000,000 but Boss Tweed went to prison where he died.

The haughty John Jacob Astor III never offered the slightest apology for the part he had played, remaining as suave and unruffled as usual, and still smiling his superior smile. However, one of John's second cousins, Charles Astor Bristed, felt compelled to intervene and defend the family name. Unfortunately the arguments he used were more contemptible than convincing. The rich, he said, 'are prone to belong to the *parti de l'ordre* as a Frenchman would say – in other words to acquiesce to the party in power. – They say to themselves: "It is true these are terrible scoundrels. We would give a great deal to see them all hung ... but the public won't back us and what can we do by ourselves?..." Every man must make the best terms he can for himself.'

When William Backhouse Astor died in 1875 at the age of eighty-three, the family fortune had more than doubled. He left $1,000,000 to each of his surviving daughters, a paltry $30,000 to Henry who had married 'the peasant', and divided the rest of his fortune equally between his two sons. Although wills were not made public in those days, he is believed to have left John Jacob III and William B. Jr over $20,000,000 each. Nevertheless J.J. was richer than his brother because his grandfather had assigned him one half of the Eden Farm as opposed to William and Henry's quarter shares; and the Farm, north of 42nd Street and west of Broadway, was becoming almost as valuable as a gold mine. Old William made his eldest son's position clear as head of the family by bequeathing him crown and sceptre in the form of the Founder's portrait and French plate.

Like the family Founder, William Backhouse believed first and foremost in kith and kin, so the sum total of his philanthropies totalled only $500,000, most of which went to the Astor Library to which he had already given $400,000. Although the majority of American newspapers praised 'the landlord of New York' for his hard work and unpretentious appearance, the *Express* jeered at 'a millionaire's mite' and Appleton's *Journal* insisted that 'the people of New York had a right to expect a noble and handsome bequest to the City'. Even the London *Spectator* felt impelled to enter the arena with a series of rather fatuous observations. 'There is in the career of Mr Astor ... a want of greatness,' it began, ending lamely with the plaintive assertion that 'living in such a country with such a family history he ought to have been more original.'

4   *The mystic rose*

Charlotte Augusta Gibbes of Carolina married John Jacob Astor III in 1847, and within a year gave birth to William Waldorf Astor.

'People seem to be going quite wild and inviting all sorts of people to their receptions,' complained young Mrs William Astor. 'I don't know what has happened to our tastes.'

Never had a city boasted so many millionaires as New York in the 1870s. Not only was America one nation, indivisible, but it was one nation eager to be developed and enriched. The post-war boom brought into Manhattan a flood of new money and a flood of new people. Thousands moved up from the defeated south and thousands more from the middle west to seek fame and fortune in a metropolis that was fast becoming a financial capital. By 1875 the population of New York exceeded one and a half million, producing scores of ebullient tycoons with money to burn.

Everyone wanted to be part and parcel of society; but what exactly was this mystical fraternity? No one foresaw that Caroline Schermerhorn Astor, John Jacob's sister-in-law, would soon grasp the sceptre and not only define society but would tyrannize over it for years. Nevertheless people regarded William Backhouse's two sons – John Jacob III and William B. Jr – as the very epitome of grandeur. Yet it would be difficult to find two brothers more unalike, one of them delighting in the *haut monde* and the other disliking everything connected with fashionable life.

J.J. was tall, thin, conceited and not very clever, while William B. was big, burly, intelligent, feckless and inclined to drink too much. J.J. worked at the Astor Estate Office while William spent most of his time at Ferncliffe, the magnificent estate he had bought near Rhinebeck on the Hudson and where he spent his time developing park and farms, racing stables and conservatories. He was charming and superbly ineffective, unable it seemed to pursue any aim, even pleasure, with concentration. After graduating from Columbia near the top of his class he travelled through Turkey and Greece and went to Egypt where he journeyed further up the Nile than any other tourist had ever done. Some people said that his life had been blighted by his father who always gave brother John Jacob precedence over him. He was not encouraged to work in the family business because John was there; and when he raised a country regiment to fight in the Civil War, his father forbade him to take part because he was unwilling to risk two sons and John had already joined McClellan's staff.

William's marriage to Caroline Schermerhorn, a big-boned, plain-featured girl with a mass of black, wavy hair, came as a surprise. For such an unconventional man to find himself mixed up with a lady who adored society and bubbled with self-confidence, struck people as very odd for she was the antithesis of her suitor. No doubt this was what William liked. Caroline had positive ideas on almost everything, particularly on how life should be organized, and he was only too happy to leave the details in her capable and diplomatic hands. Obviously she had married unambitious William Backhouse for his money and not because she loved him, for she did not complain when he retired to the country, shaking his head over the inadequacies of city life. She was thankful that he did not insist on her company, and always praised him extravagantly in his absence. William not only spent a good deal of time following his horses on the race-track but every winter cruised to Florida in his yacht the *Ambassadress*. Each year they spent a few months together, and William professed to be fond of his children. However, he was disappointed that at the end of ten years Caroline had produced only four daughters. She refused to admit defeat and in 1864 gave birth to a son whom she named John Jacob IV.

Charlotte Augusta Gibbes, the wife of John Jacob Astor III, on the other hand, produced a boy within a year of her marriage. She named him William Waldorf and he proved to be her only child. As he was sixteen years old when his cousin, J.J. IV, was born, there was not much to draw the two families together save for Charlotte Augusta's warmth and gaiety. Of all the Astor women she was the most generous, independent and likeable. She was on the board of several hospitals and gave time and money to the Children's Aid Society. Every summer she sent hundreds of poor boys out of New York to work on farms in the middle west. And during the Civil War she had answered critics who reminded her that she was a daughter of South Carolina by raising and equipping a regiment of coloured soldiers to fight for the North. 'When you look at this flag,' she said as she presented their colours to them in New York, 'remember that it is an emblem of love and honour from the daughters of this metropolis.'

If Charlotte Augusta had been born fifty years later she would have been the leader of café society. Nimble-witted and imaginative, she liked the company of writers and artists, and did not hesitate to rebel against unfair decisions. She was so indignant when she learned that Edwin Booth was ostracized for being the brother of Abraham Lincoln's assassin that she invited him to dinner and seated him on her right. Although actresses were barred from ballrooms, she held a reception for Madame Ristori, the celebrated Italian tragedienne. Some of her innovations were less successful. She introduced literary teas on Mondays, pretentiously named *causéries de lundi*, to which forty society matrons were bidden on the understanding that they would be prepared to read a poem or a story written by themselves. This venture proved to be a flash in the pan, for each week fewer people attended until there was no one left either to recite or to listen.

It would be wrong, however, to depict Augusta as a blue-stocking, for she had a frivolous side as well and loved balls and jewels and fine apparel. When her husband bought her a palace at Newport she gave a ball every year, and Harvey O'Connell describes how she always appeared wearing $300,000 worth of diamonds 'which hung from her ears, ringed her wrists and fingers, clustered around her throat, fell to her bosom, belted her waist and crowned her hair in a blazing tiara....'

Nevertheless it was odd that Charlotte Augusta should have married the conventional John Jacob, while the conventional Caroline, the member of a well-to-do Dutch colonial family, married the defiant William B. Jr who abhorred the trappings of high society. And perhaps it was even more odd that although the two brothers had nothing in common and disliked each other intensely, the two sisters-in-law, despite the difference in their characters, were devoted to each other. Charlotte Augusta watched Caroline's attempts to dragoon society with warm-hearted amusement; and Caroline returned the affection by christening her third daughter Charlotte Augusta – a name which, thirty years later, would scandalize the whole of America.

The two ladies were gregarious and liked entertaining but Caroline took exception to the fact that newcomers of whom she had never heard sometimes wrote to her asking to be included in her invitations. According to Mr Willis, the editor of the *Home Journal*, social success was simply a question of following the right pattern. People with money who took the trouble to live in the right place and do the right things found no problem in entering the citadel. They must, he explained, 'keep carriages, live above Bleeker [a landmark near the Battery], subscribe to the opera, go to Grace Church, have a town house and a country house, give balls and parties'. This made them 'fashionable folk' and fashionable folk automatically belonged to society.

This sweeping assertion, as sophisticated people knew, was a blatant misrepresentation. In Europe the leading families had risen by royal favour or feudal service and were plentiful enough to dominate the trickle of newcomers. But in America it was more the other way around. The old 'colonial' families could not muster more than a few hundred people whereas the hordes of *nouveaux riches* thrown up by the new age of railways and trade, steel and stock manipulation, threatened to be both overwhelming and decisive. What, indeed, was one to do with this embarrassing plethora of millionaires who, at the insistence of wives and daughters, were pounding menacingly at the portals of polite society?

Caroline Astor reflected the outlook of the Old Guard when she drew the line at adventurers like old Commodore Vanderbilt who had begun his career as a Staten Island ferryman. After the discovery of gold in California, Vanderbilt built a railway from Manhattan to the west. By 1852 he had accumulated $1,000,000. However, his excessive interest in female company together with his bluff manners did not endear him to the snobbish 'Faubourg St Germain' group – as the colonial families liked to term themselves – so, just to exasperate his detractors, the Commodore impishly built the world's largest steam yacht, the *North Star* – a ship of such overwhelming luxury that even the Tsar of Russia felt chagrined. But this masterpiece was not enough to melt the hearts of social New York, so the Commodore lived in splendid isolation in Washington Square, ostracized, but merrily unrepentant and, of course, surrounded by ladies.

Another ostracized, and far less happy, millionaire was A. T. Stewart whose fabulous department store was one of the show places of Manhattan. He was ignored because, 'in England, you know, people look down on "tradesmen".' Stewart was the world's most successful merchant and, next to William Backhouse, the largest landowner in New York. He built himself the grandest and most costly residence in the city – a vast white marble mansion on 5th Avenue, only a stone's throw from the two Astor houses, and here he lived, unmarried, lonely, in magnificent drawing rooms where no one ever called to see him.

Ward McAllister as depicted in Town Topics *of 11 January 1894. His promotion campaign made Caroline Astor the undisputed Queen of New York society.*

Other *nouveaux riches* newcomers succeeded in wangling invitations to respectable houses and even in gaining admission to the best clubs, much to Mrs Astor's displeasure. She was upset by the stories she heard, for some of these people were guilty of unpardonable crimes. At dinner one hostess served the wrong sorbet with the wrong flavour; another gave two consecutive brown sauces; still another imported a *troupe* from the Opera Bouffe to entertain the party and allowed them to dance the vulgar can-can.

Although the Astor name was synonymous with riches, John Jacob maintained, irksomely, that birth and breeding were more important than money. Indeed, he became so critical of the newcomers being admitted to the Union Club that he led a revolt which resulted in the foundation of a far more impregnable bastion, the Knickerbocker. John Jacob's sister-in-law, Caroline, shared his concern. In 1871 she was planning to bring out her daughters and was determined to prevent them from meeting the wrong people.

And at this providential moment, when her anxiety was paramount, forty-four-year-old Ward McAllister swam into her ken. McAllister was a well-known but impecunious southerner from Savannah, Georgia, grandson of a Supreme Court Justice and a cousin of the dashing Sam Ward who had married the elder sister of the two Astor brothers, Emily, who had died many years before. Although Ward McAllister was a qualified lawyer he never practised, preferring instead to devote his time to the niceties of society. When his lawyer father went to San Francisco in 1849 to entrench himself with the gold rush speculators, Ward was given the task of entertaining the firm's business friends. He was said to have done well, but he must have overlooked a number of prospective clients for his motto was: 'Only invite nice people.'

Ward McAllister disliked hard work and was fascinated by society. He was married to a dim, well bred woman who had a little money and he decided to make a Grand Tour of Europe to study the membership and manners of the fashionable world. Although his trip strikes one as remarkably uninspired, apparently he regarded it as a great success. In Windsor he did not manage to catch a glimpse of Queen Victoria, but had dinner with her chef who opened a door in the castle and allowed him to take a peep at the Queen's table set for dinner. In Italy he made friends with the Grand Duke of Tuscany's English physician and by engaging the latter's professional services managed to secure invitations to the Duke's fortnightly balls at the Pitti Palace. Then he travelled to France where he settled down for the winter at Pau. Here he set to work studying the national cuisine and perfecting his knowledge of the great wines.

When he returned to America he was determined to carve out a position of power for himself as a social arbiter. He bought a small place at the new resort, Newport, and soon demonstrated his aesthetic sense. When he was making arrangements for an afternoon reception, he looked out of the window at his empty fields and suddenly decided that they were unbearably mournful with no livestock on them. So he rented animals from the neighbouring farm for the day – 'an entire flock of

Southdown sheep, and two yoke of cattle, and several cows'. These parties were so successful that later he boasted: 'I map it out as a general would a battle, omitting nothing, not even a salt spoon, see to it that I have men on the road to direct my party to the farm.'

People liked Ward McAllister's flair and by the 1860s he had become a person of considerable importance in New York. He organized a series of 'Cotillion Dinners' at Delmonico's expensive new restaurant at 5th Avenue and 14th Street. The guest list, by subscription, was limited to one hundred people, which apparently made them an instant success. The Earl of Rosebery, a former British Prime Minister, appeared at one of these functions. He had been given canvas-back duck five nights running. 'You Americans!' he protested to McAllister. 'You Americans have made a mistake. Your emblematic bird should have been a canvas-back, not an eagle.'

Ward McAllister did not meet Mrs William Astor until 1872 when, as he tells us in his memoirs, this 'great personnage ... had daughters to introduce into society, which brought her prominently forward and caused her at once to take a leading position. She possessed great administrative power and it was soon put to good use and felt by society. I then for the first time was brought into contact with this *grande dame* and at once recognized her ability, and felt that she would become society's leader, and that she was admirably qualified for the position.'

Mrs Astor had the money and the organizing ability: but Ward McAllister had the ideas. He believed that New York should take a leaf from Almack's Club, that tight little London coterie of a bygone day whose ladies had arranged balls to which only the leading families were invited. McAllister had often insisted that it took four generations to make a gentleman, but now in the midst of the Astors, he put aside that observation and stressed instead the importance of money 'in vast quantities'. 'A fortune of only a million is respectable poverty,' he pronounced. And he went onto advise his readers not to waste their time on a man who relies 'solely on pedigree ... who has the aspirations of a duke and the fortune of a footman'.

After daily discussions with three leading clubmen, McAllister organized a Ball Committee of twenty-five patriarchs who would have the right to invite five gentlemen and four ladies to every party; and this, of course, gave them 'the right to create and lead society'. This small Olympian band included the two Astor brothers – John Jacob and William; two Astor collaterals; a Schermerhorn and two Schermerhorn relations; a Jones, a Rutherfurd, a Goodhue, a van Rensselaer, a King, a Phelps and, of course, Ward McAllister, 'We wanted the money power,' he explained, 'but not in any way to be controlled by it.' Although he did not spell it out, the control was to lie in the hands of the American Queen and her first minister.

The patriarchal balls were subscription balls, yet the fact that they were small and select made them an instant success. 'You could ... see at a glance that they embraced not only the smart set, but the old Knickerbocker families as well,' wrote McAllister. 'Applications to be made Patriarchs poured in from all sides; every influence was brought

The ball given every January by Caroline Astor. Caroline receives her guests in the centre, dressed in black. To her right is her daughter Mrs Orme Wilson, and talking to the gentleman on the left is her sister-in-law, Charlotte Augusta, the wife of John Jacob Astor III.

to bear to secure a place in this little band and the pressures were so
great that we feared the struggle would be too fierce and engender too
much rancor and bad feeling, and that this might of itself destroy them.'
However, McAllister saved the situation by suggesting another series of
parties called the Family Circle Dancing Class to which the disgruntled
could be invited and pacified.

The subscription parties, however, were only a rehearsal or, as
someone put it, 'a weeding-out pace for the greatest social event in
history, the party that broke more hearts than any other event before or
since – Mrs Astor's Ball'. Life could have no more bitter mortification,
wrote Elizabeth Drexel, one of the fortunate ladies who attended the
parties, than not to receive the slip of cardboard: 'Mrs Astor requests
the pleasure ...' 'There remained only one course open to them – to
hide the shameful truth from their friends,' continued Elizabeth.
'Doctors were kept busy during the week of the ball recommending
hurried trips to the Adirondacks for the health of perfectly healthy
patients, maiden aunts and grandmothers living in remote towns were
ruthlessly killed off to provide alibis for their relations ... any and every
excuse was resorted to.'

The ball was always held on either the first or second Monday in
January at her home, 350 5th Avenue: and as the great ballroom could
not accommodate more than four hundred people, the guest list did not
exceed that number. However, Ward McAllister felt it derogatory to
admit that the Queen was obliged to consider such mundane limitations
as floor space, so he told the press: 'Why, there are only about four
hundred people in fashionable New York society. If you go outside that
number you strike people who are either not at ease in a ballroom or else
make other people not at ease.'

Fastidious exclusion seemed to have a magical effect and Mrs Astor's
fiat was accepted as final throughout the country. Those who were
bidden to the ball were members of society; those who were excluded
were not. 'Elected to supremacy,' wrote Lloyd Morris, 'she became the
Mystic Rose about whom the greater and lesser saints revolved in their
fixed orbits.... She transformed society into a secular religion. You
could well say of her, as Henry Adams later said of the Virgin of Chartres
that, without the conviction of her personal presence, men would not
have been inspired....'

On the night Mrs Astor's house at 5th Avenue and 34th Street blazed
with lights and all the magnificent rooms were banked with hothouse
flowers. Servants in blue livery, copied line for line from the livery worn
at Windsor Castle, relieved the guests of their wraps and directed them
through a wide hall into one of the three connecting rooms where their
hostess awaited them.

Mrs Astor usually received alone, standing in front of a portrait of
herself painted by Carolus Duran. Although she was a large woman with
a plain face, her dignity was so imposing, her jewellery so spectacular,
that she gave an impression of awe-inspiring grandeur. Magnificently
gowned by Worth, she usually wore a satin skirt embroidered with
pearls, and a bodice and train of dark velvet. In those days a lady was

The painting of Caroline
Schermerhorn, Mrs William
Backhouse Astor, by Carolus
Duran, before which she usually
received her guests at her annual
patriarchal balls.

expected to display her good fortune and Mrs Astor glittered with so many diamonds that she resembled – as Harry Lehr once put it – a walking chandelier. On her black pompadour hair, later covered by an even blacker wig, rested a diamond tiara adorned with diamond stars, around her throat lay a triple necklace of diamonds, at her breast the famous diamond brooch known as Marie Antoinette's 'stomacher', and from her corsage a spray of diamonds that flashed like fireworks.

Mrs Astor greeted her guests with queenly graciousness, after which they went to the large art gallery which served as a ballroom. Although the pictures were not greatly admired they were costly and plentiful – 'the spoils of civilization' as Henry James put it. At one end of the room, which ran the length of the house, was a priceless, porcelain mantle-piece, at the other a statue of Psyche collected by the absent William on one of his journeys abroad. In a small balcony, banked with orchids, Lander's orchestra in Astor-blue uniforms, played its expensive music while the four-hundred Chosen Ones greeted each other as though they had not met most nights of the season. However, this night had a magic of its own. The focal point of the gallery was a divan half-way down the room, against the wall, known as Mrs Astor's 'throne'. Later, from this vantage point, surrounded by a few friends whom she wished to honour, the hostess would watch the intricate figures of the cotillion being danced. The fact that there was only space for a handful of ladies to sit with the queen made this honour so exclusive that it was passionately desired. Guests spent the whole year trying to establish themselves in her special favour, and when their hopes were unfulfilled some of them lost all control. At one party, Mrs John Drexel was so mortified at not being invited to the throne that she walked through the whole gallery sobbing loudly. How could anyone explain to this lady that she was so massive she occupied seats for two and thus made her presence quite impossible?

The ball was only one of the entertainments dispensed by Mrs Astor. On Mondays and Fridays she attended the opera at the Academy of Music on 14th Street. This auditorium was deplorably deficient in boxes – not even enough to accommodate the patriarchs – and the wives of millionaires anxious to be seen there because Mrs Astor made this evening fashionable, were said to offer as much as $30,000 for a box. Mrs Astor was not particularly partial to music for she never arrived before the end of the first act, and sometimes left soon after the second inter-mission. On these nights she moved on to Delmonico's where all sorts of gaieties were taking place, including the Patriarch's Ball and The Family Circle Dancing Class. On other days she entertained at home giving innumerable receptions and teas, but the weekly dinner party was the most sacred of her rites. The table was illuminated by golden candelabra and decorated with hundreds of *Gloire de Paris* roses; a gold service was used, unique in America, and said to be worth over $75,000. A superb French chef presented the gargantuan repast. Emily Astor's one-time husband, Sam Ward, was the most famous gourmet in New York, and his menus were studied with care. The most surprising fact about these dinners is that they took only three hours to consume.

MENU OF A DINNER GIVEN BY SAM WARD

Little neck clams

Montracher

Potage tortue verte à l'Anglaise

Potage crême d'artichaut

Amontillado

Whitebait

Filets de bass, sauce crevettes

Rauenthaler

Concombres

Timbales à la Milanaise

Filet de boeuf au madère

Pommery sec

Selle d'agneau de Central Park, sauce menthe

Moet & Chandon Grand Cremant Imperial Magnums

Petits pois, Tomates farcies, Pommes croquettes

Côtelettes de ris de veau à la Parisienne

Cèpes à la Bordelaise

Asperge froide en mayonnaise

Sorbet au Marasquin

Pluvier rôti au cresson

Château Margot

Salade de laitue

Fromages varies

Old Madeira Charleston and Savannah

Bombe de glace

Fraises

Pêches

Gâteaux

Raisins de serre

Café

Cognac & Liqueurs

Mrs Astor was not an unkind woman. She was loved by her children and admired by the small group to whom she gave her friendship. If, as Frank Crowninshield once claimed, she was 'the most portentous force ever to influence American society' she was also the most determined force ever to apply her mind to it. She embraced her mission in life with an almost mystical fervour. Her aim was to *preserve* society by saving it from the hands of the barbarians – after all, society represented the best elements of the nation, did it not?

Yet her ascendancy was not maintained by accident. The truth was that her parties were more luxurious, more attractive, better arranged, than anyone else's. Even *Town Topics*, which preferred criticism to praise, went into raptures over one of her Newport balls.

When Mrs William Astor turns on the entertainment faucet the opalescence is sure to be dazzling. The experienced lady has a way of invariably beating the last comer in all social competitive exercises. Her ball last Monday night was an improvement upon every similar function of the season and she stands in her pride today the embodiment of the great Newport idea – pleasure at any price.... Mrs William Astor is by this time a professional ball-giver and we are as much entitled to expect a fine affair at her hands as we are a worthy stage production at the hands of Henry Irving. The Monday night ball was entirely Astoresque. You cannot go much beyond that in the way of praise.

Quite apart from her expertise, Caroline Astor possessed a priceless asset: a total lack of maliciousness. Always dignified, always reserved, a little aloof, explained Elizabeth Drexel, 'she gave friendship but never intimacy. She never confided. No one ever knew what thoughts passed behind the calm repose of her face. She had so cultivated the art of never looking at the things she did not wish to see, never listening to words she did not wish to hear, that it had become second nature to her.' She met the jeers of her detractors and the tears of rejected social aspirants with the stoicism of a martyr. No one could persuade her to recognize the Harrimans or the Goulds and people said that J.P. Morgan and John D. Rockefeller preserved their dignity by never trying for her favour.

As for her absent husband, Mrs Astor had nothing but loving concern. 'Dear William,' she would murmur, 'he has been so good to me. I have been so fortunate in my marriage.' William meanwhile, was flitting from luxurious Ferncliffe to an unknown destination in Minnesota where

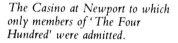

The Casino at Newport to which only members of ' The Four Hundred' were admitted.

he indulged in long bouts of heavy drinking; and from there to Jacksonville, Florida, where he also indulged in long bouts of heavy drinking but with the added pleasure of living on his yacht and entertaining the local people. He founded the Florida Yacht Club and became its first Commodore. Indeed, he gave so much pleasure that the Governor, in an effort to make him a permanent fixture, invited him to join his staff. William declined, but donated a large sum of money to finance a state military expedition. Apparently the object was to root out hostile Indians who were said to be hiding in the Everglades; but nothing was ever heard of these desperate characters who finally were dismissed as mythical.

The Governor tried again, giving Astor a grant of 80,000 acres near Jacksonville, but William's interests remained sea-bound. He sold the *Ambassadress* and bought the largest steam yacht in the world which he named *Nourmahal* 'Light of the Harem'. When people tried to find out from Caroline Astor what her husband was doing, she never lost her composure. 'Oh he is having a delightful cruise. The sea air is so good for William. So sad that I am such a poor sailor,' she would add, 'for I should so much enjoy accompanying him.'

If William Astor disliked New York he found the newly-created Newport even more tedious. Here his wife entertained at her marble palace, Beechwood, ridiculously referred to as 'a cottage' while her brother-in-law and sister, John Jacob Astor III and Charlotte Augusta, offered hospitality only a stone's throw away at Beaulieu, a copy of a great French château.

The same faces at the same extravagant balls, sometimes costing as much as $200,000, whiled away the time. Ward offered a welcome change with his picnics, known as *fêtes champêtres* while the Horseshoe Piazza at the Casino, and the Clambake Club were novelties in themselves. But the most serious occupation, at least for the ladies, was the fashion parade every afternoon at three o'clock. When the *haute monde* rolled down Bellevue Avenue in strict order of precedence – no carriage would dare to pass another carriage of superior rank – the towns-folk lined the streets to stare at the extravagant display of feminine attire.

Different dresses for every occasion, eighty or ninety in a season, worn once or twice and put aside [wrote Elizabeth Drexel]. How they swished and rustled!... Parasols to match every dress, enormous flopping feathered hats assorted to every costume. White gloves to the elbow, three or four new pairs every day, priceless lace ruffles at throat and wrist, yards of lace flouncing on underskirts, thousands of dollars worth dragged over the Casino terrace.

Although their clothes came from Paris they did not follow the French fashion, at its height under Napoleon III, of dressing their dolls in priceless lace and encasing their tiny feet in shoes made by the great Parisian bootmakers.

Not only Mrs Astor but society women in general were expected to fight a rearguard action to prevent newcomers from crashing into the sacred circle. 'A few women,' observed a society reporter, 'seem to head the concourse like sheep and there is a most riotous struggle of getting in and keeping others out.' There was no way for unsuccessful

This photograph illustrates very clearly the problem at Newport – the shortage of men! John Jacob Astor IV is the gentleman sporting the white trousers.

aspirants to hide defeat, for outsiders were not permitted to bathe at Bailey's Beach, to berth their yachts at Hasards, to join the reading room, or the Casino Club. Their thoroughbreds might carry off the prizes at the Horse Show, but not a single society leader would be at home when their wives called.

Those who belonged, however, considered Newport a delicious summer spot. The greatest drawback was the shortage of menfolk, as husbands were so busy making money in New York they were seldom present. However, even this insoluble problem melted away when the United States Navy opened a war college and torpedo station at Newport in 1880. Ward McAllister tried to take the credit by insisting that he had suggested the idea to the government.

Although William Astor was one of those who never appeared in Newport, he frequently made unexpected visits to New York. When his eldest daughter, Emily, announced her engagement to James Van Alen, son of the general who had commanded the Van Alen Cavalry during the Civil War, William was furious. He loathed the 'exquisite' personality of General Van Alen who fancied himself as a great beau, always kissing ladies' hands, a gardenia in his button-hole. 'Damned if I want my family mixed up with the Van Alens,' said William belligerently. Unfortunately the comment was carried back to the soldier who promptly challenged his deprecator to a duel.

William was horrified at the thought of risking his life, particularly over a Van Alen. Nevertheless he was obliged to appoint a second. The latter was thrilled by the drama and spent hours with his opposite number discussing weapons and rules of procedure. But after consulting the code of honour, William decided that Van Alen had no right to satisfaction. His second at last grasped the fact that the duel had been abandoned, and realized that if he did not extract Astor from the controversy a scandal might develop. He therefore persuaded William to retract his statement in a written apology. The general was pleased, Astor settled $400,000 on his daughter's betrothal to Van Alen and even agreed to attend the wedding. However, the day after the ceremony he left for Florida for a much-needed recuperation.

Meanwhile the vigilant Mrs Astor was hard at work. With the skill of an expert politician she beat off constant attempts to undermine her authority. Appraised of the local gossip by Ward McAllister, she was quick to discipline members of the Old Guard who criticized her behind her back. She simply forgot to send them invitations; then, when she felt that the necessary rebuke had been effective, she re-bestowed her goodwill without comment. McAllister credited her with 'a great power of analysis', and insisted that she understood the importance of 'the new element' – by which, of course, he meant 'the new money' – 'recognizing it and fairly generously awarding it a prominent place'.

By the 1880s the most serious challenge to Mrs Astor's leadership was coming from the Vanderbilts. When old Commodore Vanderbilt died he left his son, William H. Vanderbilt, $90,000,000, but Mrs Astor still refused stubbornly to have anything to do with members of this family. They had 'manipulated railroad stock' she said, and although she did not understand in the least what it meant, she had a distinct impression that their machinations were far from gentlemanly. The two Vanderbilts accepted their ostracism philosophically although William H. Vanderbilt, in a final attempt to impress society, built himself a house on 5th Avenue that stretched all the way from 56th to 57th Street.

However, William's two sons, William K. and Cornelius Vanderbilt, were of a different ilk. They enrolled behind the banner of Willie K.'s wife, Alva, a spirited lady born plain 'Smith' from Mobile, Alabama, who was determined to breach Mrs Astor's citadel. In 1882 Alva invited Richard Hunt, the most fashionable architect of the period, to build her a mansion that would make the whole of New York sit up and take notice; she did not care whether it was French, Italian, Moorish or Bavarian, as long as it exceeded the splendour of the Parisian palace built ten years earlier by Mrs Jones, a member of the Old Guard, or the marble mausoleum of A.T. Stewart.

Mrs William K. Vanderbilt, Alva, who was the only real challenge to Caroline Astor's supremacy in New York society.

She gave Hunt $3,000,000 to carry out her commission and the palace rose on 5th Avenue opposite her father-in-law's establishment. It was modelled on the Château de Blois with some embellishments taken from the Jacques mansion at Bourges. It was the forerunner of Hunt's relentless drive to impose European culture on rootless, and often ephemeral, American millionaires. Only Louis H. Sullivan, who believed in architectural functionalism, was rude enough to prophesy that William K. Vanderbilt could not possibly live in his new house, 'morally, mentally or spiritually, that he and his home are a paradox, a contradiction, an absurdity, a characteristically New York absurdity; that he is no part of the house, the house no part of him'.

Mrs Astor also thought Mr William K. and his house an absurdity, but Ward McAllister felt that the Vanderbilts were too rich to ignore, and without a word invited them to the Patriarchs Ball. Mrs Astor attended the party but she did not allow her first minister to present his guests to her. Alva Vanderbilt bided her time and in January 1883 announced she would inaugurate her new house in March with a fancy dress ball. It soon became clear that it would be the most stupendous affair ever seen in New York, and for six weeks no one thought or talked of anything else, while the great costume-maker, Lanouette, kept 150 dressmakers working day and night to fulfil orders.

Mrs Astor's youngest daughter, Carrie, joined with some friends in perfecting a star quadrille for the occasion which they practised at the Astor mansion. However, when this delicious piece of information was brought to the attention of Alva Vanderbilt the latter seemed genuinely upset. As much as she would like to invite Miss Carrie Astor to her party, it was quite impossible as she had never met either the young lady or her mother. Mrs Astor was very fond of her daughter so she did not give the matter a moment's hesitation. She pinned on her hat, called for her carriage, and drove to the Vanderbilt house. Her blue-liveried footman jumped out and carried Mrs William Astor's card to Mrs William Vanderbilt's footman in maroon livery. An hour later the Vanderbilt footman in maroon livery called at 340 5th Avenue and placed in the hands of the Astor footman in blue livery the last of 1200 invitations to the ball.

The ball lived up to the highest expectations. The costumes were not very ingenious but unbelievably costly. Alva Vanderbilt appeared as a Venetian princess, and there were the usual queens, ranging from Elizabeth of England to Marie Antoinette of France. More original was the Duc de Morny, ousted by the collapse of the Second Empire, posing as a courtier of Louis xv; and Mrs Cornelius Vanderbilt in white satin trimmed with diamonds representing the spectacular new invention 'The Electric Light'.

Mrs Vanderbilt did not try to wrest the crown from Mrs Astor; she was quite content with the role of lady-in-waiting. Indeed the great ladies who dominated New York were glad to accept the queen's authority for she was never aggressive, never tyrannical, and was blessed with remarkable common sense. Of course all the ladies at her court were very much in the public eye. They were national figures, characters, from a fairy story, for they lived on a scale that even Russian grand dukes found impressive. Their jewels, their yachts, their palaces, servants, clothes and carriages were of breathless interest to the thousands of Americans who dreamed of success in the same terms. As Hollywood was in its infancy, and the stage not yet respectable, these social figures had few competitors in the field of glamour. Newspapers ran daily columns on their activities while the public flocked to the weddings of their sons and daughters in such thousands that battalions of police had to be on hand to maintain order. They lived up to what was expected of them by breathless extravagance and preserved themselves as a coterie by exercising a merciless exclusion.

Opposite The announcement of the first night of the Subscription for Faust *at the Metropolitan Opera House on 22 October 1883. The 'Met' was built at the instigation of Alva Vanderbilt and all fashionable – and not so fashionable – society could be seen there.*

METROPOLITAN
OPERA HOUSE.

MR. HENRY E. ABBEY,	· · · · · ·	Director.
Acting Manager,	· · · · ·	MR. MAURICE GRAU.

MONDAY EVENING, OCTOBER 22, 1883,

INAUGURAL NIGHT

AND

First Night of the Subscription,

WHEN GOUNOD'S OPERA OF

"FAUST."

Will be presented with the following Cast :

FAUST,	· · · · · ·	Sig. ITALO CAMPANINI
MEPHISTOPHELES,	· · ·	Sig. FRANCO NOVARA
VALENTINO,	· · ·	Sig. GIUSEPPE DEL PUENTE
WAGNER,	· · · · ·	Sig. CONTINI
SIEBEL,	· · · · ·	Mme. SOFIA SCALCHI
MARTA,	· · · ·	Mlle. LOUISE LABLACHE

(Who has kindly consented to assume the part at short notice. Her first appearance.)

AND

MARGHERITA, · · · Mme. CHRISTINE NILSSON

Musical Director and Conductor, · Sig. VIANESI

WEBER PIANO USED.

Mason & Hamlin's Organ Used.

All the above Operas performed at this House can be had in every form, Vocal and Instrumental at G. SCHIRMER, No. 35 Union Square, Importer and Publisher of Music.

The Scenery by Messrs. Fox, Schaeffer, Maeder, and Thompson.
The Costumes are entirely new, and were manufactured at Venice by D. Ascoli
The Appointments by Mr. Bradwell.
Machinists, Messrs. Lundy & Gifford.

NIGHTLY PRICES OF ADMISSION :

Boxes, holding six (6) seats..	$50
Orchestra Stalls...	6
Balcony Stalls..	3
Family Circle (reserved)..	2
Admission to Family Circle...	1

Seats and Boxes can be secured at the Box Office of the Metropolitan Opera House, which will remain open daily from 8 A. M. to 5 P. M.

Doors open at 7.15. | **Performances at 8 precisely**

Gunerius Gabrielson & Son, Florists to the Metropolitan Opera House.

Opera Glasses on Hire in the Lobby.

L. F. Mazette, Caterer.

Parties desiring Ices can be supplied by the Waiter, in Corridor.

Business Manager	· · · · ·	Mr. W. W. TILLOTSON.
Treasurer	· · · · ·	Mr. CHAS. H. MATHEWS.

The craving for glamour was met by the opening of the citrus-coloured Metropolitan Opera House in 1883, a few months after the Vanderbilt Ball. The old opera house was inadequate because it had only eighteen boxes, and the failure of pugnacious Alva Vanderbilt to secure one of them inspired her to raise the money and direct the building of 'the Met'. When at last the new temple of music opened, dubbed by the irreverent 'the new yellow Brewery on Broadway', there were so many boxes that everyone who could afford to pay was accommodated. All sorts of people of whom Mrs Astor did not approve poured into the Golden Horseshoe: George F. Baker, William Rockefeller, Jay Gould, and even rough men from California who had made their money in gold and railways like Darius Mills and Colin Huntington. However, the queen assented graciously when it was explained to her that their patronage was essential to meet the financial deficit.

Soon the lower tier of boxes became known as the Diamond Horseshow for here the richest ladies were given seats. On the opening night a diagram of the boxes and their occupants was distributed with the programmes so that the people in the orchestra could have a good look. All opera glasses were trained on Box 7 where regal Mrs Astor sat, blazing in her famous jewels, and Box 6 where Mrs William K. Vanderbilt glittered in equally costly splendour. The observers could report to their friends next day that the feud between the two families was definitely over as with their own eyes they had seen Mrs Astor smile at Mrs Vanderbilt.

However, there were other sights to be seen, particularly where jewellery was concerned. Every lady with a few millions at her disposal donned her most spectacular dress and her most costly gems and sallied forth to be eyed by the populace. The only worrying problem was how to wear the precious stones so that everyone in the vast audience could see them. Mrs John Drexel found a way out of the dilemma by devising a sort of Sam Brown belt. Her jewels were reset on a wide band which she wore around her waist, diagonally crossing her imposing bosom and shoulders. Mrs Frederick Vanderbilt was even more original. She had been told that Venetian beauties of the Renaissance liked to toy with a single jewel. So she walked majestically through the lobby with a string of pearls that went to her ankles, kicking before her a huge uncut ruby.

Although the *grandes dames* of New York were not much interested in events outside their narrow world, the opening of the Metropolitan Opera happened to presage a series of sensational new architectural triumphs. In 1884 Whitelaw Reid's Tribune Building was complete, eleven storeys high surmounted by a campanile that dominated the skyline. This was followed by a revolutionary edifice at 50 Broadway known as the Tower Building. Although the law demanded that the weight of the building must be supported entirely by the thickness of the walls, a young architect, Bradford Gilbert, designed his Goliath to rise thirteen storeys on a plot twenty-one feet wide. He was erecting it, he said, on the principle of 'standing a steel bridge structure on end'. After months of waiting, he received official permission to proceed but the man in the street thought the venture quite mad. The first seven storeys were built on a steel frame, but the next six were to be of brick.

In 1886 Mrs Astor's one and only son, John Jacob IV, was driving along Broadway in an eighty-mile-an-hour gale. The Tower Building had reached a height of ten storeys and he saw crowds gathered a safe distance away, to watch the crazy edifice crash to the ground. Apparently the architect, Mr Gilbert, was on the way to the building at that very moment. Gilbert climbed a ladder to the tenth floor and lowered his plumb-line. There was not the slightest vibration: his half-finished structure was perfectly safe. Although no one realized it at the time, his victory ushered in a new age. The era of the skyscraper had begun.

John Jacob IV was fascinated by the technical strides in Manhattan and spent much of his time dreaming about the future. His mother was also interested in the future but from a narrow and strictly mundane aspect: the welfare of her children. Despite her husband's objection to Emily's marriage to James Van Alen, she had encountered no opposition in marrying off the other three girls. Helen had become the wife of James Roosevelt whose father lived at Hyde Park, an estate bordering Ferncliffe. Her third daughter, Charlotte Augusta, had married a southern gentleman, John Drayton, while her fourth daughter, Carrie, became the wife of Orme Wilson, a brother of Grace Wilson who later married Cornelius Vanderbilt.

Mrs Astor's remaining task was the most difficult of all, for now she had to find a wife for her son and heir. This unfortunate young man was pursued by every ambitious mother in New York, although *Town Topics* commented unkindly that although he was 'the richest catch of the day' it was questionable 'whether ... he could earn his bread by his brains'. Early in 1890 Jack Astor, as he was called, attended a ball in Philadelphia given by fashionable Mrs Willing, proud possessor of a beautiful daughter, Ava. And a few months later Mrs Willing brought Ava to New York to attend a Patriarchs Ball. The New York families who had hoped to ensnare the twenty-eight-year-old millionaire began to talk of the Willings as 'quite common', and the society in which they moved as 'loud and brazen-faced'. The Willings promptly retaliated by finding genealogical experts to declare that Ava Willing was a descendent of Alfred the Great, Henry I of France and Henry I, Edward I and Henry IV of England, through Mrs Willing's forebears, the Philadelphia Lloyds.

Whatever Ava Willing's ancestry her beauty was beyond dispute; tall and slim, with an ivory skin, dark hair and huge dark eyes, she was regarded by many as the most ravishing young lady that America had ever produced. Apparently Jack Astor shared this opinion for the engagement was announced at the end of 1890, and the wedding took place a few months later. The nation was thrilled by the fairy-tale match and followed the voluminous newspaper coverage all the way to the wedding and beyond.

Half a dozen specially chartered trains carried family and guests to Philadelphia. The 'Four Hundred' arrived almost in its entirety. 'New York,' reported the *New York Times*, 'practically took Philadelphia by

Ava Willing met Jack Astor early in 1890 and by 1891 they were married. The public loved the romance and the wedding was one of the events of the year.

storm today. Its Four Hundred invaded the fashionable quarter of the town and it capitulated. Not content with carrying off the hand of its wealthiest marriageable son, John Jacob Astor IV, the greatest belle of the foremost family of the Quaker City, Miss Ava Willing, the wealth and fashion of New York came ... to give the fashionable heart of the city an air of gaiety and animation entirely foreign to it.'

The bride was a sensation in a silver dress made by Worth. She wore a diamond lover's knot, four inches high, a gift from Mrs Astor, while her veil fell from a sensational diamond tiara given by the groom. 'An ideal wedding,' proclaimed the *Herald*, 'in which there was never a hitch.' Alas, all the hitches were to come later.

The first years of the gay nineties brought Mrs Astor nothing but trouble – odious publicity and utter mortification – and was the worst period of her entire life. 1890 seemed to be the lull before the storm. That was the year her widowed brother-in-law, John Jacob III, followed his wife,

Charlotte Augusta, to the grave. The *New York Times* seemed to have forgotten its angry attacks on John Jacob for his outrageous connection with the notorious Tweed ring and announced the millionaire's death with astonishing headlines: 'THE END OF A PLACID AND USEFUL LIFE FULL OF GOOD DEEDS'.

His heir, forty-one-year-old William Waldorf, inherited a fortune estimated at somewhere between $50 and $80,000,000, but apparently the money was not sufficient to overcome his natural spleen, for he at once took the opportunity of picking a quarrel with his Aunt Caroline. He was a strangely disgruntled man, and had always been annoyed by the fact that his own mother, Charlotte Augusta, had refused to take her place as leader of society and allowed Caroline, the wife of a younger brother, to wear the crown. But whenever he raised the subject, his mother only laughed and said: 'Not for me, thank you'. However, now that his parents were dead, the initiative passed to him. How dare Aunt Caroline sweep about in her imperious manner without a word of deference to his Mary, the rightful First Lady? As for Aunt Caroline she

After the death of his father, John Jacob III, William Waldorf soon quarrelled with his Aunt Caroline, queen of New York society. William Waldorf felt that, as the eldest son of the eldest son, his wife Mary had the prior claim to this throne.

simply regarded William as 'a prickly sort of person', and saw as little of him as possible.

The truth was that William Waldorf was frustrated and unhappy. He was the first Astor to dream of a political career, and his failure to reach Congress permanently embittered him. He put his toe into the water in 1877, at the age of twenty-nine, when he was elected to the New York State Assembly. The *Herald* was delighted that young men 'of wealth and culture' were willing to accept 'the responsibility of public life'. But Astor was less concerned with responsibility than in following the Republican lead. He voted for a bill to reduce official salaries; for the use of convict labour on the Dannemora railway; for the quashing of the investigation of Republic intrigue in the coal combine.

However, he was merely cutting his teeth, for two years later, when the Republicans promoted him to the State Senate, consisting of thirty-two men, he startled his supporters by introducing a Bill to reduce the fare of the Elevated railway (the 'El') from ten cents to five cents. This impertinent suggestion cut across the interests of Jay Gould and August Belmont and stung the El lobbyists into furious activity. A five cent fare, they wailed, would so increase traffic that 'the iron rails would have to carry 18,000 tons of animal matter daily, and that would make the rails

The Elevated Railway in New York photographed in the 1890s. In 1879 William Waldorf proposed that the fare on the 'El' should be reduced from ten to five cents, but his Bill was defeated in the State Senate.

red hot and shake the structure to pieces in two years'. Even talk of the 'Red menace' entered the dispute. 'In these days of communism should the Legislature encourage the spirit of spoilation by breaking a sacred contract with the Elevated?'

The Senate defeated the Bill and Astor embraced another cause. He introduced a measure to remove the unsightly Croton River Reservoir from 5th Avenue and 42nd Street. This time the Bill passed the Senate but floundered in the Assembly. Astor was noted for his vindictiveness and now his dander was up. Normally the unanimous consent necessary for the passage of Bills on the third reading was a mere formality; but Astor arrived in the chamber carrying a list of the assemblymen who had voted against his reservoir motion. And he simply refused to give his consent to a Bill bearing any of his opponents' names. The turmoil was unprecedented, and although William Waldorf lived to fight another day he scarcely endeared himself to his colleagues.

Many of them complained of his haughty aloofness but the truth was that he suffered from acute shyness. He found it almost impossible to be what people called 'a good mixer'; even entering a room required an heroic effort. Yet this strange, nervous, introverted man craved to be a member of the United States Congress. Although he dreaded the ordeal of an important election campaign he convinced himself that the work in Washington would be so exhilarating it would make the effort worthwhile. He had no difficulty in getting the right backing as the Astor family had always supported Ulysses Grant, and Grant's close friend, Roscoe Conkling, controlled the New York Republican machine.

In due course William Waldorf stood for the Seventh Congressional District and both Grant and Conkling appeared on his platform. The district was a working-class area bounded by the Bowery and Houston Street, and included many Astor slums, but Conkling was certain that generous gifts of money would overcome the disadvantages. Obediently the dollar bills fluttered on to the campaign table. Soon a thousand 'boys' were mobilized and supplied with torches, and sent to Germania Hall to cheer for Astor. William Waldorf stressed his German descent and told his audience that when he got to Washington he would try to secure a better wage for manual workers. Astor's managers begged him to call on his tenants in the slum area but William W. stubbornly refused and afterwards people claimed that this had lost him the election. Out of a total vote of 23,000 he was defeated by only 165 votes.

Nevertheless Astor had earned the respect of the party bosses who were deeply impressed by his lavish expenditure. So a while later when Congressman Morton of the Fifteenth Congressional District was appointed Minister to France, the Republican machine once again turned to Astor. This time the nomination looked like certain victory, for the Fifteenth was a 'silk stocking' area. However, the Democrats were determined to give William Waldorf a run for his money and appointed Roswell Flower, a millionaire stockbroker to oppose him.

The press dubbed the campaign 'The Golden Canvass' and the country followed the proceedings with rapt attention. The *New York Times* declared hesitantly that Astor was the lesser of two evils, but the *New*

York Sun proclaimed that the financial exactions imposed upon the two men were 'preposterous'. Astor was ready, the paper continued, to 'engage in unbounded and corrupt expenditures'. 'Apart from his money Mr Astor is one of the weakest aspirants who ever sought the suffrages of a New York constituency. He has been tried in the Legislature and proved himself the most partisan, the most narrow-minded, the most selfish of representatives.'

William Waldorf was appalled by these attacks. He had always regarded himself as a high-minded man who wished to serve his fellow citizens – not, as the papers insisted, 'an unscrupulous millionaire aspiring to office'. At that time William's father had tried to pacify him by explaining that he had been caught up in a battle between Tammany Hall and the Republican machine. 'Take whatever trick you can,' he counselled, 'but always remember to keep smiling.'

Poor William Waldorf found himself quite unable to follow this advice. First of all the campaign was a nightmare. Colonel Marshall, his personal aide, insisted that they spend their evenings in the saloons buying the chaps beer and cigars, but the press always found something to complain about: Astor shook hands with his gloves on; Astor did not drink his beer; Astor should unbend – 'take his coat off and help the bar man' – as one paper put it. Of course Mr Flower was a target as well, but somehow he seemed to get more amusement out of the contest, splashing money about and lambasting 'rich landlords who batten on slum property'.

After a horrendous campaign in which Astor's wealth, Astor's record, Astor's personality, Astor's extravagances, all came under sustained attack, Astor was defeated. Although the *New York Telegram* claimed that 'running for office in this city is about the most expensive amusement going', Astor had not found much fun in it. He was disgusted by the flagrant way his legislative record had been twisted and misrepresented, and by the personal attacks on his birth and breeding. Indeed the campaign had obliterated his desire for public life. His father had been right in maintaining that democracy was a farce and that gentlemen should have nothing to do with politics. The editor of the *New York Times*, Mr Raymond, even managed to jeer at him for not fighting again. 'If a rich man goes into politics and a ruffian says he lies or calls him "an old pocketbook" or threatens to "warm him" at a primary meeting he goes straight home, has a good cry with his wife, vows he will never touch politics again, says the country cannot last very long....'

Fortunately Astor did not have much time to brood over the inadequacies of democracy, for President Arthur rewarded him by appointing him Minister to Italy. At least this was a life for a gentleman, for he lived in the Rospigliosi Palazzo, which had seven reception rooms and an enormous ballroom, and where he was able to entertain lavishly. His wife, Mary, was a great favourite, pronounced by Queen Margarita to be 'the most beautiful woman in Italy'. The diplomatic work was not too arduous, he had plenty of time to collect wonderful works of art, and even wrote an historical novel about Cesare Borgia

Opposite (above) This peaceful picture of Broadway, New York in 1835 bears little resemblance to the hustle and bustle fifty years later. Drawn and etched by Thomas Horner, aquatint by John Hill.

Opposite (below) The slum district of New York. The long interiors of the tenements had common walls with next-door houses, and the only windows were front and back.

Overleaf New York city in 1860. The population of New York had expanded rapidly in the 1850s when immigrants from central Europe began to pour into the metropolis.

Central Park in winter, a Currier and Ives print of 1862.

entitled *Valentino*. Unfortunately this delightful life came to a close after eighteen months when Grover Cleveland defeated Arthur as President.

Five years after William Waldorf returned to America his father died leaving him the Astor plate which was always bequeathed by eldest son to eldest son, signifying that the owner was head of the family. W.W. took his new position seriously and in the summer of 1891 decided that the moment had arrived to have a show-down with his Aunt Caroline. He installed his wife at Beaulieu and gave several parties at which he openly criticized his Aunt's Olympian ways; people were only too glad to carry the tittle-tattle straight to the queen. Mrs Astor was not leader of society for nothing; she knew how to buckle on her sword and fight. Her calling cards said 'Mrs William Astor', but the time had arrived for a change. William Waldorf must realize that she alone was head of the family; and not only head of the family but head of society by dint of an unerring leadership of twenty years. She therefore had new cards engraved simply saying 'Mrs Astor'; and at the same time asked her friends in future please to write to her as 'Mrs Astor, Newport'. Her politeness concealed a steel-like determination, for when the patroness list for the Casino Ball appeared with her name as 'Mrs William Astor' she wrote a blistering letter of protest to the chairman, saying that she had been insulted.

William Waldorf's wife, the gentle, shy, Mary Paul of Philadelphia, had no stomach for this sort of fight, but William insisted, giving instructions that his wife also was to be addressed as 'Mrs Astor'. Although the press fastened on to 'the Astor feud' and made the most of it, the main outcome was total confusion about the mail. Mary Astor had no hope of displacing her aunt. Everywhere the great Caroline went, she was flattered and fêted and given the place of honour at her host's right.

William Waldorf finally tired of the quarrel and at the end of 1891 took his wife to Europe. But the society magazines refused to let the feud drop and *Town Topics* made a remarkably inaccurate forecast. The journal declared on 7 January 1892:

In the little fuss existing between the two houses of Astor, I must continue to believe that *the* Mrs [Mary] Astor, now in London, has the best of the situation ... and I cannot help seeing that the young lady is bound to be victorious in the end.... When the right moment arrives she will return to these shores with great *éclat* and as the richest and best equipped matron on New York she will at once be recognized as the leader of society ... and when she does come then we will see fun.

The truth was that *Town Topics* was gunning for Mrs Astor. The magazine was owned by Colonel William D'Alton Mann, a kindly-looking old gentleman with a long white beard, a clerical frock coat and a red bow tie, who made a speciality of blackmail. He collected disreputable tidbits about the well-to-do. His chief Newport correspondent, for instance, gained access to the homes of Newport's leaders by posing as a musician, while other reporters picked up salacious gossip from servants or disgruntled climbers. Most of this information was never printed, as the Colonel derived a handsome income from money paid for his silence. People who refused to contribute to his well-being became a target for vilification. It was amazing how many prominent men pacified the Colonel with 'interest free loans'. When Mann's secrets were revealed because of a law-suit, twelve prominent New York millionaires were named as having contributed to the Colonel's welfare. They included J.P. Morgan, William C. Whitney, William K. Vanderbilt, James R. Keane, and John W. Gates, who had provided Colonel Mann with over $200,000.

But *not* Mrs Astor. This lady had courage and character, and refused point blank to give the Colonel a penny. As a result, when the news about her daughter became public, Mrs Astor was *Town Topics'* main target of attack. The scandal broke on 18 March 1892, when the *New York Sun* told avid American readers that Charlotte Augusta Astor, the wife of James Drayton, had left her husband and run off to Europe with another man.

The Astors, of course, had known for some time that a crisis was approaching. Charlotte had fallen passionately in love with Hallett Burrowe, a next-door neighbour in Bernardsville, New Jersey, and the son of a well-known director of Equitable Insurance. For once, William Astor came back from Florida, joined his wife and tried to exert an influence. He told his daughter bluntly that if she persisted in seeing Burrowe he would cut her out of the $850,000 he was leaving her in his will.

Charlotte was too much in love to heed such threats and suddenly sailed for England to keep a rendezvous with her lover. Before she left she arranged with her bank to make Drayton an annual payment of $12,000 for the children. Drayton accepted the money but hired detectives to follow her in London. They soon reported that Burrowe was staying at the St Pancras Hotel in the company of a brown-haired lady with a fair skin and innocent blue eyes. Apparently friends of the abandoned husband urged him to save his face by taking some dramatic action. So he rushed to Europe and challenged Burrowe to a duel. As duelling was forbidden in England, Drayton suggested they meet in Paris. But Burrowe clung to a pose of complete innocence and replied by saying that he was unaware of any 'subject for discussion'. 'I gave you your choice of behaving for once in your life like a gentleman,' persisted Drayton, 'and you did not choose to accept it. Do you or do you not care to meet me in Paris for matters impossible to settle here? Yes or no? Your obedient servant. J.C. Drayton.'

Town Topics wrote with incredible smugness on 24 March:

It is pleasant to note that society at large is genuinely shocked by the scandal and that the sympathy of everyone is with the husband. So long as we are capable of distinguishing evil and deploring it I suppose we are not yet so bad as were those Romans who, in the ultimate days of their degeneracy could not tell virtue when they saw it.... The American respect for a pure woman is as high as it ever was and when an impure one is exposed there are few of us who do not feel the blow, striking as it does straight at the face that sustains honourable society.

How did the letters that revealed the scandal find their way to the *New York Sun*? Many people believed that Burrowe had sent them, not for money but to encourage Drayton to divorce his wife. Unfortunately, gentlemanly instincts seemed to be in short supply on both sides. Although Burrowe finally accepted the challenge and the two men appointed seconds, the seconds recommended that the matter be referred to a French Court of Honour presided over by the Duc de Morny. In the investigation that followed, it was revealed that Drayton was not only living on the $12,000 a year bestowed by his wife, but had received another $5000 from his Astor in-laws to keep the matter quiet – which, of course, he had not done. The Duc de Morny therefore pronounced that Drayton had no right to challenge his wife's lover. 'There is no longer any honour where there has been traffic, where honour has been conditionally sold.'

Town Topics would not admit that the injured husband was wrong in any way, as this might help the Astors. 'No one who has known Drayton,' the journal asserted angrily, 'can for a moment imagine him receiving from the Astors any money.... As for Andrew Scholl and the Duc de Morny who were called upon to give a scientific opinion of the propriety of a duel ... Scholl is utterly untrustworthy ... and de Morny is a rake of the shallowest description.'

Colonel Mann's failure to extract blackmail money from Mrs William Astor continued to excite him. And when the *Sun* described Mrs Astor as a woman 'whose goodness of heart and charity towards others has endeared her to thousands', *Town Topics* burst out with a fury of a tropical storm:

Like a great many others Mrs Astor may be charitably inclined in a sympathetic way, but neither she nor any member of her family has ever been charged with any excess of character where it cost a dollar. That a woman who has never done anything except give caterers' dinners to friends in her own set should be flattered by a sentiment (goodness of heart and charity toward others!) which is carved on the pedestal of the statue of our martyred President is ridiculously grotesque.

A month later, in April 1892, William Astor went to Paris to be near his daughter, and while staying in a hotel near the Rue de la Paix he had a fatal heart attack. His body was sent back to New York for burial, but even these lugubrious circumstances failed to modify the tone of *Town Topics*. It not only jeered at the dead William for his ineffectiveness, but suggested that amatory dalliance was a trait that his daughter had inherited from him:

The death of Mr William Astor has not robbed New York of a personality of great importance. His place in society was indicated by the activity of the lady who bore his name rather than by his own admixture.... Even his face and form were relatively unknown while every *gamin* could point out Mrs Astor in a throng of pleasure-seekers, but few could have identified the thirty or forty-fold millionaire. To the last, I believe, Mr Astor went his own gait, as the Scotch put it, and got out of life, I fancy, all the substantial delights that vast wealth could procure. I should say that some of his tendencies were inherited by Mrs Coleman Drayton whose troubles caused her parents no little

Below *Caroline Astor's French château at 840 Fifth Avenue caused a sensation when it was put on display to the public. Richard Hunt, the celebrated architect, designed the white stone Renaissance palace which cost $2 million to build, while the furniture, much of which was copied from the Petit Trianon, cost another half-million.*

uneasiness. I question though whether they impressed him as profoundly as some of my contemporaries would have their readers believe.

Nevertheless, William had been sufficiently impressed to alter his Will. When this testament was read, Charlotte learned that her father had carried out his threat and transferred the fortune intended for her to her children.

These difficult years revealed Mrs Astor in her true colours as a woman of outstanding character. Not only had she refused to be blackmailed by Colonel Mann, but now she refused to be influenced by the criticisms of her unhappy daughter, Charlotte Augusta. Indeed she fought for her with elemental protectiveness and in 1894 even invited fashionable Newport to a reception in Charlotte's honour. Some of the guests, given the chance of a lifetime to return the snubs they had suffered from Mrs Astor, declined, but Mrs Astor presented an impassive countenance and people wondered if she had noticed.

At the same time she persuaded her son Jack to reinstate his sister in her inheritance, although there was nothing she could do to prevent Drayton

Below *Caroline gave an inaugural ball in February 1896, and after receiving the guests seated herself on her customary throne in the centre of the long gallery which served as a ball-room.*

from retaining custody of the four children. As far as society was concerned, the great Mrs Astor was carefully feeling her way. A short while later she carried her zeal for her daughter a stage further by taking Charlotte, unannounced, to a reception at which Bishop Horatio Potter was present. Afterwards, when the good prelate heard that Charlotte had been among the guests, he was deeply distressed to think that he had shared the room with such a notorious woman. Eventually Drayton divorced Charlotte 'on cruel suspicion of marital infidelity'; and eventually fickle Charlotte, who had abandoned her lover, married a rich Scotsman, George Ogilvy Haig.

Mrs Astor's anxieties were not yet over, for at the end of 1892 William Waldorf Astor made more trouble for his aunt. He announced that his father's house, which stood next to Aunt Caroline's on 5th Avenue at 34th Street, would soon be torn down to make way for a splendid new hotel, the Waldorf; and within a few months of his statement a demolition crew arrived and began to dismantle J.J. Astor's famous residence. The noise and dust and rubbish-strewn pavements were insupportable, and after consulting her son Mrs Astor sent for the celebrated architect,

Richard Hunt, and asked him to build her a new citadel at 5th Avenue and 65th Street – a double palace with one half for herself, the other half for her son and daughter-in-law.

Mrs Astor inaugurated her new French château at 840 5th Avenue in February 1896 by giving her first ball in six years. Much water had flowed under the bridge since 1890. Charlotte's scandal had galvanized the nation, while another daughter, Helen Roosevelt, had died very quietly and very suddenly in England. And although husband William Astor had been more shadow than substance, now that he was gone she missed his unexpected home-comings and his quixotic loyalties. She had even lost her faithful counsellor, Ward McAllister, who breathed his last in 1895. Unfortunately this celebrated social arbiter had run into trouble in 1890 by producing a rather self-important little book, *Society as I have Found it*. McAllister was lampooned by the press while the nation guffawed. *Life Magazine* published a cartoon of a policeman reporting to his captain with two drunks in evening dress: 'What's that you've got, O'Hara?' 'Society as Oi have found it, sorr!' Nevertheless, Mrs Astor remained loyal and gave McAllister the sort of funeral he would have liked, with an Astor and a Vanderbilt as two of his pall-bearers.

Mrs Astor's Renaissance palace won national acclaim when it was put on display a few days before she moved in. Richard Hunt's white stone masterpiece had cost her son $2,000,000 and perhaps another half-million for the furniture, much of which had been copies from the Petit Trianon. Although the Furniture Workers' Union alleged that many pieces had been smuggled into the country, no one was in a mood to heed such ill-natured complaints. Each room was decorated in period style, and all the reception rooms done in various combinations of white and gold. The magnificent art gallery ballroom ran the whole length of the house while the rococo *salon* with its Trianon furniture boasted a carpet made of peacock's tails. The dining room was considered a triumph of elegance in ebony and gold.

Thousands of sightseers crowded into horse-drawn buses to stop first at Mrs Astor's old house at 34th and 5th Avenue, to hear of past glories within the sombre brownstone walls, then up the Avenue to No. 840 where they gazed at the latest Medici triumph. If New York was America's social capital, 840 5th Avenue was New York's White House. The public felt that it was a fitting residence for their queen and speculated among themselves whether or not her doorknobs were made of gold and inset with diamonds.

On the night of Mrs Astor's ball, the guests marvelled at the furnishings and commented on Richard Hunt's use of pastel colours. Somehow the decor seemed to suggest a lighter, less ponderous era. Even sixty-five-year-old Mrs Astor had a re-upholstered look, for she had abandoned her dark velvet for a gown of palest grey satin. Nevertheless once again the crown was firmly on her head and she intended to make sure that it was kept there.

'It's outrageous,' the great Mrs Astor's son, John Jacob IV, exclaimed to the press in the autumn of 1894, 'that a man can commit such an offence and not be punished. If he goes free hundreds of other people may take it into their heads to do the same thing!'

Mrs Astor had not yet moved uptown to her new palace but was still living, greatly inconvenienced, in her old red-brick house at 34th Street, next door to that new hotel, the Waldorf, which her disobliging nephew had just completed. A woebegone tramp had been attracted by the bright lights and stood for some time watching the carriages clattering up to the hotel entrance and the resplendent doorman bowing out the occupants – men in evening dress and top hats, accompanied by glamorous actresses with painted faces. After a while, the tramp's interest waned and he moved along. But as he passed the large house next to it he saw a light coming from the basement door which was ajar. Being a curious soul, he walked in and suddenly found himself in a comfortable, empty bedroom. He was tired and had nowhere to go so he lay down and went to sleep. The bedroom belonged to the Astor laundress, but she was away for the night so the tramp was not disturbed until the servants found him in the morning. They called the police and he was arraigned before a magistrate.

Times were hard in the spring of 1894. The stock market had crashed six months earlier and now there was an economic depression and widespread unemployment. The vagrant had not committed any crime, so the magistrate fined him five dollars for entering a private house. Unfortunately the tramp could not pay and was sent to jail. The case received a good deal of publicity with Mrs Astor's son assuming the role of family spokesman. 'It does not seem right,' John Jacob IV complained, 'that a man can enter a house and only be fined five dollars. My mother is frightfully alarmed over the matter and something must be done to punish him so he will not repeat the offence.'

The public apparently did not share the Astors' concern, for while the newspapers moralized on rich and poor, on the right of a landlord to evict and the right of a tramp to sleep, an unknown citizen stepped forward and paid the tramp's fine. Jack Astor was horrified by this intervention which he regarded as utterly anarchistic. 'I am at a loss to understand why anyone would want to let him get away,' he fumed. 'Imagine escaping with only two days in prison! A great injustice has been done.'

Meek and mild Jack Astor was under the thumb of his domineering mother and his aggressive wife Ava. Apparently these two ladies refused to let the matter drop, and despite public opinion, which was wholly on the side of the tramp – now known to the world as Mr Garvey – goaded John Jacob IV into pursuing the luckless offender. The Astor family filed new charges; the tramp was picked up in a Bowery lodging house and brought to court where he was charged with attempted burglary. Astor appeared on the witness stand followed by his butler, his footman and his laundress. Locked up in The Tombs, Garvey found plenty of sympathizers, while Jack Astor made himself known to thousands of newspaper readers as a humourless, arrogant, purse-proud plutocrat lacking the smallest grain of magnanimity, and even worse, too stupid to see the harm he was doing to his 'class'.

Food was sent into Garvey and another unknown benefactor offered to pay his bail, but the tramp declined saying that it was raining and he had nowhere to go. It was discovered that he was not quite sound mentally because of a spinal injury, but the power of Astor money was so potent that Garvey was sentenced to one year in the penitentiary. No doubt he was relieved to be fed and lodged free of charge and removed temporarily at least from the cruel world.

Jack Astor had a bad press which was well deserved, for he was a man who cared for nothing, not to mention the fact that very few people cared for Jack Astor. Cold-hearted, weak-minded, he was distinguished by an almost complete absence of personality, a being no one would have noticed had it not been for his millions. Outwardly he observed the correct forms, chief of which was a deep traditionalism. He served as a vestryman for Trinity Church to which he donated six bronze doors. But the gift was his mother's suggestion for he rarely responded to charitable appeals.

Perhaps his blunted, almost stunted, nature stemmed from his unsatisfactory childhood. Neglected by his Florida-bound father, the elusive William, and adored by his mother who nevertheless managed to squeeze him into the wrong mould, Jack was an awkward, ungainly youth, too diffident to establish himself as head of the family. He did not dare to challenge his forceful mother, and his egocentric wife made it clear from the start that the only thing she admired about him was his bank account.

As a boy, Jack seemed to offer promise for the future. He had a mechanical bent and took a keen interest in the innovations thrown up by science, but it would never have occurred to his mother to send him to a Technological Institute. Jack's role in life was mapped out the moment he was born. Trained as a crown prince who one day would assume a leading position in American society, his school had to be St Pauls; his college had to be Harvard; his work no other than to look after the family property at the Astor Estate Office.

He loved Ferncliffe and had laboratories and workshops fitted out where he spent most of his time experimenting with some form of steam power. He invented a marine turbine engine, and an extraordinary gadget known as a 'vibratory disintegrator' designed to obtain gas from peat. His most successful tool was a pneumatic road improver capable of blowing dirt off the roads, which he demonstrated at Ferncliffe. In 1893 he submitted it at the World's Columbian Exhibition at Chicago where it won first prize. However, there was little demand for this invention as eventually dirt was eliminated in a more practical way by covering roads with asphalt. The following year he gave his contemporaries even more of a sensation by writing a science fiction book entitled *A Journey In Other Worlds*, which Appleton published. The story opened in the year 2000 with Colonel Bearwarden, President of the Terrestrial Axis Straightening Company, supervising the pumping out of the Arctic in order to put the globe on an even keel. An audience in New York could see by kinograph, a form of television, men working thousands of miles away in Baffinland; and they could see Dr Bearwarden lecturing on the progress of the work. The Aleutian Islands had been blown up to permit the Japanese current to warm the Arctic.

The book was enlivened by highlights filling in the years between 1894 and 2000. Flying machines and high explosives had been invented which made war so terrible that the expected holocaust had never come. New York had over 14,000,000 inhabitants; electric automobiles made speeds as high as forty miles an hour; underground trains sped under Manhattan; railways were run by magnetism; marine ships raced across inland seas; canals were heated in winter. Most important of all, scientists had discovered a force, the direct opposite of gravity, known as 'apergy' and composed of a new form of electricity. Apparently Elijah and Christ had used it, which explained the mysteries of the Bible.

It was surprising that a man with such a bizarre imagination should have been such a dull companion. When he was not living in his strange, futuristic world, his imagination seemed to evaporate and he was transformed into an utterly commonplace creature without a spark of originality or charm or compassion. As one of his friends remarked: 'When Jack descended from the interstellar spaces to consider mundane affairs, orthodoxy bounded his mind in politics, religion and business.' When the Republican party was out of power, Astor felt that America was facing anarchy, and when property owners were treated irreverently that the country was on the verge of a revolution.

Although it still was a great thing to be an Astor, the critical tone of the press foreshadowed the irreverent new world that was approaching. The two brothers who had never liked each other – John Jacob III and William Backhouse Jr – had died within twenty months of each other in 1890 and 1892, and left their only sons and heirs, J.J. IV and William Waldorf, estates jointly reckoned to be worth anything from $100,000,000 to $200,000,000. Cousins Jack and Willie were even further apart than their fathers had been, divided not by quarrels but by mutual dislike.

Despite the sixteen years that separated them, they should have banded together to withstand the slings and arrows of their outrageously large fortunes, for Americans were growing increasingly critical of inherited wealth, and particularly of the Astor men who no longer made any pretence of toiling or spinning. It was still alright to make a large fortune, but not alright to sit back and merely collect it from Manhattan property rises. The son of a tycoon was one thing; but idle, fourth generation descendants of the family founder quite another.

The press began to go out of its way to search for chinks in the Astor armour, often belittling the heirs quite unfairly while the more scurrilous sheets resorted to jeers at anything the heirs undertook. No doubt men of stronger character and more equitable temperament would have overcome the disadvantages of their patrimony, but neither cousin found much happiness in life. Indeed, it would be difficult to decide who suffered most from the Astor name and the Astor money: Willie, who flounced off to England after newspaper attacks on his brief political career, not to mention the publicity from his duel with Aunt Caroline; or Jack, who became known as 'Ava's henpecked husband' and whose attempts to achieve something on his own always seemed to flounder.

Yet these two frustrated millionaires found it impossible to get together – except over one business venture. When Cousin Willie's new hotel was rising next door to Aunt Caroline's house, Jack threatened to build stables alongside the Waldorf, a suggestion which caused a furore of indignation and was luckily abandoned. Then someone introduced the brilliant idea of building a second hotel – a sort of annexe – on Mrs Astor's land, which could be joined to the Waldorf, forming the greatest hostelry in New York. Although the cousins were divided by such deep animosity that even the red-brick Astor Estate Office on West 26th Street was partitioned into two sections, the prospect of financial gain accomplished the impossible, and the two men reached agreement.

The opening of the fabulous Waldorf-Astoria in 1897 marked the beginning of a new concept in living. The mission of this sensational establishment, a wit declared, was to bring exclusiveness to the masses. The public – particularly the female section – had always been avid to know how millionaires lived, but up till now could only assuage their hunger by devouring the gossip columns. Now the days of vicarious excitement were over, and the real world was spread before their eyes. The hotel, intellectuals explained, was a national university ready to teach the amenities of high social life to eager candidates. And it was far more magnificent than any château built by an Astor or a Vanderbilt; more costly, more spacious, more ingenious. And it belonged to anyone who cared to walk in and who had the money to pay. 'It was a vast, glittering irridescent fantasy [Lloyd Morris wrote] that had been conjured up to infect millions of plain Americans with a new ideal – the aspiration to lead an expensive gregarious life as publicly as possible.'

The hotel boasted 1000 rooms and 750 private bathrooms. On the ground floor there was a promenade which became world famous as 'Peacock Alley'. This was a 300-foot corridor made of amber marble, running along the 34th Street side. Furnished with luxurious sofas and chairs where spectators could sit undisturbed and watch the continuous parade of beautiful, overdressed ladies. Each day, it was claimed, over 25,000 people walked along this passage.

The genius who ran the Waldorf-Astoria was Mr George Boldt, a Philadelphia hotel-keeper who leased the new enterprise and at once began to introduce the public to 'marvellous ways of living and luxuries hitherto unattainable'. One magnificent reception room gave way to another, but the most important quarter was the Palm Garden where ladies and gentlemen were only allowed to dine if attired in full evening dress. A table here was almost as much in demand as a box at the opera and had to be booked weeks in advance.

Boldt was a stickler for rules, particularly where his staff were concerned. He would not employ waiters unless they could speak German and French as well as English; and he suddenly pronounced that all those

The Palm Garden Dining-room of the Waldorf Astoria, (above) photographed in 1902. Not all New York society could enjoy the luxury of one of the most expensive hotels in the world, as these New York street vendors (top right) could testify.

who served him must be 'clean-shaven'. In an age of beards and side whiskers this edict caused an uproar, – even Mr Boldt had a bushy moustache. But Boldt answered the protest by extending his dictum to the cab drivers who waited to convey the hotel guests around the city. By this time there was such a furore that the Governor of New York entered the fray. New Yorkers, he said, had the right to cultivate any sort of facial foliage they wished. However, the prestige of the Waldorf was so great that Boldt won an easy victory over the Governor's appeal for personal liberty.

If Boldt was a national figure, his chef, known simply as 'Oscar of the Waldorf', was even more famous. The $10,000 a year which he was reputed to receive was regarded as so astronomical that people refused to believe it. No one, they insisted, could be paid that much to run a kitchen. However, Oscar was as inventive as Boldt. He made after-theatre suppers so fashionable that his rooms were crowded with all the richest men and the most glamorous musical comedy stars. Lilian Russell and Edna May were often there, squired by J.P. Morgan. Oscar also developed a cosy rendezvous where Wall Street operators could recuperate after the close of the Stock Market. Here he administered to such tycoons as Charlie Schwab and Henry Clay Frick.

The most spectacular affair ever to be held at the Waldorf took place soon after the hotel opened and was a private occasion – a ball given by the Bradley Martins. This couple had been *nouveau riche* long enough to be accepted. They had been attending Patriarchs Balls for twenty years and finally received invitations from Mrs Astor herself. In 1896 Mrs Martin became deeply distressed by the financial depression that her newspaper told her was gripping the country. At the end of the year, in a burst of patriotism, she decided to alleviate the hardships of the poor by giving a sensational stimulus to trade. She therefore sent out 1200 invitations to a fancy dress ball to be given at the Waldorf-Astoria on 10 February 1897. The guests were asked to array themselves for presentation to Louis xv in Versailles.

Newspapers not only in the United States but in England regaled their readers with descriptions of the costly preparations. On 4 February *Town Topics* wrote:

Future generations will date every event in relation to the Bradley Martin ball.... Not only in clubs, in drawing rooms, in hotel restaurants and cafes, but in hundreds of workshops of costumers, milliners, dressmakers and perruquiers, in the newspaper offices and factories and business offices, people can be heard discussing the coming event.

A week later, on 11 February 1897, the same magazine had a hint of scandal which undoubtedly gave Colonel Mann a chance to collect some blackmail: 'Incredible as it may seem confidential applications were made to Mr Boldt by several well-known men and women who had not been invited, to be allowed to disguise themselves as waiters, ladies' maids and even chamber maids, so that they could see the show.'

When the great night finally arrived the *New York World* described the ladies who stepped out of their carriages as representing 'a delirium of wealth' with 'enough diamonds to fit out all the crowned heads of Europe and have some over for Asia and Africa....' Mrs Astor arrived in a costume designed by Worth and copied from a Van Dyck portrait but she still managed to look exactly like Mrs Astor. The host appeared as an unrecognizable Louis xv, and Mrs Bradley Martin as an aptly frivolous Marie Antoinette. Jack Astor wore an uninteresting courtier's costume that could have done for any country, but as Mrs Martin selected him to be her partner he won the title of King of the Ball.

Afterwards criticisms of the ball assumed the proportions of a tidal wave. Mr Martin was said to have spent a quarter of a million dollars. Clergymen and editors denounced the entertainment as an unpardonable example of the heartless behaviour of the rich, while Oscar Hammerstein produced a burlesque on the 'Bradley Radley Ball'. The final blow fell when the State of New York doubled the Bradley Martins' tax assessment, causing the couple to flee from America and to take up residence in gracious England.

People soon had other things to think about, as war with Spain was threatening. Jack Astor often cruised to the Caribbean on the magnificent yacht, the *Nourmahal*, left to him by his father. On these trips he developed an interest in Cuba and as early as 1896 announced with the fervour of an English imperialist that the United States ought to appropriate the island.

I should like the Republican platform better, [he said in a lordly manner] if it were more strongly in favour of the annexation of Cuba. I look upon the matter as an important one owing to the resources of the island and its commercial relations with the United States. They have gold mines in Cuba and iron mines of hematite ores which scientists have pronounced the best iron ore in the world.

When war with Spain, inspired by tendentious and inflammatory news-paper stories, was finally declared in 1898, thirty-four-year-old Astor hurried to Washington to offer his services. Theodore Roosevelt was Assistant Secretary of the Navy and one of Astor's trustees, Douglas Robinson, was conveniently married to Roosevelt's sister. The right strings were pulled and Astor met President McKinley and Secretary of War General Miles. He placed the *Nourmahal* at the government's disposal and made a gift of a mountain battery complete with artillery-men, costing $75,000, for use in the Philippines – also under Spanish rule. He was suitably rewarded with an appointment as Inspector General which carried the rank of lieutenant-colonel. As usual, he was attacked for being a rich man. The army was furious that 'money' could elbow their own candidates out of coveted appointments, and a man named Dooley published a satire on Astor's new office which apparently turned annoyance into merriment. The *New York Times* castigated Astor's appointment as 'without relevancy to the good of the service'.

Astor's first assignment was to accompany the Chief of Staff on an overcrowded transport bound for Cuba. Through field glasses he watched the Battle of San Juan Hill in which Theodore Roosevelt's cavalry, known as the 'Rough Riders' played an active part. He even got caught in rifle fire and was lucky enough to escape unwounded. Later he caught malaria sleeping on wet grass under a tent, but he was not ill enough to be sent home. So he remained to witness the destruction of Cervera's fleet (again through field glasses) when this unlucky admiral steamed out of Santiago Harbour on 3 July 1898. The admiral's entire fleet was destroyed, 500 men killed, wounded or drowned, and 1,700 taken prisoner. John Jacob Astor was despatched to Washington with messages, where he was given leave to recover from his illness.

Meanwhile the Astor battery sailed to the Philippines in one of the most outrageously aggressive missions in American history. The United States coveted the Philippines as 'a great prize that will give us the Eastern trade'. 'Our Asiatic squadron should blockade and, if possible, take the Philippines,' announced the Assistant Secretary of the Navy, Theodore Roosevelt, as early as 1897, a year before the war actually began. The programme was faithfully followed. The American navy sank the Spanish fleet outside Manilla during the first two weeks of the conflict; and although the Philippines government immediately set itself up as an independent state, the American army arrived to force the island into another half-century of colonial rule, a fact deeply resented to this very day.

The military campaign came to an end in three short months and once again Washington became a hotbed of officers and politicians battling over promotions and honours. In New York, the Murray Hill Republican Club suggested Theodore Roosevelt as Governor and John Jacob Astor as a Congressman. Boss Croker, an Irish-born politician who had made a fortune out of bribes and risen to the head of

In 1898, Jack Astor volunteered to fight in the Spanish-American War. He was made Lieutenant-Colonel and accompanied the Chief-of-Staff to Cuba where he saw Roosevelt's cavalry – the 'Rough Riders' – in action at San Juan Hill.

Tammany Hall, bluntly opposed the idea. 'I will stick to it that Astor is an ass and that an ass even though an Astor has no business in Congress.'

Mrs Astor was delighted to have her beloved son home in one piece and dismissed Tammany Hall's ungracious comments as the inevitable effulgence of rough Democratic circles. Some ladies complained of their sheltered lives but she, for one, preferred restrictions to insults and was particularly happy to have found a charming Lord Chamberlain to take the place of the departed McAllister – no other than society's newest favourite, Harry Lehr. Although in those days homosexuals were not classified, probably not even recognized, the witty, socially ambitious Harry had married the heiress Elizabeth Drexel, informing her on their wedding night that he would never sleep with her but would always see that she was invited to the right parties! Needless to say this aspect of his life was not known to Mrs Astor, who only saw him as a blond, plump, witty young man with a slightly mincing gait, eager to arrange her cotillions, to buy the favours for her guests and to help her in a dozen small but essential details.

Harry loved the stir that the presence of the great Mrs Astor always created, particularly when he was acting as her escort and could become part of it. Like other *grandes dames* of the Victorian era Mrs Astor never dined in public. But when Louis Sherry opened his exclusive new restaurant in 5th Avenue, Harry Lehr persuaded her that the time had come to break new ground. One Sunday evening she swept into the restaurant on Lehr's arm 'in white satin with the tiniest hair dress and her famous pearls'. 'I could hardly believe my eyes,' gasped one reporter. 'What are we coming to?' exclaimed another. 'Mrs Astor at Sherry's *table d'hote*! ... the very ultra people dining and breathing the same air as those of the "middle classes".... I never dreamed it should be given to me to gaze on the face of an Astor in a public dining room.'

Mrs Astor prided herself on her ability to change with the times. She was well aware that a new era was dawning and even took a close look at her guest list, searching for the necessary dash of 'Bohemianism'. When she ran into Elsie de Wolfe (later Lady Mendl) she said proudly, 'I am having one of those new parties, too.' When asked who was supplying the Bohemian element, she answered with perfect repose, 'Why, Edith Wharton and J.P. Morgan'.

John Jacob and Ava shared Mrs Astor's great new double house on 5th Avenue and 65th Street, and although Ava made a point of getting on well with her mother-in-law, she stretched out both arms to greet the onrushing ideas of the onrushing century. She always had a train of admirers eager to accompany her wherever she went, and often had dinner in the Waldorf-Astoria Palm Garden. 'I finally decided that Mrs John Jacob Astor ... was the most beautiful woman I had ever known,' wrote a society reporter, Mrs Harrison, who gazed at her across the crowded room. 'Sir William Orpen must want a good deal when he shouts from Paris that he has never had a perfect model. For at least twenty years society has had a flawless beauty ... not only a beautiful face but the *tout ensemble* arms, wrists, hands, ankles and a brilliant distinction, quite unforgettable.'

Sometimes Ava was audacious enough to visit a restaurant in Chinatown where she knew the *maître d'hôtel*, and to disappear into a back room to spend the evening playing mah-jong with the champion players. On one such occasion, when she had sent her servants away on a holiday, she walked into the Waldorf at midnight and asked for a room. As it was strictly forbidden to give unescorted ladies rooms after dark – and as no one knew or recognized her – she was refused. Apparently she then made such a scene that Mr Boldt was aroused from his slumbers, pulled on his clothes and hurried down to offer Mrs John Jacob Astor his abject apologies. After that the rules were changed.

Ava loved to entertain and her balls in New York and Newport were always glittering affairs. She also loved sports and encouraged her husband to commission the famous Stanford White to build an athletic complex at Ferncliffe. It was a large white building with two imposing wings, wonderfully complete, consisting of an indoor tennis court, two squash courts, a sixty-five-foot-long marble swimming pool, a rifle range, a bowling alley and a billiard room. In the winters, Ava often went to Switzerland for winter sports and was one of the first ladies to go down the Cresta. Later she raised the money for the Colony Club, a revolutionary venture launched in 1907 as 'a social and athletic club for ladies'.

Ava's swirling, tempestuous life with her houses and travels and dances and games and friends did not leave much time for her only son, Vincent, nine years old in 1900. Ava had always dreamed of a golden boy, as lean and fleet-footed as a Greek hero, and Vincent was the antithesis of her hopes. Angular and clumsy, she could not bear the sight of his unbalanced body, nor of his huge hands and feet that were always knocking things over. 'Stupid!' she would flash at him in front of a room full of people.

It is not surprising that Vincent preferred his father, who introduced him to the most glamorous of all playthings: the newly invented and far from perfected motor car. Soon the Astor garage at Ferncliffe was stocked with eighteen cars ranging from a red runabout for Ava to a seventeen-horse-power Bentley racer. That summer at Newport Jack and a few other millionaires, William K. Vanderbilt, O.H.P. Belmont and Harry Payne Whitney, staged a number of races on the beach at Newport, and several weeks later someone organized an obstacle race in which a dozen cars careered wildly around dummies of horses, dogs, children and policemen. Ava rode with Harry Lehr and Jack with a neighbour, Mrs Ladenburg. Although the contestants decorated their vehicles with everything from stuffed eagles to hydrangeas, Jack Astor's very plain, very expensive car won the race.

A few months later Ava rode down 5th Avenue with her husband – this time little Vincent was allowed to come as well – in a surrey with a steam engine under the seat. Crowds gathered on the sidewalks to wave them on but suddenly the seat became unbearably hot. The engine had caught fire, and there was no alternative to the ignominious decision to

Jack Astor was a keen driver of that new invention, the motor-car. His garage at Ferncliffe was stocked with 18 cars. Here, he is at Newport.

leap out of the burning vehicle. However this contraption was not as dangerous as the electric car 'the size of a 5th Avenue stage' which John Jacob bought in 1901 for service at Ferncliffe. He was driving around the estate with young Vincent when the car suddenly overturned, no one knows quite how or why, catapulting the passengers on to the grass verge and 'bobbing around until the engine stopped'.

He had even more mishaps with the *Nourmahal*. In 1900 it richocheted off New Hamburg Reef in the Hudson and had to be beached. He cashiered the captain but the new skipper fared just as badly, for a few weeks later, while racing against J.P. Morgan's *Corsair* – through New York Harbour of all places – he ran into a ferry. The fate of this captain is unknown, but the next man to take the job had an even worse experience for in 1901 at the Americas Cup Races Astor's yacht rammed the Vanderbilt boat, the *North Star* (a new version of the old Commodore's yacht) and the Vanderbilts promptly sued him for $15,000.

It was now widely believed that the *Nourmahal* had a jinx and it was not easy to find captains. Nevertheless Jack Astor persevered, and in 1902 had the ship remodelled. She was changed from a bark to a three-masted schooner rig and her speed raised to seventeen knots. The interior was redecorated and that marvel of the day, electricity, installed in saloons and cabins. The dining room was redesigned to accommodate sixty guests although with the *Nourmahal*'s record it was considered unlikely that the host could persuade sixty people to come aboard. When the vessel was finally completed she carried aboard a forty-two-foot steam launch – the fastest gig in New York waters, a private launch, a steam gig, a gasoline messenger launch, and six lifeboats. And as Astor was impressed by stories of modern pirates said to be lurking in Mediterranean and Caribbean waters, the yacht was also equipped with four Hotchkiss rapid-firing guns. However the greatest danger came from aggressive landmarks. In 1904 the *Nourmahal* was on the rock again, this time at Brenton's cove at Newport. As usual the captain was dismissed, although it was later proved that the buoy placed to mark the danger was out of position.

The *Nourmahal* was not the only thing running aground, for after thirteen years the Jack Astors' marriage seemed to be heading for the rocks. Ava continued to sparkle at every lighted candle and Jack continued to follow her about like a bedraggled and slightly bad-tempered spaniel. In 1902 Ava gave birth to a second child – this time a daughter, Alice – and friends hoped that the marriage had taken a turn for the better. But soon after, Ava was off alone on a trip to England, and when she came back she could talk of nothing but the newest craze: bridge. According to Harry Lehr's wife, Elizabeth Drexel, Jack Astor scarcely saw his guests at Ferncliffe, for Ava Astor filled the house with bridge players who, from the moment they arrived, would have their noses glued to the table.

Their host [Elizabeth wrote] who detested bridge and was far more at home going at top speed in his new racing car or at the helm of his yacht in a storm than in his own drawing room, shambled from room to room, tall, loosely built and ungraceful, rather like a great over-grown colt, in a vain search for someone to talk to. He was not even permitted to enjoy the Mignon-Welte pianos which he had installed all over the house, for a few minutes after he had turned one on a footman would appear, ... 'Mrs Astor asks you to stop the music, sir. She says it is disturbing the bridge players....' And he would sigh and turn it off. He was not particularly fond of music, but the mechanical system of the pianos interested him; it offered a temporary diversion at least.

He would go up to his room and dress faultlessly for dinner, come down, prepared to talk and entertain his guests, and find everyone scurrying upstairs to make a hasty, last-minute toilet. Of course they would all be late, which annoyed him intensely, for he made a god of punctuality; and the probability of a spoilt dinner ... did not improve his temper for he was a notable epicure. The house party would come down to find him, watch in hand, constrained and irritable.

Dinner was not an enjoyable meal for him. Never a brilliant conversationalist at the best of times, he would be wanting to discuss what Willie Vanderbilt's new car was capable of doing, or whether the chef Oliver Belmont had brought back from France was really better than his own. And instead he had to listen to interminable post-mortems – 'You should have returned my lead....' It was the same thing next morning. He would come downstairs ready for church in cutaway coat and immaculate topper, only to find rubbers in progress already. So he would sit alone in the front pew, come back to lunch off a tray in the study and return to New York in the afternoon, a lonely man in spite of all his acquaintances.

No matter how difficult the relations between the John Jacob Astors, a divorce was unthinkable – at least for the time being. Old Mrs Astor was in her seventies and it would not be right to darken her remaining years.

Instead, Jack Astor tried to pass the time by involving himself in the problems of the Astor Estate Office. He did not run the business himself, as three previous generations of Astors had done, but instead appointed

competent men to work for him: Charles Peabody, Philip Kissam and Charles Southmayd, the eminent family lawyer.

This was a sensible move as Astor real estate had become big business. In 1900 the family was reckoned to be receiving rentals that grossed $9,000,000 a year, while the Estate was estimated to be worth $200,000,000 compared to the $40,000,000 of only twenty-five years before – 'the most phenomenal growth ever recorded for such a fortune'. Burton Hendrick, a contemporary writer, prophesied that the Astors would be worth a billion in 1920 and eighty billion in 2000, and he called the Estate 'the world's greatest monument to unearned increment' or more explicitly 'a first mortgage on Fate itself'.

This seemed no exaggeration at the time. The Thompson farm which ran along 5th Avenue where the Waldorf-Astoria now stood had been bought by William Backhouse for $35,000 and was worth $35,000,000, a thousand times what he had paid for it. And the twenty-four-foot lots along 39th Street were valued at $200,000 each, lots that formed only a fraction of the farm land which the first John Jacob Astor had bought in 1803 for $25,000. And now that the American aristocratic families were leaving their brownstone houses on Lower 5th Avenue, Tiffany's and Gorham's were moving in and paying $36,000 a year for a fifty-foot front.

Yet there were plenty of problems as well, for three quarters of the Astor income came from the hundreds of tenement houses owned by the Estate, and these slum dwellings had become a target of constant and widespread reproach. In 1894 the City of New York established a Tenement House Commission to look into the situation and a young Danish writer, Jacob Riis, began to shock people by his descriptions. 'In the Astor tenements on Elizabeth Street where we found 43 families living

In the 1890s the slum tenements (left and right) owned by the Astors – but usually sub-let to contractors – became more and more of a reproach to the City of New York authorities. The report of the Commission established in 1894 prompted Jack Astor to follow the example of his cousin, William Waldorf, and sell some of his tenement buildings.

in rooms intended for 16, I saw women finishing 'pants' at 30 cents a day,' he wrote. Carefully this report measured the three rooms, each of which often housed a family; one was 14 by 11 feet, one 7 by 11, the other 7 by $8\frac{1}{2}$. Only one flat in this tenement had one family in it, three had two each, twelve had a family in each room. The building was one of the notorious 'dumbells' with a dark, narrow, evil-smelling, airshaft. Of all kinds of slum dwellings, said the Tenement House Commission of 1894, 'It is the one hopeless form of tenement construction. It cannot be ventilated, it cannot be well lighted, it is not safe in case of fire.' At 260–270 Elizabeth Street there had been no water for a month because the pipes were frozen. John Jacob Astor couldn't know that because he was not responsible for maintenance. That had been entrusted to an Italian undertaker as lessee, who openly boasted of the profitability of housing people below as well as above the ground.

Jack Astor decided to follow the example of his cousin William, who was selling many of his slum properties. In 1900 he disposed of some fifty tenements in the 5th Avenue district for which he received $850,000. His decision to rid himself of the worst tenements came in the nick of time for in 1901 the City set up a new department to enforce laws that were on the statute books but never observed. In 1902 the committee reported that Astor property still had courtyard lavatories, long forbidden; and that forty years after the passing of fireproofing regulations Astor tenements were still ignoring the law. On Avenue A and East 4th Street the department ordered several tenements evacuated for sanitary reasons.

Of course, many of the buildings that drew the sharpest condemnations were still run by sub-landlords who had put up their own houses; but as they had to pay rent to the Astors as well as paying back their mortgages, they were hard pushed to make a living.

A contemporary journalist, Harvey Sutherland, explained: 'When the Astors buy land they keep it . . . if they do not get the price they think they ought to from a piece of property they let it lie idle rather than scale down the rent. Or they let you pull the house down and build on a 21-year lease, at the end of which the Astor Estate has all the ground rent on the house you have built. . . . It behoves a Gould or a Vanderbilt to have all his wits. An Astor needs but sit tight and collect his rents.

Even though New York's first skyscraper, the famous Tower Building, had withstood gale-force winds, the Astor Estate did not embark on a more daring building programme. The truth of the matter was that slum property still commanded the largest returns. As Americans were coming to realize, quantity was far more profitable than quality in every sort of venture, from toothpaste to sleeping space. Although for prestige purposes the Astors occasionally put up an imposing giant like the Exchange Court on Broadway, from a business point of view nothing was more lucrative than a crowded tenement. As the city grew in population, rents doubled and tripled and quadrupled and property values increased as much as one thousand per cent; the Astors' decision to resist speculative innovations was not only understandable but also thoroughly good business.

Although William Waldorf had settled in England he maintained an interest in New York, and in 1900 had the Hotel Astor built in Longacre Square.

Nevertheless, William Waldorf was fascinated by hotels; and, although he now lived in England, in 1900 he directed the building of the Astor Hotel in Longacre Square hoping to make the area fashionable so that the land values would rise. Luck smiled on this venture for the subway – which the Astors had blocked for years – suddenly leaped forward, running up East Side from City Hall to Grand Central Station, westward across 42nd Street to Longacre Square, then northward on Broadway to 145th Street. The underground opened its Longacre station in 1904 the year Astor opened his new hotel; and shortly after he opened his new hotel the *New York Times* decided to take advantage of the amenities and to move its offices into the area. Longacre was renamed Times Square and Jack Astor hastened to compete with his cousin by building a second hotel, the Knickerbocker, across the way from the Astor. Both hotels proved so prosperous that William W. financed the exclusive Netherland on 5th Avenue at 59th Street and Jack Astor countered with the St Regis on 5th Avenue and 57th Street. 'These amazing Astors,' wrote an admiring Frenchman, 'could stroll from Broadway or Fifth Avenue stretching out their arms hither and yon, saying "Mine, all mine!"'

Meanwhile, America's ageing but tireless queen continued to carry out her functions as society's leader. Although her annual ball was still the most important social event of the year, the new generation complained that cotillions were boring and hoped that someone would provide amusement. Mrs Astor's lord chamberlain, Harry Lehr, could not resist pranks and encouraged Mrs Stuyvesant Fish, a lady of impeccable lineage, to give all sorts of ludicrous entertainments in the name of diversion. One evening a baby elephant wandered around her ballroom distributing peanuts; another time her guests arrived dressed like dolls and were told to talk baby-talk; still another evening she organized a dinner for one hundred dogs at which the owner of the canine guest of honour presented his bitch with a jewelled collar worth $15,000. Other cruder and richer hosts bettered Mrs Fish's innovations by spending hundreds of thousands of dollars transforming ballrooms into lakes and forests. One man gave a ball at which all the guests arrived on horseback; another presented the gentlemen at his dinner party with cigars wrapped in $100 bills instructing them to smoke the banknotes as 'the taste was delicious'.

Mrs Astor refused to lower her standards. Although she was well aware of the turbulent waters swirling around her, she did not even get her feet wet. Her only innovation was to give an interview to the press, which she did with considerable effect.

I am not vain enough to believe that New York will not be able to get on without me, [she told the American people]. Many women will rise up to fill my place. But I hope that my influence will be felt in one thing, and that is, in discountenancing the undignified methods employed by certain New York women to attract a following. They have given entertainments that belonged under a circus tent rather than in a gentlewoman's house.

When Mrs Astor gave what proved to be her penultimate ball in 1904, she invited 1200 people. The 'Four Hundred' had faded into history for, as everyone knew, society was the exact number Mrs Astor cared to make it; and Mrs Astor favoured the number her ballroom could most comfortably hold. However, the event provoked acute disappointment as the public liked to see Caroline applying the whip to the arrogant rich. 'SHE LETS BARS WAY DOWN AND ASKS EVEN THE EDGE OF THE FRINGE OF SOCIETY', one disillusioned headline informed the world.

However, her last banquet did something to restore her reputation for exclusiveness. She gave a dinner for Prince Louis Mountbatten to which she asked only seventy-nine people, excluding even the Vanderbilts. This caused more of a newspaper stir than the actual event but this time the newspapers were deeply satisfied. Even *Town Topics* had realized the futility of beating against an impregnable wall and now, after ten years of quarrel, showered the old lady with fulsome compliments. 'Because Mrs Astor could not accommodate more than 80 persons in her dining room when she entertained Prince Louis on Tuesday night the newspapers jumped to the conclusion that the high priestess of *haut ton* was going to restrict society more narrowly than ever before. What nonsense! Mrs Astor does not give herself airs about social position and exclusiveness.' One can imagine the writer of this surprising sentence pausing and taking a deep breath before ending with the words: 'Few realize how simple and unaffected she is.'

Although *Town Topics* had changed its tune, the younger generation began to make fun of the old lady. If the new age was less pompous, it was also crueller and more vindictive and it became a sort of game to link her name in marriage with all sorts of people ranging from Harry Lehr to Alexander Clarke, her French doctor. Even more embarrassing were the practical jokes. In Paris an unknown wag sent out engraved cards in Mrs Astor's name inviting four-hundred leading lights, including cabinet ministers and ambassadors, to dinner. But the public did not think these capers funny. Over the years they had come to venerate the old lady for her superb dignity, a commodity that often seemed in short supply.

However, there was one Astor 'tease' – harmless to the great dowager who probably never heard of it – which became a minor classic with the years. The idea was conceived in 1896 when Frederick Head, a quixotic lawyer who practised in Chicago and as a hobby amused himself by weaving improbable stories about famous people, attended a dinner and sat next to Miss Olmstead, the daughter of Frederick Olmstead, who had designed New York's Central Park. Apparently Miss Olmstead told Mr Head that her father had bought a small island off the coast of Maine, near Penobscot Bay; and soon they were talking about the notorious eighteenth century pirate, Captain Kidd, who operated in these waters and was said to have buried treasure along the coast which had never been found.

This was enough for Head's fertile imagination, and before long he had produced a masterly work, sober, well-documented, so persuasive in invention and so conscientious in detail it was difficult to believe it could be a fabrication. It told how John Jacob Astor had become America's richest man. Entitled *A Notable Lawsuit* it was read in 1896 to a small literary society in Chicago who were completely spellbound. Kidd had buried his treasure in a strong-box on Dere Island, an Olmstead possession; a French fur trapper, Jacques Cartier, employed by Astor had found the box in 1801 and taken it to his master; John Jacob had sent the box to London and sold the contents for over a million dollars. From that moment Astor had never looked back.

However, in 1892 the Olmstead family (so the author claimed) sued the descendants of John Jacob Astor for the original sum appropriated from their land, plus the compound interest for one hundred years, which amounted to five million dollars. Apparently lawyers were now discussing the matter and it looked as though there would be a settlement out of court.

Although Mr Frederick Head died in 1914, members of the Chicago Literary Club, not to mention the Rowfant Club in Cleveland, continued to discuss the brilliant little story and every twenty years or so a copy was produced and re-read to the club. The reader will find the tale reproduced in the appendix of this book, partly because it is a *tour de force*, partly because rumours persist to this very day that the Astor fortune derived, mysteriously, from Captain Kidd. Indeed, when the present writer began this biography a well-known New York advertising man kindly sent a photostat copy of *A Notable Lawsuit* as something 'worth investigating'.

It is doubtful if the great Mrs Astor ever heard of *A Notable Lawsuit* and even more doubtful that she would have found the contents in the least amusing. In 1905 she gave what proved to be her last ball, and although no one knew that the end was approaching the accounts have a faintly nostalgic flavour. *Town Topics* wrote on 12 January:

After half a century of social activity Mrs Astor again stood before society, looking regal in a magnificent Marie Antoinette constume of the deepest shade of purple velvet, both the skirt and bodice trimmed with a rich shade of pale blue satin, embroidered with gold paillettes. Her jewels were superb. She wore a massive tiara that seemed a burden upon her head, and she was further weighed down by an enormous dog collar of pearls with diamond pendant attachments. She wore also the celebrated Marie Antoinette stomacher of diamonds and a huge diamond corsage ornament. Diamonds and pearls were pinned here and there about the bodice. She was a dozen Tiffany cases personified.... After the cotillion Mrs Astor slipped away and retired.

At the end of the year Queen Caroline had a stroke and retired from active life. There were rumours that she sometimes wandered through her white and gold reception room greeting guests who long ago had departed from the world. When she died in 1908 the silver plaque on her casket bore the simple inscription: Caroline Webster Astor. Mrs Astor was dead. And when the coffin slid into its cold resting place an epoch went with her.

Within thirteen months of Mrs Astor's death the John Jacob Astors were divorced. The news came like a clap of thunder for the press had no inkling that it was even pending. The announcement on 9 November 1909 was a *fait accompli*; the decree had been granted, the case was closed. Apparently, the day before, judges and legal advisers had travelled to an unknown town in upper New York, known as New City. The party consisted of Supreme Court Justice Mills, Referee Charles Young and two lawyers – Lewis Ledyard for Colonel Astor and Henry Taft, brother of the President, for Mrs Astor. Mills climbed on the bench, Taft presented the motion and the Justice quickly confirmed the Referee's report. Taft then asked that the papers be sealed and it was over.

The press howled with fury at being cheated of the best society story in a decade. 'Such proceedings tend to confirm the popular impression,' said the *Sun*, 'that there is one law for the rich, another for the poor.' It even provoked one of Mills's fellow Justices to lash out at the determination to protect 'the names of the people involved' and accuse him of 'favouritism'. But Mills replied stoutly: 'I order the paper sealed on account of the children.' No one bothered to point out that as the rich and privileged automatically became front page news, unlike more humble people, it was only fair that some consideration be shown to bring them into line with ordinary mortals.

In January 1911 Jack Astor gave a huge ball at 840 5th Avenue. He had redone the house, restoring it from a double to a single residence. He had ripped out the grand staircase, which society beauties had loved, and made a central courtyard; turned the dining room into a study and one of the reception rooms into a dining room. He received his guests flanked by the redoubtable Mrs Ogden Mills and Mrs Douglas Robinson, a sister of Theodore Roosevelt. That evening he paid noticeable attention to a pretty eighteen-year-old girl, Madeleine Force, whom he had met on one of his cruises to Bar Harbour, Maine. She was chaperoned by her large, buxom mother, referred to behind her back as 'La Force Majeure'.

No one took the romance seriously because Madeleine was considered most unsuitable, pretty in an uninteresting schoolgirlish way, younger than Jack's son, Vincent, and, most unforgiveable of all, she was the daughter of a Brooklyn shipping clerk. However, Jack's friends became anxious that summer when Astor took mother and daughter cruising on his new boat, the *Noma*. Before the trip was over the engagement was announced, and the marriage took place a month later, in September 1911.

In the autumn Astor brought his bride to New York to introduce her to the fashionable world, but society turned its back. So he took her on a long journey to Egypt and France. By March she was pregnant and they decided to return to America. Jack booked passages on the world's newest and largest luxury liner, the *Titanic*, which was about to make its maiden trip across the Atlantic. Although the streamlined giantess was known as 'the unsinkable ship', when Lord Rothschild was asked to join the syndicate arranging the vessel's insurance, he declined.

The vessel was four days out and nearing Newfoundland when in the early hours of 15 April, at 2.30 in the morning GMT, it ploughed full steam into an iceberg that should not have been so far south. Captain Smith, duly impressed by the importance of all Astors, informed the Colonel what had happened before the other passengers were told. According to one eye-witness, when John Jacob handed his pregnant wife into a lifeboat he asked second officer Lightoller if he could accompany her, explaining that she was 'in a delicate condition'. 'No sir,' Lightoller replied, 'No men are allowed in these boats until the women are loaded first.' Although it was obvious even then that there would not be enough boats for everyone, Astor assured his wife that he would follow soon. Later Madeleine said that she protested at leaving him but he shook his head and told her she must go. 'To please me,' he added gently.

John Jacob Astor, the man without a heart, had found happiness at the end of his life: at last he cared for another being. He was icily calm as the end approached. Apparently a barber standing near him on the deck begged him to put on a life-preserver and jump. 'I am not going to jump,' he said. Slowly the great ship foundered then suddenly turned almost perpendicular before diving to its watery grave.

On 15 April the fantastic story began to reach New York in a series of excited wireless snatches, frequently so garbled as to be nonsensical.

The *Titanic* had struck an iceberg and was 'down at the head and putting women and children into lifeboats'. That was all. In those days amateurs were allowed to use the ether at will and the air was so crowded it was impossible to get confirmation from London. The White Star Office in New York knew no more than anyone else. The editors could not believe that the unsinkable had sunk, and finally decided to print the rumour as rumour and not to play it up.

The *New York Times* was the only New York paper to commit itself fully. On 16 April the public awoke to read the following banner headlines:

TITANIC SUNK FOUR HOURS AFTER HITTING ICEBERG
866 RESCUED BY CARPATHIA PROBABLY 1250 PERISH
ISMAY SAFE MRS ASTOR MAYBE NOTED NAMES MISSING

Very few people had heard of Ismay, the managing director of the White Star Line (news of his safety was printed as a rebuke), but everybody knew about the Astors. A smaller headline announced that John Jacob Astor was abroad, another that his heir, Vincent Astor, had called at the White Star Office and had left weeping. There was no more news as the rescue ship *Carpathia* refused to answer the shoal of queries that descended upon her. The *New York World* protested:

CARPATHIA LETS NO SECRETS OF THE TITANIC'S LOSS
ESCAPE BY WIRELESS

The *Evening News* was even blunter:

WATCHERS ANGERED BY CARPATHIA'S SILENCE

Later the captain explained that he was saving his wireless for official traffic and private messages between survivors and their families.

So it was not until the morning of 19 April, three and a half days after the disaster, and twelve hours after the arrival of the *Carpathia* in New York harbour, that the full story was known. One of the survivors was the *Titanic*'s wireless operator, Harold Bride, who gave the *New York Times* an exclusive account underneath these headlines:

745 SAW TITANIC SINK WITH 1595 HER BAND PLAYING
HIT ICEBERG AT 21 KNOTS AND TORE HER BOTTOM OUT
I'LL FOLLOW THE SHIP LAST WORDS OF CAPT SMITH
MANY WOMEN STAYED TO PERISH WITH HUSBANDS

All the newspapers carried front-page stories about the Astors:

Colonel Astor Went Down Waving Farewell to His Bride
Goodbye Dearest I'll Join You Later On
Vincent Astor Still Hopes
The Titanic's Rescued Tell of Colonel Astor's Heroism As Ship Went Down
Mrs Astor Pulled Oars in Titanic's Life Boats

Twenty-year-old Vincent Astor, now head of the American family, met his pregnant, nineteen-year-old stepmother with two doctors, a trained nurse and a secretary. A week later John Jacob's body was recovered and early in May a service was held at Rhinebeck.

When the Will was read it was revealed that Madeleine had relinquished her dower rights in the Astor Estate for an outright settlement of $1,695,000. A trust fund of $3,000,000 had been set aside for her unborn child. She also had other pecuniary advantages but they were conditional upon her not marrying again: the income from a $5,000,000 trust, use of the 5th Avenue house, and 'Beechwood' in Newport.

Astor's daughter, Alice, was given a trust fund of $5,000,000 to be hers absolutely when she reached the age of twenty-one, but to revert to Vincent if she died childless.

The remainder of the fortune went to Vincent and was appraised at $87,000,000, the first time that the public had ever had an exact accounting of the wealth of an Astor. $63,000,000 was in real estate, and $24,000,000 in personal property including stocks and bonds.

For once the newspaper could not complain about the Astors' lack of support for their main charity, the Astor Library, founded by the first John Jacob Astor, as it was no longer under the family's control. When the two Astor brothers had died in 1890 and 1892, John Jacob III had left the usual sum of $400,000 to the library, just as his father and grandfather had done before him. But when William Astor died two years later he left only $50,000, making it plain that the family had no intention of becoming the library's main support. So in 1895 the trustees of the Astor, Tilden and Lennox libraries got together and decided to pool their rescources in an attempt to create a major New York Public Library of which the Astor Library would serve as the reference division. Andrew Carnegie gave $5,000,000 to build branches in all parts of the city and work was started on the central building at 5th Avenue and 42nd Street. It was finished in 1911 just twelve months before Jack Astor's death; and it still stands today as the world's greatest reference library.

Jack Astor's philanthropies amounted to less than $50,000 – a few small bequests to trustees and employees, and $30,000 to his old school, St Paul's. Some people tried to explain his lack of generosity – mean even by Astor standards – by suggesting that he had left nothing to charity because of the new property tax levied by the State of New York. Although the tax seemed mild at 3·7 per cent it cost the Astor estate over three million dollars.

6 The first English Astors

MR. ASTOR

PEOPLE are asking themselves whether Mr. Carnegie could be right in urging Mr. W. W. Astor to shoulder the responsibilities of his unique position and place himself at the head of the movement for the reunion of the English-speaking race. Mr. Astor has great advantages for playing such a part. He has wealth without envy, he comes of a good breed, he has the sense of responsibility—all that is good. He is also not without ambition, social and journalistic, as his recent adventures prove. But whether he is man enough for this other work time alone can show.

Previous page *Andrew Carnegie decided to back William Waldorf in a get-together peace forever move but his suggestions came to nothing.*

William Waldorf Astor did not make a public statement when the cousin he disliked went down in the Titanic. He had been living in London for over twenty years and on the morning that the news broke spent his day in the usual way, barricaded behind the heavy doors of his wonderfully ornate office on Victoria Embankment.

William Waldorf was forty-two-years-old in 1890 when his father died and he stepped into his shoes as America's richest man. He was rumoured to have inherited $300,000,000 but more conservative estimates put the figure at $175,000,000 and reckoned that even on this accounting his annual income from Manhatten rents could not be a penny less than $6,000,000 a year. A big burly fellow with brilliant blue eyes and a sweeping moustache, he seemed custom-built to revel in life – yet his looks belied his morose, shy and almost pathologically sensitive nature. Indeed he seemed devoid of all the usual Astor characteristics for he hated business and loved the arts. He was widely read and a connoisseur of beauty ranging from sculpture to women. He gave generously to charity and spent prodigious sums on restoring the wonderful old houses that he bought. He had the best chef and the best cellar in England.

Even his faults had nothing Astoresque about them but seemed to be strictly his own. He was cantankerous in a way that none of his forebears had been. Abnormally quick to take offence, he frequently imagined slights where none had been intended. He was no mean opponent, for his most impressive talent was to phrase his replies in words absolutely bound to infuriate. No doubt this came from hours of silent brooding over how to get even. When he had taken his wife and three children to live in England after his battle with Aunt Caroline in 1891, he had announced, with a throw-away line well-calculated to incense the whole United States: 'America is not a fit place for a gentleman to live.'

Later, he made things worse by elaborating in a voice of sweet reasonableness: 'America is good enough for any man who has to make a livelihood, though why travelled people of independent means should remain there more than a week is not readily to be comprehended.' In the 1890s Europe was a paradise for rich men, abounding in unspoilt scenery, beautiful houses, fascinating company. The fact that William Waldorf had hit upon an essential truth seemed to upset the Americans more than the basest lie. The uproar which followed only shows how great the power of self-deception can be, how great the rivalry of the new world for the old. As Mrs Trollope had pointed out fifty years before, Americans revered money; now they were humiliated to think that their richest man, whose name was a household word, had abandoned them.

However, William Waldorf not only had a streak of perverseness but liked to tease. And on 12 July 1892 every paper in New York, except for James Gordon Bennett's *Herald*, printed the front-page news that William Waldorf Astor had died of pneumonia in his house in London. True, some of the papers were uneasy about the story as servants at Astor's home, Lansdowne House (rented not owned), denied the report of his death, saying that he had a slight cold but was recovering. On the other hand the Astor Estate Office in London had put out the announcement of his demise and Astor's lawyers in America had contributed moving tributes to the dead man as artist, writer, lawyer and politician.

The Philadelphia *Public Ledger*, in deference to one of the city's daughters – William's wife, Mary Paul – wrote in exaggerated terms: 'His nature was kindly, his manner simple, unaffected, sincere. He had many friends who admired him for his learning, his talents, and the noble qualities of heart which were his most distinguished characteristics.' The *New York Tribune*, although supposed to be one of his most loyal supporters, struck a disagreeable note. 'The death of William Waldorf Astor, though not an event of great and lasting significance whether in the world of action or the world of thought, will be generally deplored.'

The next morning all the papers with the exception of the *Herald* had the humiliating task of informing their readers: 'w.w. ASTOR IS NOT DEAD.' The *Tribune* obviously had a guilty conscience for it noted sourly that Astor 'would enjoy the rather remarkable distinction of reading his own obituary notices'. An investigation took place but nothing could be discovered apart from the fact that the hoax had started in W.W.'s office and that W.W. was believed to think the whole affair very funny. The London press tried to reach Astor but failed as his movements were shrouded in mystery and his servants had instructions, on pain of instant dismissal, to give no information to the press. This prompted one journalist to send a story to the *New York Tribune* that Astor's mind was affected, an allegation that was promptly denied by the *Associated Press* which described the millionaire as a sort of recluse. 'The Astors have always lived a peculiar life here; they know few people and live in solitary state at Lansdowne House.' Although Astor had a mania against talking to the press, he was far from alone at this time. William Waldorf's eldest son, another Waldorf, was at Eton, his second son, John Jacob, at an English preparatory school, and his daughters, Pauline and Gwendolyn, at London day schools. The children were encouraged to bring their friends home in the holidays and William Waldorf periodically gave large and pompous dinner parties. It was one of the few periods in his life when he was surrounded by people.

However, in 1894 his wife Mary died and although the marriage had never been an outstanding success, he admitted that he missed her gentle, consoling presence. Perhaps for this reason his life became increasingly active. In 1893 he had bought the *Pall Mall Gazette*, an evening newspaper directed by John Morely, E.T. Cook, and William Steed, all ardent reformists. (Steed was famous for his crusade in 1885 against child prostitution.) Although these men believed that their ideas contained a panacea for all ills, the new proprietor called them together and told them that the paper would no longer reflect Liberal opinions. It would be 'a paper written by gentlemen for gentlemen' and as such, strictly Tory. Needless to say the management walked out *en bloc* which is what Astor wanted. Soon after, he engaged Mr Harry Cust, a Tory MP and heir to the Earl of Brownlow, as his new editor. According to H. G. Wells, Cust's knowledge of literature and the world was 'manifest as his manners were charming'. Cust collected a brilliant high-spirited staff, displaying aristocratic disregard for expenditure suitable to the proprietor's income. Fleet Street, cynical though it was, was amazed by Cust's office which was established in a magnificent suite of rooms appropriate for a royal reception.

Astor was eager to contribute articles to the paper, but Cust fobbed him off by arguing that his ideas were more suitable for a literary magazine. Astor agreed and founded the *Pall Mall Magazine*, 'a handsome thing, entertaining but not frivolous, refined but not weak'. The first issue included a poem by Swinburne and an article on Madame Recamier written by himself. The literary magazine was followed by the *Pall Mall Budget*, a woman's journal specializing in sewing and cooking and happy hints for housewives; in the few months before his wife's death, it became her favourite reading. One of its chief contributors was H.G. Wells who supplied the magazine with science fiction articles and later told how he earned the incredible sum of one thousand pounds a year.

Astor could not find business premises that suited him, so he bought a house on Victoria Embankment and spent $1,500,000 demolishing the rooms and halls and rebuilding them. The outside of the building was

The private house on Victoria Embankment which William Waldorf converted into the most luxurious office in the world at the cost of $1,500,000. He did not neglect to install the world's most sophisticated burglar alarm system which, at the touch of a button, automatically locked every door, thus providing a severe handicap for intruders.

made of Portland stone. Inside the floors were inlaid with marble, the ceilings covered with allegorical paintings, and the staircase decorated with statues modelled after the figures in Astor's romantic novels. The great hall, on the second floor, was seventy feet long and had a hammer-beam roof in Spanish mahogany.

The building contained two bedrooms and bathrooms, a *pied à terre* where Astor occasionally received his lady friends. Otherwise the house consisted of a series of resplendent rooms which were used as offices. Outside a large plaque said 'Astor Estate Office'; inside two real estate officials dealt with his Manhattan property. A large gilded weathervane on the roof depicting Columbus's ship suggested that the fortune had come from the New World.

However, as Astor was a nervous man and lived in constant fear of assassination (the fault of a drunken fortune-teller, some people said), the building not only had its classical delights, but was equipped with the most modern burglar-proof devices that could be procured. In case Astor should be disturbed by an unexpected sound, he could press a button in bedroom or study which automatically locked every door in the house. Apparently a tradesman was once trapped by this manoeuvre and to his horror saw that there were no handles on the doors. Apart from this precaution, the ground floor windows were heavily barred; there was only one outside door which guests and servants had to share; and on the owner's bedside table two loaded revolvers were always ready for use.

Astor also acquired a fine house on Carlton House Terrace overlooking St James's Park and a superlative country estate on the Thames which he purchased from the Duke of Westminster. The first Cliveden had been built in 1661 by George Villiers, the second Duke of Buckingham, of whom Dryden wrote:

> Stiff in opinions always wrong
> Was everything by starts nothing long

In the eighteenth century Frederick, Prince of Wales, son of George II, rented the house for a short period and amused himself by watching boat races, plays and musicals. Apparently *Rule Britannia* was first played there in the Prince's grassy amphitheatre overlooking the river.

The house was destroyed by fire in 1795, rebuilt, bought by the Duke of Sutherland, and again gutted in 1848. The new house which stands today was designed by Sir Charles Barry, architect of the House of Commons. It was a gigantic and lordly creation, more like an Italian palace than an English country house, with a commanding view of the Thames. Although some people criticized its proportions, no one could fault its wonderful rolling land: the wooded walks, the exquisite groves, the hanging gardens above Cliveden Reach, which constituted the loveliest half mile on the Thames. Astor willingly paid the Duke $1,250,000 for the property which included the house and much of the furniture. Later, the Duke asked him to return several art treasures which had been included by mistake and Astor obliged. But when Westminster demanded the Visitor's Book containing the famous signatures of two hundred years, the purchaser flatly refused.

For generations the public had been accustomed to boating along the Thames and picnicking in the woods of the Cliveden estate; and sometimes walking parties stopped and peered through the iron-grilled gates at the end of the drive. But Astor hated the public, so he pulled down the gate, forbade the boating parties to land and threw a huge stone wall around the property, surmounted by jagged bits of glass. He even enclosed a spring of water which had been open to the public for years, and despite numerous requests refused to allow sightseeing parties, even once a year, to enter the grounds to see the world's largest fountain 'The Fountain of Love' which he had bought in Italy for $250,000. The three statues were made of Sicilian marble and showed a woman battling with Cupid; the last statue showed her recumbent.

The democratic English were indignant. 'No reasonable man,' one old gentleman wrote, 'wishes to prevent American or citizens of other States from inhabiting our country. But if they wish to do so, their first duty is to show decent respect for the customs of their adopted country. Failing this it becomes a duty to ask if there is no way to teach them good manners.' Apparently there was no way at all, but London's *jeunesse dorée* found the whole thing funny and referred to Waldorf Astor as 'Walled Off Astor'.

Criticism did not seem to trouble this strange millionaire. The Prince of Wales, the future Edward VII, adored rich men and he beamed upon Astor, which was enough to encourage William Waldorf to give vent to the most outrageous and spiteful acts. Once, when he gave a concert at his town house, Carlton House Terrace, he spied a gentleman that he did not know. He went up to him and said: 'I have not had the pleasure of your acquaintance and I must ask you to leave. I will insert a notice in the newspapers about this.'

The unfortunate man was Captain Sir Berkley Milne of the Royal Navy who had been brought to the party by Lady Oxford with whom he had been dining and who assured him that the host would be delighted. Despite Milne's written apology and explanation, Astor inserted a paragraph in the *Pall Mall Gazette* of 6 July 1900: 'We are desired to make known that the presence of Captain Sir Berkley Milne of the Naval and Military Club, Piccadilly, at Mr Astor's concert last Thursday evening, was uninvited.'

Sir Berkley's friends were furious, the navy felt that it had been personally insulted and the Prince of Wales went out of his way to make amends by inviting poor Captain Milne to the royal box at the theatre the next night. William Waldorf departed for Marienbad to take the cure untroubled by the storm he had caused. The *Saturday Review* declared hotly that Astor was unworthy of 'untying the latchet' of the Captain's shoe. 'We only regret that the gallant servant of Her Majesty so far forgot his dignity to accept a second-hand invitation to the house of the purse-proud American whose dollars could not save him from the contempt of his countrymen.'

The members of the Carlton Club, led by the Prince, demanded an apology which Astor had printed in the *Gazette* explaining not very truthfully that the incident had been caused by a misapprehension.

'Explanations of a completely categorical kind now show that Sir Berkley Milne's presence was due to a misunderstanding that entirely absolves him from any individual discourtesy.'

Astor's rudeness seemed to grow with the years. He gave enormous dinners but often went to bed and left the party to fend for itself. Other times he told guests that he expected them to leave not a minute later than one o'clock. And at Cliveden he drew up schedules and timetables that he expected everyone to follow. After lunch one day he asked each lady how she planned to spend her afternoon. One replied that she had some letters to write. When she had finished them she strolled into the garden but a servant ran out saying as tactfully as possible that Mr Astor expected people to follow the schedules they had settled upon. ' "In that case you may call the carriage," she said. "I shan't stay a minute longer." "I'm sorry, Madam, but Mr Astor doesn't allow the carriage to be called at a time that has not been appointed." ' By now she was so angry that she carried her bag down the road to Taplow and hired a hansom-cab to take her to the station.

Nevertheless Astor could command whatever guests he liked, and made a point of collecting royalty as such people were used to time-schedules. Before Edward VII's coronation he invited the Crown Prince of Roumania and his British-born wife, Princess Marie, to stay at Clive-den, accompanied of course by a considerable suite. There the future Queen Marie met William Waldorf's eldest son, Waldorf, and his daughter, Pauline. Later, in her memoirs, she described the weeks at Cliveden as '*absolute* happiness' and her meeting with Waldorf 'as the starting point of a very dear friendship which has meant much in my life'.

For once the autocratic father remained apart and allowed the young people to enjoy themselves. Usually his pernickity, humourless nature seemed to be engulfed by a cloud of black melancholy which was all pervasive. As a boy he had been inquisitive and high-spirited, but his harsh upbringing had darkened his mind and destroyed his zest for life. His mother, the Southern belle, Charlotte Augusta, who had such advanced ideas about Negroes and slum children, totally neglected her only child. He was turned over to governesses who not only managed to frighten him but to give him a neurosis from which he never re-covered. Years later he wrote to a lady friend:

I was myself brought up severely and kept upon a pitiful allowance. If I had not the benefit of conventional rules I lived in an atmosphere of sinister religion filled with hobgoblins that people believed in sixty years ago and that I taught my children to make merry over when they were young. I was a mis-chievous little animal and everybody kept telling me I was so bad. The hellfire sermons of my childhood the like of which no congregation out of Scotland would listen to today frightened me silly and I knew those red hot things were being made ready for *me*.

Astor's spartan childhood, his cold, uninteresting home life, the unfair taunts about rich men in politics, combined to make him equate his native land with unhappiness. His most exciting years had been spent in Rome where he had spent hundreds of thousands of dollars on paintings and marbles. He had become famous overnight when he bought the entire balustrade of the Villa Borghese, 'a beautiful and massive structure in stone, complete with fountains and statues, in all some two hundred yards long'. The one which nows stands in the Borghese gardens in Rome is a replica, for Astor had the original sent to England and put up at Cliveden.

Although for a long time Astor felt that he would never recapture the pleasures of Rome, he was now beginning to enjoy England, even to bask in long periods of contentment that battled successfully with his morose nature. Under these circumstances it is not surprising that in 1899 a paragraph in the *Gazette* announced that William Waldorf had become a naturalized Englishman. It is difficult today to understand the resentment of the United States in losing this contentious millionaire. Yet we are told that a jeering crowd surged up Broadway carrying an effigy of Astor placarded 'THE TRAITOR'. The popular press inveighed against him as 'the richest man that America ever owned and that disowned America'.

Astor never seemed to be able to resist pouring oil on a fire that had already become a conflagration. When he heard that a group of Americans living in London were thinking of buying the battle flag of the USS *Chesapeake*, famous for her brave but unsuccessful stand against the English in 1807, he stepped in and bought the *Chesapeake* flag himself. But instead of sending it back to America, as the others had planned to do, he presented it to the British Royal United Service Museum. The *Chesapeake* had provoked an immense outcry in 1807: and now, ninety-two years later, the gale became a hurricane. American newspapers referred bitterly to 'this man whose wealth comes from the country he has repudiated' and talked about his 'outrageous act' and 'mortal insult'. One newspaper coupled him with Benedict Arnold who had also renounced his citizenship. Henry Cabot Lodge who was in England on a visit, even wrote to President Theodore Roosevelt: 'I had a long talk with Balfour. [future Prime Minister] I was interested to find that he resented Astor's conduct about the flag as much as we and has the same opinion.'

Astor continued on his way unperturbed. When the Boer War broke out the following year he made such generous donations to his adopted country that the English were openly grateful. He gave $100,000 to the army for quick-firing batteries; $100,000 to Oxford, where his son, Waldorf, was an undergraduate; $100,000 to London University; $50,000 to Cambridge; and many large sums to hospitals. Americans were astonished by his gifts as this type of generosity was not an Astor characteristic. Some people said that he was angling for a peerage, but although English governments have always been ready to send rich philanthropic gentlemen to the House of Lords, the honour was not forthcoming. Perhaps the outburst in the American press introduced a note of caution into Tory thinking for there was no point in gratuitously stirring up bad feeling between the two countries.

Whatever the truth of the matter, the character of this strange man seemed to defy analysis and some people clung to the view that he was not quite right in the head. Indeed his political opinions which he published in the *Pall Mall Magazine* seemed both muddled and childish, for he longed for a feudal world in which men with the most property were automatically regarded as the most valuable citizens. He declared bitterly that America's Founding Fathers felt it 'democratic and virtuous to be poor, and aristocratic and un-American to be rich'. In this difficult milieu his poor grandfather, he said, had had a hard struggle to accumulate his millions. Then, in what seemed to be a non-sequitur, he went on to lament that most of America's 'fine, old families' had fallen by the wayside and become 'mere tillers of the soil', ending with the pronouncement (another non-sequitur) that even in the days of Benjamin Franklin certain thinkers questioned the wisdom of submitting complex problems to the decisions of the multitude. What is this all about? Apparently Astor was arguing that an oligarchy of rich men is the best form of government; and if they cannot be rich at least they can be aristocratic.

As far as Astor himself was concerned, he was both. The *Pall Mall Magazine* published a wonderfully elaborate genealogical chart showing that William Waldorf was descended from the Spanish Counts of Astorga, one of whom in medieval times had fought the King of the Almoravideo of Morocco. Later, some of these Astorgas moved to France. But one of them, styled Jean Jaques d'Astorg, fled from Paris at the revocation of the Edict of Nantes and took refuge across the Rhine. And this Astorg was the ancestor of the butcher Astor.

Needless to say the new family tree created considerable amusement. *Town Topics* published a letter from the current Comte d'Astorga at Pau ridiculing the genealogical table as 'an appalling mixture of facts some of them actually turned upside down'. Nowhere in the family records, he said, was there a Jean Jacques d'Astorg born in 1664 who fled to Germany. At this same time an American genealogist, Lothrop Withington, made inquiries and declared that no member of the d'Astorg family had left France over the revocation. On the contrary, they enjoyed high honours under His Most Catholic Majesty's protection. The *New York World* welcomed the whole affair as deliciously funny but claimed that the Prince of Wales was finding Astor and his pretentions a bit of a strain. 'Not Mr Astor,' he is reported to have said as he drew his pencil through the name which was submitted as one of the proposed guests for a weekend, 'Not Mr Astor, he bores me.' This of course was a most unlikely story as royalty was well able to protect itself from unwelcome repartee without resorting to such gaucheries.

At this time in his life, Astor had plenty of interests to occupy him. He had always been interested in the 'curious arts' and now wrote a series of stories about the occult, magic stones, birds with human souls, soothsayers and sensational transformations. 'The Ghosts of Austerlitz', 'The Red Dwarf of Rabenstein' and the 'Wraith of Cliveden Reach' were some of his tales which were later published in a book called *Pharaoh's Daughter and Other Stories*. No doubt Astor's preoccupation with the supernatural induced him to buy Hever Castle in Kent where Anne

Boleyn had lived before marrying Henry VIII. After the King beheaded poor Anne, people claimed that the Queen's unhappy spirit wandered through the rooms and on windy nights, in an oak panelled chamber where Henry had courted his bride, one could hear doleful love songs sung in a minor key. Astor invited the Psychical Research Society to investigate Anne's ghost but although members of this curious group kept watch through Christmas week for several years running, they never heard the mournful lays.

Astor was believed to have spent the truly staggering sum of $10,000,000 on restoring Hever Castle, which had not been lived in for many years. First of all, in order to drain the marshland and create a lake, he changed the course of the River Eden and threw a new bridge over it. He then built a model farm with piggeries done in expensive oak, cowsheds adorned with chocolate and white tiles, and a dairy whose floor was a mosaic made by workmen imported from Italy. He also built a Tudor village where his guests could be housed, connected to the castle by a bridge. He constructed a deer park, laid out magnificent Italian gardens, and around the entire property erected a twelve-foot wall to keep sightseers from looking in. A crusty old English gentleman wrote:

I can hardly bear to tell of the things that this man did to Hever Castle in Kent: of the diverting of a river, the bringing of fully grown trees and rocks to mask from public gaze a castle which was historic but long had been a farmhouse to which any courteous stranger might be admitted. He built on to it and altered it and had costly sham antiques made and then enclosed the whole within high walls and huge electrically-operated gates so that when his motor car came, the door opened silently and closed smoothly and swiftly almost upon the back of the car as it entered.

A photograph by E.O. Hoppe of Nancy Astor wearing the $75,000 tiara with the Sancy diamond in front, given to her by her father-in-law as a wedding present.

Astor was engrossed in the renovation of Hever when two of his children became engaged. His only daughter, Pauline (his second daughter, Gwendolyn had died of tuberculosis in 1902), fell in love with an English county squire, Colonel Herbert Spender-Clay, and his son and heir, Waldorf, with a lady from Virginia who was keen on fox-hunting. She was Nancy Langhorne, the divorced wife of Robert Shaw of Boston, and the mother of a five-year-old son, Bobbie. Astor was disappointed with both choices. He would have liked Pauline to marry a peer and although he did not mind Waldorf marrying a divorcee, he would have been happier, if she had not been an American. However, he hid his disappointment and as a wedding present gave Nancy a $75,000 tiara containing the famous Sancy diamond. On Waldorf, he bestowed Cliveden and then went off and bought himself a magnificent villa at Sorrento in Italy.

William Waldorf Astor may have been autocratic and remote, yet he was wonderfully generous as far as his children were concerned. Although parents are always blamed for not surmounting the barriers between themselves and their progeny, in this case it is surprising that his eldest son, Waldorf, on whom he bestowed his wordly goods with such abandon, made so little effort to draw closer to him. Pauline, even

Waldorf Astor, photographed about the time of his marriage to Nancy Langhorne in 1906. Four years later he was elected Member of Parliament for Plymouth.

after her marriage, often went to stay with her father, and deeply impressed other members, of the family by the patience with which she read aloud to him – usually at luncheon and dinner and usually on his favourite subjects, Napoleon and Cesare Borgia. His second son, John, was genuinely fond of his father but was seldom in England. After leaving Oxford (where he became racquets champion of England) he was commissioned in the Life Guards and went abroad; in 1911 he became ADC to the Viceroy of India.

Waldorf might have got to know his oligarchic father better, but his approach to life, already liberal and reformist, discouraged him from making the effort. He had inherited his share of the Astor inhibitions and perhaps his shyness and modesty helped make him an outstanding success at Eton. Despite being an American, he had captured such coveted

The grand ballroom of the Astor Hotel, which was built by William Waldorf in Longacre Square, later renamed Times Square.

positions as President of Pop, Captain of the Boats, and Captain of his House. Unfortunately he strained his heart rowing and had to give up this sport when he went to Oxford, but he managed to make up for it by representing the university at polo. He also became Master of the Drag and hunted with the Bicester. His concern with horses deepened into an interest which absorbed him all his life. Indeed, it was here in the unlikely atmosphere of Oxford University that he used his father's princely allowance to lay the foundation of a first-class racing stable.

It was sad that he could only see in his father the differences that separated them, not the parental generosity that had made life so agreeable for his brother and himself. The truth was that William Waldorf

was basically an intellectual whose interests lay in the world of thought and beauty, while his son Waldorf was absorbed by politics and the betterment of the human race. His grandson, Michael, wrote:

My father recognized the fact that William Waldorf's attitude to affairs had been aristocratic, as well as autocratic. William Waldorf paid scant regard to what other people felt or thought of his behaviour. He had remained imperiously a law unto himself. My father did not applaud his attitude. Being American by birth he did not fit into the English aristocratic pattern. Being Puritan by inclination he did not wish to. He wanted to succeed in a life of public service and made amends, as he saw it, for his father's negligence in this respect.

Waldorf's daughter-in-law, Nancy, may not have found the old man's dictatorial outlook congenial, but she was impressed by his intelligence and proud of the fact that she always got on with him. However, on one occasion she was so frightened when he appeared that she ran to her room and stayed there until she learned that the expected storm had not taken place after all. When William Waldorf gave Cliveden to his son, he told Nancy that he would never return to the house which he had owned and loved and refashioned. She therefore threw herself into redecorating with enthusiasm. Christopher Sykes writes:

She not only swept contents away but attacked the very edifice itself. From the hall she ordered a mass of stone antiquity to be removed; Roman statues and busts and stupendous wine jars and sarcophagi.... She had the entire floor of the hall, an Italian mosaic stone design, dug up and replaced by comfortable parquet, and another of her father-in-law's favourite importations removed at the same time: an Italian ceiling in the dining room, painted under William Waldorf Astor's personal direction, representing an Olympian banquet.

'The keynote of the place when I took over,' Nancy explained, 'was splendid gloom. Tapestries and ancient leather furniture filled most of the rooms. The place looked better when I had put in books and chintz curtains and covers and flowers.'

The blow fell when her first child, William, was born in 1907. The old man was so delighted that he forgot his vow never to visit Cliveden again and sent a message announcing his imminent arrival in order to see the baby and greet his son and daughter-in-law. They awaited the ordeal with trepidation, but when Nancy saw his car drive up she lost her customary pugnaciousness and fled to her room. 'I am in bed,' she said over her shoulder, 'and I mustn't be worried.'

Apparently Mr Astor surveyed the changes without comment. Even the disappearance of his beloved mosaic floor, the obliteration of his cherished ceiling, evoked no angry remarks. Having looked, he said to his son: 'The first joy of possession is to change everything around and remould it nearer to the heart's desire.' And when Nancy received him in her bedroom he was charm personified. 'He came up to see me and the baby and was very gentle and sweet to us. He gave me a beautiful silver cup to commemorate the child's birth. I said "If I have seven sons, will you give me a cup for each one of them?" He said he would, but I never got the cups.' Nancy did not have seven sons, but two years after

Bill's arrival, she gave birth to a daughter, Phyllis, known as Wissie and in 1912, 1916, and 1918, produced David, Michael and Jakie'.

When Nancy moved into magnificent Cliveden, only twenty miles from London, she at once became a figure of intense interest, particularly to Englishmen who could not believe their luck in having a vastly rich *châteleine* who was both beautiful and hilariously amusing. She was a pocket Venus, small, graceful, with a delightful oval face and brilliant blue eyes brimming with fun. No one had ever seen anything quite like her before. In Edwardian England the hour-glass figure with the full bosom and the tiny waist was the epitome of feminine grace; certainly not the boyish shape of a ravishing hoyden who laughed at everything, including sex. Indeed her irresistible looks and her irrepressible personality not only blazed the way for a new species of woman but seemed to have the effect of shattering English reserve like an explosion in front of a plate-glass window. Even the redoubtable King Edward VII heard reports that made him eager to see what she was really like.

A gracious request was conveyed by telephone from Windsor, and on the same rainy day King Edward VII drove over with a party of intimates including his long-standing favourite Mrs Keppel and his new favourite Mrs Willie James. The rain stopped, the sun came out in a burst of King's weather, and the great royal guest found his visit so 'agreeable' that he would not go until eight o'clock to everyone's great inconvenience.

But royalty was not enough for Nancy. What she sought in society was excitement – to meet and to know the leading personalities of her time. She began by scooping up a handful of Lord Milner's 'Kindergarten', a name given to the brilliant young Oxford graduates hand-picked by Milner when he was High Commissioner of South Africa. Milner not only trained his protégés, but imbued them with his own passionate desire to weld the Empire into an indissoluble entity protected by inflexible ideals. Among her new friends in this group were Bob Brand, who later became her brother-in-law; Geoffrey Dawson, a future editor of *The Times*; Lionel Curtis, a huge man with bushy eyebrows who was a member of All Souls; and Philip Kerr, later Lord Lothian, who became Nancy's lifelong friend – probably the closest friend of her life.

She certainly had a profound effect on the Kindergarten. [wrote Brand] ... She had many weapons available for the task, beauty, wit ... incomparable courage, great wealth which she used and which Waldorf delighted she should use, with great generosity. She had money of her own but she used to say: 'I didn't marry an Astor to spend my own money.' ... Reason was not a weapon she cared to use much, if at all, but she certainly had a very powerful intuition which worked like a flash. Her charm was such that we all fell easy victims. She liked our society because she was full of desire to do things in the world.

What did the dynamic American have in common with the modest, self-effacing Waldorf? Was it, people asked, only the attraction of opposites? Not entirely it seems, for hidden behind the worldly facade of both was a streak of puritanism that nourished deep religious beliefs. Nancy had been reading and re-reading the Bible since the age of fifteen. As a girl she suffered from poor health which was put down to an unstable

A photographic portrait of Nancy Astor by Alice Hughes. Nancy combined beauty with almost outrageous vitality.

nervous system. Periodically she was forced to retire to her bed for several weeks at a time, and in 1914 when she was desperately trying to recover her spirits, her sister, Phyllis, visited her and suggested that she study Christian Science. Nancy warmed to the idea, sent for a practitioner and before the week was out had become a convert. She immediately made up her mind to win over Waldorf who not only suffered from a weak heart and rheumatism but lived in fear of tuberculosis, the disease from which his thirteen-year-old sister, Gwendolyn, had died. Waldorf had great faith in medical science and when he took his children to Scotland in his private train, he always had a cow aboard so that they could drink fresh, tubercular-free milk. Nevertheless after several years of relentless pressure from Nancy, Waldorf succumbed and became a Christian Scientist. He also joined his wife in her battle against alcohol which stemmed from her unfortunate marriage to the bibulous Robert Shaw. Together they became life-long teetotallers.

Fortunately they did not inflict their views on the guests who flowed through the Astor houses in profusion – Plymouth, Sandwich, Jura, and, of course, No. 4 St James's Square, London. 'Here Mr and Mrs Astor used to entertain on a very large scale,' explained their butler, Edwin Lee, in a description of life before the First World War.

Dinners between 50 and 60 were very frequent and probably two or three balls for anything up to 500 or 600 would be given during the season....

A fairly large staff was kept in both London and Cliveden but most of us used to travel between the two. At that particular time we had a very fine French chef who was considered one of the best in the country and a very nice man to work with. He had five girls working with him. We also had a stillroom where all the bread and cake were made. Baking was done at Cliveden twice a week. The head stillroom maid used to travel between London and Cliveden. One under stillroom maid was kept in either place. There was a very large staff of gardeners and stablemen kept at Cliveden, between 40 and 50 gardeners and about 10 or 12 stablemen. All the lawns on the pleasure grounds were mowed by horses with leather boots strapped over their iron shoes. In the house at Cliveden there was a housekeeper, 6 housemaids, 6 laundry maids and always one or two left in the kitchen apart from the travelling staff, also an Odd Man who used to look after the boilers, carry coal, answer the telephone – a most useful man in every way.

Old William Waldorf Astor did not make more than his one, fleeting visit to Cliveden, but he was delighted to hear reports of the grandeur of the young Astors' life; equally he deplored their teetotalism which he regarded as 'a sin against nature'. Nevertheless he continued to bask in his daughter-in-law's warm attentions and for many years Waldorf and Nancy remained in his good books. Journalism continued to be his chief preoccupation and in 1896 he decided that Harry Cust, who had edited the *Pall Mall Gazette* for four years, would have to go: Cust did not seem to understand the elementary fact that the man who paid the bills called the tune.

Unfortunately, the paper suffered from Cust's departure and went into a decline, where it remained for fifteen years. In 1910, W. W. decided that the only man to revive the moribund gazette was the brilliant J.L.

Garvin, editor of London's most respected Sunday newspaper, *The Observer*, owned by Lord Northcliffe. Young Waldorf undertook the negotiations and learned that the only way the Astors could obtain Garvin's services was to buy *The Observer* and to employ him as editor of both journals. Old William Waldorf did not turn a hair. He simply nodded and bought the Sunday paper. Four years later he turned it over to his son.

During the last ten years of his life, William Waldorf has often been depicted as a lonely old man, eating and drinking in splendid solitude. However, his love letters to Lady Sackville-West (whose daughter, Vita, married Harold Nicolson) show that occasionally he found diversion in amatory pursuits. This particular lady was married to Lord Sackville-West, and although Astor had known her for many years, the romance did not begin until July 1913. In a letter written from Hever Castle on 20 July, before he left for Marienbad, he tells her how happy he is and says: 'For anything I may have said or done amiss in that splendid hour's excitement I entreat your forgiveness.' He asks for her photograph and assures her that he always destroys letters. 'I take away with me an infinitely delightful remembrance and I kiss your hand....'

From Marienbad he wrote often, sometimes two or three times a day. The letters show an attractive side of his nature that was usually hidden, and gives one a new insight into his character. In his first letter he tells her that he 'left England so happy and yet deeply sorry to go'. And then, with schoolboy flirtatiousness, refers to the 'hidden meaning' of Cupid. 'In all the history of Olympus and the affairs of the Immortals Cupid was always sent to say "yes", and never once to say "no".' He tells her that for years he has been afraid of her, 'by which I mean fearful of displeasing you, for to have done so would have pained me dreadfully'.

Four days later he is trying to assure her that if they are discreet and careful no one will be hurt by their romance.

As you rightly say it is cruel and wicked to give pain to another but this could only happen if our game had been stupidly played.... You bid me reassure you. The trouble comes from servants for they set people talking.... My butler-valet Fooley has been with me 13 years. He has seen many things and has always been discreet.... The only suitable rendezvous I know of in England is in my office, a little palace on the Embankment where I live in solitude. *La ci darem la mano!* Without at present attempting details I would show you how to arrive veiled and unnoticed and as I alone should let you in and out none but we could know.

Before he ends his letter he says: 'That momentous Saturday was the psychological hour for which you and I have unconsciously waited ... what wonderful things awaken at the meeting of the hands.'

And on 2 August he writes:

A woman in the flower of her prime – like yourself – needs a romantic attachment. Without it, the heart grows cold. It is as necessary as daily bread and not even Knole and four acres at Hampstead can take its place. It is the consciousness that someone thinks of you, desires you, longs for the touch of your beautiful body that keeps the heart warm.

Lady Sackville apparently was a woman who blew hot and cold for she told him flatly that she could never come to his retreat on the Embankment. And although she had decided to join him at Interlaken, it would have to be a 'picnic without refreshments'. He wrote on 8 August:

I do not comprehend why all we have said is suddenly to go for nothing, but it is part of a philosopher's life to meet puzzling subjects. *Chose bizarre!* After calling my attention to the notice *Trespassers Will be Prosecuted* you write, 'Oh my dear, if only you were here!' I cannot help wondering what 'iced lovemaking' may be. But I shall be so happy to take your dear hand in mine again that I shall have no other thought than to please you in all things.

Before ending he acknowledged her letters of the 1st, 2nd and 3rd. 'On the 1st you do not seem quite sure about *Trespassers Will be Prosecuted*, and it fills me with wicked delight to think that perhaps before the year is out we may use that notice to light the fire.'

Although this promising romance budded, it never seemed to blossom and it finally faded away. There are a few letters written by Astor from England; then a very cross letter in which he replies to a note from her saying that her husband does not approve of his being a godfather to her grandchild because people might talk. 'The consideration of the world's opinion has not suggested itself to me. But I at once see the force and correctness of Lord Sackville's view....' This letter was signed 'W. W. Astor' and here the matter ended sadly and coldly.

William Waldorf's eldest son Waldorf, had been elected Member of Parliament for Plymouth in 1910. Yet as soon as war was declared he volunteered for the army. His bad heart prevented him from passing the medical examination and after making two or three attempts to enlist, in the end he saw that there was no alternative but to perform some routine job in England. He so hated being at home while his friends were undergoing the horrors of the trenches that he insisted on a 'disagreeable job'. As a result he was made an inspector of army camps with the task of saving waste. Needless to say he provoked the sarcasm of senior officers who assumed that he had wangled a safe job – and he thus achieved the mortification of the soul if not the flesh! Eventually he accepted an appointment as an army inspector for ordnance factories and served in this humble capacity for two years. In the autumn of 1914 he offered Cliveden as a hospital, but the British Army decided that the house would be too difficult to convert. The Canadians, on the other hand, received the gift gratefully, ignored the house, and transformed the covered tennis courts into wards.

Meanwhile William Waldorf's youngest and favourite son, J.J. was serving with the Life Guards in France. In the Battle of Ypres his arm was broken in two places by a shell which drove fifteen pieces of metal into his body. While he was recuperating in England, he began to see a good deal of Lady Violet Mercer-Nairne, widow of a brother officer who had been killed in the same battle in which Astor had been wounded. Lady Violet was a daughter of the Earl of Minto, pretty, charming, agreeable – just the sort of woman William Waldorf would

Opposite (left) *The portrait of William Waldorf Astor by Sir Hubert von Herkomer, which hangs in Cliveden.*

Opposite (right) *William Waldorf became famous overnight when he bought the entire balustrade of the Villa Borghese and had it moved to Cliveden.*

Overleaf *William Waldorf was believed to have spent $10,000,000 on restoring Hever Castle which had not been lived in for many years.*

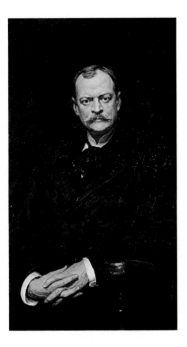

Right *The Honourable John Jacob Astor V pictured in 1922 standing on the drawbridge of Hever Castle with his wife, Violet, and their eldest son Gavin, now Lord Astor of Hever. J.J. was William Waldorf's youngest and favourite son.*

The courtyard at Hever Castle.

like his son to marry. So with no more ado he wrote an ante-nuptial agreement that probably has never been equalled for splendid generosity. If Lady Violet would marry his son within six months she would have $30,000 a year for life and $4,000,000 on the day of the wedding, all of which would be deducted from J.J.'s Trust. After the wedding the bridegroom rejoined his regiment and was wounded again. At Cambrai an explosive shell shattered his leg which had to be amputated. In appreciation of his gallant service, Astor was commissioned a major, a title which he used proudly for many years.

During this period old William Waldorf fidgeted about wondering what he could do to help. His personal life had come to a standstill. His daughter-in-law, Nancy, wrote:

He could not go to Vichy where he took a cure every year. He could not go to Sorrento where he had a villa he loved. It was then that Lord Farquar suggested that he take a peerage and go to the House of Lords. It would occupy him and give him a chance to be of some use to England. We were never consulted or told. . . . Waldorf wrote to his father bitterly opposing the whole thing. His father, who, I think, had never had anyone openly disagree with him before, was very angry. He asked me did I agree with Waldorf and I said I did. So he wrote a codicil to his Will, cutting Waldorf off. All the money that would have come to my husband, went to his sons when they came of age.

This assertion was only partially true. Two trust funds composed of stocks and bonds, jointly valued at $25,000,000, had been set up in 1916 and this was the money to which Lady Astor was referring. Instead of distributing the funds between John and Waldorf, they were given to John and to Waldorf's children. However, William Waldorf's major trust, which he established in 1919, estimated to be worth $50,000,000 (the value of his Manhatten real estate), was divided equally between John and Waldorf.

William Waldorf only appeared in the House of Lords twice; once in 1916, when he was made a peer and took his seat; again in 1917 when he received his viscountcy. A new coat of arms was designed for him with a falcon in the place of honour – the same falcon which had graced the shield of an Astorga in the Middle Ages. In America Astor's cousin, John Chaloner, wrote a sonnet containing the lines:

> Bravo Cousin Willie. Punch 'em once again!
> And when you're made the Duke of Asteroid
> See that a cleaver's on your arm deployed
> A butcher's cleaver ...
> And axe and chopping block all honour give.

William Waldorf retired to a solitary life in Brighton where his interest was concentrated on the superb food supplied by his chef and the superb wine that he himself had collected. Occasionally his ten-year-old grand-son, Bill, journeyed to Brighton to spend a few days with him. He frequently wrote to the little boy. 'I have spent a week with a barrel of oysters and a superb turkey to keep me pleasant company. . . . The turkey made its appearance six times – hot, cold, mince and grilled bones. No one,' he added rather unnecessarily, 'has ever died of hunger in this house of mine.' And another time, clearly to wean the boy away from his mother's ridiculous teetotalism:

I hope that you will continue to grow fatter and wish you had a glass of red wine as I had from the age of seven, and as all my children had regularly with excellent results. I am an enthusiastic enemy of 'Dɒwn Glasses' at least as far as I am personally concerned. I should not have my excellent health today had I not used stimulants freely all my life. My other rule for a long life is to kill my doctor. It is usually the doctor who kills the patient.

Despite his buoyant optimism, he could not escape the inevitable; and on 18 October 1919, at the age of seventy-one, he moved to another world.

7 Hands across the ocean

Vincent Astor with his father, Jack, who went down on the Titanic in 1912. Vincent was devoted to this parent; so much so that when he moved into a new house in New York in 1926 he reproduced his father's bedroom exactly as it had been in the old château.

Early in 1918, about nine months before the death of William Waldorf in England, twenty-seven-year-old Vincent Astor, a lieutenant in the United States navy, returned from duty in France aboard a captured German submarine. Americans were delighted to have their reigning monarch on *terra firma* again, for Vincent's grandmother, Queen Caroline, had been dead only eleven years and the public still looked upon the Astors as their own species of royalty; indeed they regarded them with that feeling of intense awe of which only citizens of a republic seem capable.

Vincent Astor, the youngest Astor ever to head the family, first came into the public eye when his father, John Jacob Astor, went down in the *Titanic* in April 1912. The *New York Times* carried columns on twenty-year-old Vincent, who did not know for thirty-six hours whether or not his father had been saved. Later, when John Jacob's body was recovered, $2500 dollars were found in one of his pockets and a gold watch that was still ticking in another. The watch became one of Vincent's most cherished possessions.

His grief for his father was curious for few boys had had a more unhappy childhood. Although John Jacob allowed Vincent to work in the family garage he believed in bringing up children strictly. When Vincent was twelve he sent him to St George's School in Newport with an allowance of only fifty cents a week – if his marks were good. If not, the pocket money was reduced to thirty-five cents. He hated the school so much that he tried to burn it down, but apparently even this heinous offence was overlooked if one was an Astor.

When Vincent was at home he and his younger sister, Alice, lived in the huge French château at 840 5th Avenue. There, in a museum with a vast marble staircase, surrounded by priceless *boiseries* and Louis XIV furniture, Vincent was brought up by an Irish nursemaid and a German governess, neither of whom offered much companionship. When he was naughty his father punished him, and as John Jacob believed that it was his duty to be a severe parent, he either sent the boy to bed without any supper or took a strap to him. Every week Vincent and Alice, wearing their best clothes, were led through endless connecting rooms to the other side of the house to have tea with their aging grandmother. Once Alice saw a lady pianist playing Strauss waltzes in one of the outer passages and asked her grandmother why she did not ask the performer to play in the drawing room. 'Because my dear we might become friends'; and seeing Alice's puzzled expression, added with emphasis, 'and *friends*, my dear, mean *responsibilities*.'

The Mrs Astor was too old to undertake any such onerous duties. Nevertheless Vincent found that his grandmother had a gentle side where children were concerned. His grasshopper legs and enormous feet always made him self-conscious, and once when the old lady said that one could tell a gentleman by looking at his feet she saw the sudden consternation in Vincent's eye and added in a kindly way: 'Not feet, *shoes*. Shoes must always be well polished.'

Where money was involved, Vincent was never spoiled. Although he dreamed of a naval career and begged his father to send him to Anna-

Vincent Astor in the Astor Box at the Astor Cup Race, Sheepshead Bay, New York, in 1915.

polis, John Jacob refused to consider anything but Harvard. And at Harvard he had such a small allowance that he could barely make ends meet. He was furious when one of his classmates told a reporter that he had arrived at college with one hundred suits and two dozen pairs of shoes. In fact he only possessed three suits and was so short of money he could not afford a train ticket. He finally overcame the problem of transport by borrowing $40 from a friend and buying a one-cylinder Excelsior motorbike.

And now suddenly, in April 1912, newspapers were informing the world that John Jacob Astor had left an estate of $87,000,000 most of which had gone to Vincent Astor. Before the Will was read, Vincent's mother, who had been living in London since her divorce in 1909, arrived in New York. Vincent did his best to get on with his mother but he could not overcome the deep aversion he had felt for her as a child, and was relieved when she departed again for England. Years later he told a friend: 'Even when my mother was an old woman I could never bring myself to spend Christmas with her.'

Long before America entered the war, Vincent was a strong supporter of the Allies. In 1916 he got in touch with the Assistant Secretary of the Navy, Franklin Delano Roosevelt, who lived only twenty miles from Rhinebeck and offered his yacht, the *Noma*, to the government. Roosevelt accepted it gratefully and encouraged Astor's attempts to persuade other yacht owners to follow his example. The two men, who had known each other slightly for many years, became friends. Vincent then turned to another neighbour, this time a lady, Helen Huntington, and married her. Tall, with ash-blond hair, she bore a strong resemblance to the actress, Ina Claire, whom Vincent had fancied as an undergraduate at Harvard. In June 1917 Helen reported to Bordeaux for canteen work with the YMCA while Vincent was assigned to the US coastguard ship *Aphrodite*; for six months he laid wireless cables off the coast of France with a donkey-engine made out of a Ford motor.

Shortly after Vincent returned from Europe in 1919, his stepmother, Madeleine, married for the second time at the ripe old age of twenty-six. Her husband was a respectable stockbroker, William Dick. The move was welcomed by the Astors as Madeleine forfeited the income from the $5,000,000 Trust, which automatically went to Vincent, as well as the 'cottage' in Newport and the French château at 840 5th Avenue. Vincent was glad to see the last of her as he had always found Madeleine

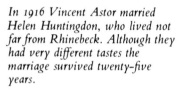

In 1916 Vincent Astor married Helen Huntingdon, who lived not far from Rhinebeck. Although they had very different tastes the marriage survived twenty-five years.

The wedding of Alice Astor to Prince Serge Obolensky in 1925 was the first of four unsuccessful marriages for Alice. She believed that she was the reincarnation of an Egyptian princess. Her chief interest was the Sadler's Wells Ballet, which she heavily subsidized.

both extravagant and silly. In 1918 she had asked the court for an increase in the $25,000 a year allotted for her baby's expenses. She told the judge that an ermine wrapper and muff had cost $250; an ermine robe $185; a mink coverlet $580. Indeed she had spent over $6000 on the baby's clothes in the past three years. The judge was unsympathetic and so was the most important trustee, Vincent Astor. Luckily Mr Dick had inherited $3,000,000 from his grandmother so he could keep Madeleine in the style to which she had grown accustomed.

Vincent and Helen moved into 840 5th Avenue with a staff of twenty servants. Every January, in remembrance of Grandmother Caroline's famous party, they gave a large ball. But times were changing and now the function was always in aid of a charity which meant that anybody who could pay was welcome. Prince Serge Obolensky, who married Alice Astor in 1925, found the residence:

...the most imposing mansion in New York if not in the New World. Facing the great hall, we passed through huge bronze gates, and came into a reception room whose walls were panelled with canvasses patterned after Brussels cartoons. Facing the entrance was a big sculptured fireplace. Beyond it lay the ballroom which was also the art gallery...statues were everywhere. The marble stairs and the enormous, heavily gilded drawing room created an impression of almost overpowering solidity and permanence....

At first glance it would be difficult to find a more ill-suited couple than Vincent and Helen Astor, yet they stayed married for twenty-five years and remained fond of each other for the rest of their lives. Helen's passion in life was music, and Vincent was tone-deaf; Helen loved Paris and Vincent never went to Europe if he could help it; Helen liked living in New York because it meant the Metropolitan Opera and the New York Symphony Orchestra and Vincent loved country pursuits and yachting. Whereas Helen was blond and statuesque and quiet, Vincent was dark and aggressive, and although he had not inherited his mother's looks, he had an arresting countenance. He prided himself on being 'One hundred per cent American', but his worst characteristic was his poor diction; he talked rapidly and had a habit of swallowing his words so that many people could not understand what he was saying.

His personality was so complex that no two people ever agreed about him. Some found him charming, others boorish, some beguiling, others menacing, some intelligent, others mentally retarded. The truth was that despite his domineering nature, despite his gusts of anger and a tendency to say the unforgiveable, he had a strong urge to use his money and energy for the betterment of his fellow beings. In 1914 he built a great public market on Astor property at Broadway and 95th Street to enable merchants to lower their prices and housewives to shop with greater ease. In a sense it was New York's first supermarket although no one had thought of the name, but unfortunately it came to grief. The fact that for several weeks it was crowded with customers encouraged the merchants to raise their prices; the buyers melted away and eventually Astor sold it to a car mart.

Other schemes were more successful. He founded a home for emotionally disturbed children at Rhinebeck, built a playground in the middle of the Bronx, and gave money to a group fighting anti-semitism in Roumania. He launched an anti-vice crusade in his own West side property, but this proved farcical. Disturbed by rumours that Astor-owned tenements were being used as brothels, he employed a group of private detectives disguised as canvassers to cover forty or fifty buildings, knocking on every door and peering inside to see if they could detect anything that looked suspicious. Many of the occupants had gone to bed and were annoyed at being disturbed, but when they gleaned the purpose of the call, irritation turned to outrage, and they chased the canvassers down the stairs, brandishing mops and brooms. Needless to say, no brothels were uncovered.

At Rhinebeck, Astor increased the size of his farm to 3000 acres and turned a third of it over to the government to use as an experimental station. The garage was still full of his father's motor cars, but Vincent's most exciting toy was a miniature railway. The tracks wound around the estate for three quarters of a mile, and the three-foot steam engine was his pride and joy. Not only was it solid enough to hold his weight, but it was strong enough to pull seven cars containing twenty-eight passengers. The engine was a perfect model that could be stoked and oiled, with an impressive instrument panel and a whistle that could be heard for a mile down the Hudson. Guests described weekends with Vincent appearing for breakfast wearing a fireman's cap and carrying an oil can with a long spout. They seldom saw him again before lunch. Some of them wondered whether he was 'all there' but came to the conclusion that he was just a trifle odd.

Even so, his relations preferred the toy engine to the real thing, for when Vincent became a director of the Illinois Central Railway he frequently rang up his friends and invited them to accompany him to Chicago. 'Why on earth would I want to go to Chicago?' one of his Chanler cousins asked, 'I don't know a soul there.' 'Oh, we won't go into the city,' replied Vincent cheerfully, 'We'll spend the day shunting around the yards and start home at nightfall.'

Invitations to cruise on Vincent's yacht were more appreciated. At the end of the war he sold the *Noma* to the government and put his father's yacht into dock for renovations. In the summer he sailed to Newport for long weekends, in the winter to the West Indies for the Christmas holidays. However, when he saw J.P. Morgan's magnificent *Corsair*, which crossed the Atlantic with the easy grace of a greyhound, he began to toy with the idea of designing a new boat. His investment of $200,000 in a syndicate to finance the making of a film, *Ben Hur*, starring Ramon Navarro, helped him to make up his mind. When the returns poured in from the most successful moving picture of the decade, he commissioned a German company in Kiel to build him a diesel-powered boat 264 feet long, with a speed of 16 knots and a cruising range of 20,000 miles.

The new *Nourmahal* cost $1,250,000 as no expense was spared. A dining room panelled in walnut ran the length of the ship, every cabin had

Vincent Astor backed Ramon Navarro in Ben Hur – *the most successful film of the decade – and made a handsome profit.*

its own bath, and the magnificent beige and gold salon was equipped with its own fireplace. There was a library for thinkers and a sun-deck for sportsmen. The ship had a crew of forty-two and cost $250,000 a year to run. Vincent looked every inch a captain as he strode about the deck, and no one was surprised when the New York Yacht Club elected him its commodore.

The yacht brought out the most dictatorial side of Vincent's nature. Although he could be affable when he chose, if anyone irritated him he took on the unpleasant and imperious air of his mother. Once a guest sent word that she was feeling seasick and would not be down for luncheon. No one knows why Astor took exception to this innocuous remark, but he did. He sent her a furious message saying that his guests were *obliged* to appear for lunch, and if they were not well they could be sick over the side of the boat. The lady in question, very white and unable to put a morsel of food in her mouth, sat through luncheon close to tears. 'You can imagine what a success the cruise was,' she commented, when telling the story many years later.

However, Astor's moods changed with bewildering rapidity and at times he even managed to laugh at himself. His elongated body and unco-ordinated limbs ending in enormous feet made him look very curious. He often wore a tie with penguins on it; his cigarettes had the same emblem; even his cuff links and wristwatch bore the outline of a penguin. When someone asked him why he had chosen this particular animal, he said, 'Because we both walk with out feet sticking out.'

His humour consisted of practical jokes arranged by himself. If he knew that a man was gambling on the Stock Market he would go to great lengths to get a list of his shares. Then he would arrange to have a wireless message sent to the *Nourmahal* from the victim's broker announcing that the market was collapsing. The businessman would try frantically (and unsuccessfully) to get in touch with the broker. For three days he would have no alternative but to listen mournfully to a succession of disastrous wireless reports spelling complete ruin for him.

Where women were concerned Astor was even more outrageous. Once he chose as his target a married lady who was in the throes of a love affair; employed someone to 'write up' the story in the style of a well-known gossip writer; then paid to have an entire page of the Sunday newspaper magazine section specially printed with the sensational account included in it. The newspaper would be delivered to the lady at breakfast. At some point in the day the yacht's wireless operator would receive an angry message from the lady's husband; and later, perhaps an even angrier one from her lover.

These jokes fortunately were reserved for weekend cruises. On longer expeditions people were expected to behave themselves. When Vincent took a party to the Galapagos Islands in the Pacific he had six eminent men aboard – and no practical jokers. They were in search of a rare *testuda portieri*, a gigantic and indigenous tortoise, as well as coral reef fish and a plant called a 'spineless cactus' which was being tested as cattle food in arid regions of the United States. On this trip the party included two directors of the Museum of Natural History, a well-known botanist, two ornithologists, the head of the New York Aquarium, and two friends to keep the host amused – Kermit Roosevelt and Suydam Cutting. The voyage was highly successful and the *Nourmahal* came back laden not only with tortoises but penguins, sea lions, fork-tailed gulls and all sorts of aquatic fauna which found a resting place in museums and aquariums in Bermuda and New York.

However, all these excursions, even the scientific ones, fell into the category of exciting holidays. Throughout the 'twenties Vincent's work consisted of reorganizing the Astor Estate Office. His managers, first Nicholas Biddle and then Gerry Chadwick and John Yates, believed that the peak in property values had been reached in the fashionable areas of Broadway and 5th Avenue. As for the slum district, from which Vincent drew the bulk of his income, they were rapidly being depopulated. Thousands were leaving New York for the Bronx which was far less crowded and at last had a good subway system. Indeed, in 1920 Astor's income from rentals which normally amounted to something between two and three million dollars, fell to the all-time low of only $799,000.

So Vincent began to unload, slowly of course, waiting for the right time and the right purchaser. The Longacre Building in Times Square went for $2,373,000; the site for the Paramount Theatre for $3,845,000; the Schermerhorn Building for $1,500,000; the St Regis Hotel for $2,600,000; and although the Knickerbocker Hotel, known as 'the 42nd Street Country Club' was retained, it was turned into an office block. The most spectacular sale was the Waldorf-Astoria, the great luxury hotel that had thrilled America only thirty short years before, blazing a new path in gracious living. It was sold to a property company for $15,000,000, half of which went into Vincent's pocket, the other half to his two cousins, Waldorf and J.J. Astor, in England. However, the buyers were only interested in the ground on which it stood. Wreckers were sent in to clear the site and before long a new giant was reaching for the sky: the Empire State Building. Altogether in the space of little more than a decade, Astor sold one half of the $70,000,000 of real estate that he had inherited; and despite the depression he managed to reap a slight profit, netting $40,000,000 from buildings valued at $35,000,000.

After that, he began investing and building in new areas. On upper Broadway at 90th Street he created the Astor Court Apartments, modelled after the Astor Concourse, a group of low-priced apartment houses in the Bronx financed before the war. He also launched a 322-acre housing estate on Long Island, at Port Washington, complete with beach huts, tennis courts and bridle paths. But his most profitable investment, as time showed, was the land he bought in the vicinity of East 86th Street and the River in what was then a neglected and derelict neighbourhood. When he rebuilt the dilapidated brownstone houses, he created a new fashionable area on the very spot where the first John Jacob Astor had had his country estate, Hurlgate.

The most nostalgic of all Astor's sales, however, was his decision in 1925 to part with the family mansion at 840 5th Avenue. Once Vincent had made up his mind to let it go, he refused to brood about it. He sold it for $3,500,000 to the Jewish society, Temple Emmanuel, who pulled it down and erected New York's most costly synagogue. Many of the paintings and tapestries and statues were put up to auction and bought by Mr John Ringling, the circus man. Meanwhile Vincent built himself a new house at 130 East 80th Street for $250,000 – 'a simple, neo-Georgian dwelling of six storeys' as a columnist put it. Here the owner reproduced the bedroom of his father, John Jacob, exactly as it had been in the demolished château; the same furniture and pictures, even the same fixtures in the bathroom.

While Vincent was paying tribute to his father in this endearing way, his mother was bitterly lamenting the destruction of 840 5th Avenue; but at the same time admitting that she had never been really happy there. As the still-alluring Ava advanced into middle age, she grew increasingly querulous. In 1919 she married Lord Ribblesdale who, in his youth, had been one of the gayest bachelors in England. He was still an amusing and attractive man, but the bride was full of complaints. She had visions, wrote her son-in-law, Prince Obolensky, of tremendous parties and a whirl of movement but 'all Lord Ribblesdale wanted was to settle down with the most beautiful woman he could find, take her out to his country place, where he could lead a quiet, gentlemanly life, and read her the classics in the evening with the great sonorous bass voice that he possessed.'

The Vincent Astor Estate at Port Washington on Long Island. It was one of the first housing estates for the rich, very grand and very profitable.

In spite of this handicap, the beautiful Ava managed to establish herself as an important hostess – if only for weekends. But even this did not

The NEW ILLUSTRATED

No. 40.   NOVEMBER 15, 1919.   VOL. 2.

LADY ASTOR'S FIGHT

(Hoppé)

The great contest at Plymouth for the honour of sending the first woman M.P. to the House of Commons, showing Lady Astor consulting Lord Astor (the late M.P.) over a map of the constituency, and the various stages of her campaign.

appease her and she continued to find fault with almost everything. Occasionally she went to Cliveden to stay with Nancy Astor whom she had met when the latter was Mrs Shaw and they had crossed the Atlantic together. Although John Jacob Astor IV and cousin William Waldorf had been at daggers drawn for thirty years, now that both were dead it was easy for John Jacob's first wife, Ava, and William Waldorf's son and daughter-in-law, Waldorf and Nancy, to become friends. However, Nancy Astor sometimes found Ava's petulance trying. In 1919, after spending a weekend at Cliveden, Ava bid her hostess goodby saying, 'Isn't life *frightful!*' Then she stepped mournfully into her Rolls Royce.

Despite her tiresomeness, Ava was responsible for completing the reconciliation between British and American Astors, for when Waldorf and Nancy visited America in 1922 she arranged that Vincent and Helen should look after them when they stayed in New York. As 840 5th Avenue had not yet been sold, they spent two nights sleeping in the suite that *the* Mrs Astor always reserved for royalty.

The royal suite was an appropriate setting for Lord and Lady Astor who received a royal welcome wherever they went. Americans were thrilled that Virginia-born Nancy had become the first woman to sit in the House of Commons, and even more impressive, that she had fulfilled the American dream by marrying one of the richest men in Europe and now was the châtelaine of fabulous Cliveden where she entertained everyone of importance from the King of England to Charlie Chaplin.

Thirty-nine-year-old Nancy Astor had become a candidate for Parliament in 1919 almost by accident. Her husband, Waldorf, had sat in the House of Commons since 1910 as member for Plymouth. He had hopes of a career in 1916 when he was appointed Parliamentary Private Secretary to the Prime Minister, Lloyd George. However, when the latter formed a new government, after winning the Khaki election of 1918, Waldorf was passed over. The owner of the powerful *Times* newspaper, Lord Northcliffe, had no liking for Waldorf, but he nevertheless blamed his own editor, Geoffrey Dawson, for not publicly urging the Prime Minister to drop 'the old Gang Tories' for newer, younger men. 'For the ungrateful and unjust treatment of your friend Astor,' wrote Northcliffe to Dawson in January 1919, 'you have only yourself to blame.' Later, some biographers attributed Waldorf's blighted political career to his elevation to the Lords but this was nonsense as members of the Upper House were not, and are not, prohibited from holding office. The truth is that Nancy Astor's entry into the political arena in a fanfare of publicity, and her retention of the world spotlight, was far more damaging to Waldorf than his removal to the Lords. He was so enamoured of his wife, so admiring of her talents, that he not only effaced himself but virtually became her private secretary, devoting most of his time and attention to her needs.

In 1919 Conservative candidates were not only expected to pay their own election expenses but to make handsome contributions to the constituency as well. The *Evening Standard* was quick to see the advantages of Nancy taking over Waldorf's constituency and on the very day that old William Waldorf died flew a kite reporting 'a rumour'. She had helped her husband in the constituency and was well known for her dash and drive and money. Furthermore female suffrage had become the law of the land in 1918, and although a beautiful Irish lady, Constance Gore-Booth, who had married a Pole and was known as Countess Markiewicz, had been elected to Parliament she had refused to take her seat on the grounds of being a Sinn Feiner. (The famous Irish poet, W.B. Yeats nursed a hopeless passion for the Countess for many years.) Why should Plymouth not have the distinction of sending the first woman to the House of Commons? In a pioneering mood, the Plymouth Conservative Association extended the invitation to Lady Astor and Lady Astor accepted.

The keynote of her adoption speech was: 'If you can't get a fighting man take a fighting woman.' With the faithful Waldorf at her side she toured the constituency in a landau hired from a local stable drawn by two sleek horses and driven by an enormous, top-hatted and liveried coachman whose name was Churchward. The horses' bridles were decorated with red, white and blue ribbons and Nancy was dressed in her most elegant clothes, wearing a spectacular pearl necklace. Whenever the carriage came upon a knot of people Nancy gave a signal, the coachman stopped, and she addressed the crowd. This was what she liked best; the noisier and more obstreperous the hecklers, the more exciting she

Nancy Astor's campaigning was nothing if not aggressive. She relished the heckling and is pictured here having a slanging match with a spectator in the Plymouth election of November 1923.

found it. Once her coachman, the good Churchward, became frightened for her safety, jumped down from the box and waded in with some growls. 'You there, behave yourselves.' But Nancy turned on him. 'Shut up, Churchward, I'm making this speech, not you.'

Sometimes they shouted at her: 'Go back to America!'

'You go back to Lancashire!'

'I'm an Irishman.'

'I knew it! An imported interrupter!'

'If I'd imported you, I'd drown myself in the sea.'

'More likely in drink.'

'I'm a teetotaller.'

'Well go and have a drink anyway. It might improve your temper.'

When people asked her questions that she was unable to answer, (something which extended to all economic subjects) she sometimes said: 'I'm not a paid politician therefore I can afford to speak the truth and declare straightforwardly that I don't know.' On other occasions she slid out of the dilemma by diverting the interlocutor. 'Let me tell you something awfully funny that happened to me. I saw a young sailor looking at the outside of the House of Commons. I said to him: "Would you like to go in?" He answered: "You are the sort of woman my mother told me to avoid."'

Prohibition had just been introduced in the United States, and many people, including Nancy's devoted admirer Philip Kerr (later Lord Lothian) urged the teetotal Nancy to come out flatly in favour of Britain following suit. But Waldorf told her that it was the one sure way to lose the election, so she campaigned as 'no pussyfooter (an abolitionist) but against drunkenness'. When the result was known at the end of November (to allow the service men's votes to be counted) she had 14,495 notes; her Labour opponent, Mr Gay polled 9,292 and the Liberal candidate, Mr Isaac Foot, 4,139. After acknowledging the cheers of the crowd, and thanking the party workers she said: 'I ought to feel sorry for Mr Foot and Mr Gay but I don't. The only person I feel sorry for is the poor old Viscount here.'

The poor old Viscount disliked the House of Lords on principle. He did not believe in an hereditary chamber and decided that the best way to bring about its demise was for young men to relinquish their titles. He therefore persuaded Jim Thomas, a Labour MP to introduce a motion in the Commons 'that leave be given to bring in a Bill to empower His Majesty to accept a surrender of any peerage'. But the motion was defeated by 186 votes to 56. Although it became law twenty years after Waldorf's death, one wonders if he would have been disappointed to see how few men cared to relinquish their peerages.

Nancy was introduced into Parliament by Prime Minister Lloyd George and a former Prime Minister, Arthur Balfour. She wore a simple black suit, a white blouse and a tri-cornered hat. These clothes are now in the Museum of Costume at Bath. She made her maiden speech on the necessity of restricting the hours that public houses were allowed to sell drink. Although the theme was very unpopular on her side of the House, she delivered the speech (which Waldorf had helped her to write) with dignity and restraint. 'I do not want you to look upon your lady member as a fanatic or a lunatic. I am simply trying to speak for hundreds of women and children throughout the country who cannot speak for themselves. I want to tell you that I do know the working man, and I know that, if anyone will tell him the truth about drink, he would be as willing as anybody to put up with these vexatious restrictions.' Although she hoped that prohibition in Britain would come eventually, she continued to claim that she was not a 'prohibitionist' as she was 'not in favour of it being imposed tyrannically' – meaning that laws without public support would not stick. On the whole she got a good press and the speech was judged a success.

Lady Astor was now famous in many parts of the world, not least in the United States where Americans found her good looks, humour and vivacity as praiseworthy as her accomplishments. As she was not educated or even politically experienced, she used her platform to champion what she knew about – women's rights. But in the flood-tide of American enthusiasm reporters began to endow her with qualities she did not possess. The fact that she was quick at repartee and specialized in a sort of friendly insolence suddenly won her the reputation of being a wit, which she was not; and dozens of sharp exchanges, entirely apocryphal, were attributed to her. However, the 'Astorisms' most frequently quoted do not suggest rapier-like thrusts. Walking along the street in Plymouth she would call up to the windows: 'Hey, you there!' and when heads began to peer over the sills she would cry, 'Come on. I'm ready for you!' 'You have enough brass to make a kettle!' called an old man. 'You have enough water in your head to fill it,' she replied. 'You pretend to know about farming,' called another, 'Well, how many toes on a pig's foot?' 'Take off your shoes, man, and count!' was the answer.

This was the sort of good-natured badinage that kept the public amused, and when she went to New York in 1922, accompanied by the faithful Waldorf, she went as a celebrity. A crowd gathered at the pier to watch them disembark. That night gangling Vincent Astor led his celebrated cousin on to the platform of the Town Hall where she made a short speech and answered questions for two hours. The *New York Times* was lyrical: '... best type of American womanhood, charming, gay, unaffected ... persuades all judgements ... messenger of good cheer'. In the Capitol, President Harding received them, the Senate invited them to a reception and the leading hostesses gave parties for them. Waldorf not only spent his time answering letters, mapping out schedules, arranging times for speeches, but actually wrote the speeches himself. And as she often spoke two or three times a day, he was kept furiously busy. Travelling by train through Virginia was a doubtful undertaking – a royal progress with no guards to fend off intruders. 'Not even with a stateroom can we get privacy,' Waldorf wrote in his diary. 'Our fellow travellers are kindness themselves but don't realize one needs to be quiet at times.' And another day: 'Crowds – guard of honour in uniform – flags – officers – swords – schoolgirls – song "Nancy Astor you are some girl" – flowers – speech – train moved on – cheers.'

Before the trip was over Waldorf himself managed to create a stir. Seated in the Astor Estate Office on 26th Street, this prince of landlords who lived on an income from New York tenements gave an astonishing interview to the press saying that in England people were determined to have better housing conditions. 'All Europe is living on the edge of a volcano...it is bad business to tolerate slums...our housing policy is in one sense uneconomic. It will cost the taxpayers money but it is cheaper than having revolutions.'

Lady Astor loved being the centre of attention and Cliveden was the perfect setting. The armistice of 1918 had brought the great house to life like the touch of a magic wand. Overnight the servants returned, overnight the corridors resounded to the noise of children and barking dogs, to the scurrying of feet of housemaids and the leisurely stride of guests, not to mention the majestic boom of the dinner gong. The weekend parties might contain anyone, wrote Walter Elliot, a frequent guest:

Henry Ford, the Queen of Roumania, Mr Charles Mellow, Jim Thomas, Philip Lothian, Bernard Shaw, Tom Jones, Edith Lyttleton, Arthur Balfour, a general, a scientist, a Christian Scientist, relations, protégés, American senators whether sober or not (this was the only category to which such licence was extended), people of High Society, people of no society, and if you were lucky indeed, one or more of the other Langhorne sisters....

I don't know which was more pleasant, to appear at tea-time in winter when the tea was set in the centre hall before the big fire, or in summer, when it was laid out with infinite details, under a pavilion roof at the end of the broad terrace. Tea, did I say? It was more like a Bedouin encampment. There was a table for tea, a table for cakes, a table for children, a table for grown-ups, a table for more grown-ups and generally a nomadic group coming and going somewhere in the neighbourhood of Nancy herself. Cushions, papers, people were mixed in a noble disarray. Nancy presided over the whole affair like a blend between Juno at the siege of Troy, and one of the leading Valkyries caracoling over an appropriate battlefield. [After dinner there were always two fires in the drawing room with guests around both.] If Nancy were in one of her wilder moods, then at one, acting, games, impersonations of everything in and out of the world, while at the other fire grave and reverend seigneurs would be exchanging views upon the Gold Standard.

Lady Astor's outstanding characteristic, needless to say, was her vitality which engulfed those around her like a river overflowing its banks. She loved everything from boating to bowls, from tennis and golf to croquet. A friend wrote:

After a long day in the House of Commons, she would return to Cliveden around seven, change into tennis clothes and play two or even three sets of single with one of her nieces, then down to the river in her cream-coloured car. She would swim across the Thames talking all the time about GOD, touch the bottom at the far bank, tell the swans to go away and swim back still talking.

Although she gave up hunting when she began to have children, she still craved the excitement that only danger can bring, and in the late twenties persuaded her friend Colonel Lawrence (of Arabia) to take her riding on the pillion of his motorbike. In November 1930 the *New York Times* informed its readers that Lady Astor was indulging in the favourite sport of English 'flappers', and had ridden with Lawrence for seventy miles along the twisting lanes of Devonshire. 'Really, Lawrence,' protested Lord Astor, 'my wife should not be encouraged to find new ways of breaking her neck!' His words were prophetic in a misdirected way for a short time later Lawrence broke his own neck on the motorbike.

Lady Astor's son, Michael, tells us that his mother was at her very best with an audience of children. At home she often entertained her family by slipping a set of false teeth in her mouth and mimicking an English country lady about to ride to hounds, or a nervous Jewish businessman, a Russian refugee, or one of the Virginia 'darkies' she had known as a girl. The children loved going into her room, lying in front of the fire and listening to her. In 1922 her son Bobby Shaw was grown up, but the young Astors were still children: Bill fifteen; Wissie thirteen; David eleven; Michael six; Jakie four. The stories from her childhood, wrote her son Michael, 'were witty and humorous with a touch of pathos which is inevitable in any Negro story. My mother acted every part with her voice, making her characters lazy and confiding, boastful or frightened. We were listening to the world of the coloured people at Mirador.'

The routine of the young Astors had its serious side for when the children were at Cliveden they had to study a Christian Science 'lesson' every morning. Lady Astor did her own lesson right after breakfast and Michael recalls the general pandemonium while this sacred duty was taking place: telephones ringing, dogs barking, interruptions from cook and nanny; not to mention the children's internecine arguments, quarrels, slaps and kicks.

William Waldorf and Nancy with David, 11, and Michael, 6. Nancy gave her five children daily readings in Christian Science which frequently developed into an hour of story-telling. Using a negro dialect, Nancy told them tales of her childhood in Virginia.

'Now keep still and listen to this, it will really help you,' my mother's religious asides were spoken in a gentle voice.... But quickly the tone of her voice would vary; a note of humour would come into it and, either to catch the interest of the child or because what she was about to read out was such a mouthful that she could not properly digest it herself, she would look up and say in the purest imitation of a Southern Negro woman, 'Yassir, I'se gonna help yew. Me and Mistah Jesus is gonna help yew.'

Not surprisingly, the children much preferred to be 'given the lesson' by their mother than their father. With the latter the 'whole episode became more portentous, and when it was finished we would leave the room knowing that we could never live up to the expectations of this good man who, at times, took such a stern and uncompromising view of life.'

It was one thing for Lady Astor to read her children the lesson; quite another to have the iron will to refuse medical aid when one of them was seriously ill. Her faith was put to the test – or perhaps one should say that it escaped being put to the test – when her twenty-year-old daughter, Wissie, was hunting with the Pytchley in Northamptonshire and had a bad fall. Wissie was staying with Ronald Tree, who was married to Lady Astor's niece, Nancy, and who was the joint Master of the Hunt. One of the riders, Henry Tiarks, saw the accident and called to Ronnie. Wissie was lying on the ground conscious but unable to move. The men unhinged a gate and carried her to a nearby house where they called an ambulance which took her to Ronnie's house, Kelmarsh. Ronnie rang Lady Astor who said that she and Waldorf would come at once bringing a Christian Science practitioner with them.

Meanwhile Henry Tiarks had called the eminent radiologist, Harold Hodgson, who was asked to come as quickly as possible – before Lady Astor arrived – with his portable X-ray. The examination was taking place when the Astors' car drew up.

Hodgson finally finished and came into the room. 'Well, it's nothing is it?' said Lady Astor. 'I am afraid you are mistaken. It's very serious indeed.' He explained that there was a structural injury to the spine in the middle of the back and recommended a thorough re-articulation by an orthopaedic surgeon.

Nancy went quite white, struggling with herself for a decision and finally came up with a compromise. The only doctor she would summon was Sir Crisp English who had operated both on Philip Kerr and herself. This was a fantastic solution for the doctor was an abdominal surgeon and quite unable to pronounce on spinal injuries. He was furiously angry at being called all the way from London, and told them to summon Thomas Fairbank without delay. When Fairbank arrived, he, too, was angry as twelve hours had elapsed since the accident, a time-lag that might prove fatal. However, he put Wissie in plaster and left, hoping for the best. Wissie's convalescence was slow and painful but after some months she could walk again. Although she had trouble with her back for the rest of her life it was what Lady Astor called a 'complete recuperation'.

The most remarkable aspect of the whole episode was that Lady Astor convinced herself that the doctors had contributed nothing to Wissie's recovery. It had been brought about by Lady Astor's faith in Christian Science. Henry Tiarks tackled her one day and asked: What about Hodgson? What about Crisp English? What about Thomas Fairbank? She flatly denied that she had seen any of them – only Sir Crisp English who said he could not help!

Lord Astor was so impressed by his wife that he gradually relinquished the idea of a political career for himself and devoted more and more time to her. Of course he had a good many obligations of his own. He was a founder member of the Royal Society of International Affairs and in 1935 became its chairman. He kept a close watch on his newspaper, *The Observer*, and although he made it a policy not to interfere with his fiery editor, J.L. Garvin (whose weekly articles were known as 'the thunderstorms'), he frequently invited him to Cliveden and had long talks with him.

But whereas London activities fell into the category of 'duty', country preoccupations were always surrounded by an air of pleasure. He loved the good earth and every morning liked to rise early and take his dogs

for a walk while the dew was still on the ground. He was particularly
fond of the fine old trees in the park which he tended as lovingly as
a gardener cares for his flowers. The White Place Farm at Cookham
(part of Cliveden) also absorbed his interest; he had one of the first tuber-
culin-tested herds and became an expert on grass seed. He learned so
much about agriculture that he later wrote a book, in collaboration with
Seebohm Rowntree, entitled *Mixed Farming and Muddled Thinking* which
received excellent reviews.

One of the outdoor hobbies which he liked best was fishing. In 1920
he had bought a large, sporting estate on the island of Jura in the Inner
Hebrides. Here, in the mouth of the rivers, he fished for sea trout. Later
he dammed the streams and made special pools where he could fish for
fresh trout. He taught his children the skills of this difficult pastime – at
least those who expressed a desire to learn.

However, his great passion was horses. He had begun his stud farm
at Oxford, but the undertaking was very far from being a rich man's
folly. He had only four or five mares which he picked up very cheaply
– indeed, his 'foundation mare', Conjure, cost him only one hundred
guineas. And when he left the university he apprenticed himself to a
vet and studied the Mendelian theory of breeding. Throughout the
'twenties he built up one of the finest stables in the world, competing
with the Aga Khan, Lord Rosebery and Lord Derby, champion owners
of champion stables. Although he never won the Derby, he came second
five times. Other races gave his horses the coveted blue ribbons. He won
The Oaks five times; the 2000 Guineas three times; the 1000 Guineas
twice; and the St Leger once.

Lord Astor's friend, the famous painter of horses, A.J. Munnings,
often came to Cliveden to immortalize his best horses. Although

*A delighted Lord Astor leading in
his horse, 'Short Story', after
winning the Oaks in 1926.
During the 'twenties he built up
one of the finest stud farms in
Europe.*

puritanical Waldorf regarded most artists as immoral, Munnings was an exception, at least until the evening when his careless talk appalled the priggish host. The men were left alone in the dining room after dinner talking about the League of Nations, Baldwin, Chamberlain, Chatham House and back again to the League. Michael Astor wrote:

My father, realizing that Munnings had been out of the talk, tried to bring him in. 'A. J. where are you going after this?' 'Brighton,' was Munning's reply. 'What's it like at Brighton?' said my father. 'Oh, you know,' said Munnings, who had been consoling himself with the port, 'a lot of old Jews lying on the beach making love upside down to a lot of young tarts.' There was a nasty hush, rendered even more silent by the stentorian tones of Lionel Curtis asking, '*What* did he say?' My father did not know about Brighton, and certainly he wished he had not tried to find out; nor did he see what course the conversation could take after this. Quietly embarrassed, he snuffed the candles on the dining room table, like an umpire at the end of a cricket match drawing stumps. We groped our way to the door in silence.

As Waldorf Astor and his brother J.J. lived entirely on the revenue from Manhattan real estate rentals, they were greatly concerned at the end of the war to find that both the United States government and the British government were determined to tax the same income. In 1919 the gross rent from the William Waldorf estate was somewhere in the region of $2,500,000. That year the two brothers paid a joint $1,680,000 to the British government and a joint $1,134,000 to the American government, a total of $2,814,000 – $300,000 more than their total income.

Old William Waldorf had advised his sons to dispose of real estate 'because there is no other way out'; and although at the time they thought he was unduly pessimistic they now seemed to have no alternative – at least until they could get a sensible ruling on double taxation. So the order went out from London to sell, something that Vincent Astor had already begun to do. They sold tenements along West 129 and 130th Streets; more tenements on York Avenue; over 1600 lots in the Bronx; the Netherland Hotel and the Exchange Court Building on Wall Street, and one half of the Waldorf-Astoria which they owned jointly with Vincent and for which they each received $3,750,000. By 1925 they had realized over $20,000,000 and still had another $20,000,000 in real estate. In the depression of the thirties the bargains seemed too tempting to miss, and once again they began to shop around for property.

However, they were still battling in the courts over taxes. Although the two governments came to an understanding about double taxation, the two brothers found themselves in trouble with the tax authorities over inheritance tax, a demand which came to about twenty per cent of the whole. The US government argued that if the two trusts set up in 1916, amounting to $25,000,000, had been established in 'contemplation of death', it was merely a blatant attempt to avoid paying the American Treasury and the assessment must be regarded as valid. Norman Davis, counsel for the Astor Estate, had no alternative but to find another, convincing reason for the establishment of the trusts, so he

Major John Jacob Astor of Hever, accompanied by his wife Violet, talking to the men of the Deal lifeboat during the Deal and Dover Election Campaign of November 1922, his second attempt to enter Parliament. This time he was successful.

argued that the Astors, far from trying to avoid American taxation, were struggling to prevent the British government from seizing their American securities and forcing them to accept in exchange British War Bonds.

The case was fought out in the American courts and in 1926 Judge Knox declared that as the trusts could be altered to suit the Astors they were not, in fact, *bona fide* settlements but, as the American government contended, dodges. However, the case was taken to the US Circuit Court of Appeals, and two years later Judge Martin Manton reversed Judge Knox's decision, claiming that the Astors could not have changed the trusts without the consent of their senior trustee, the Farmer's Loan and Trust Company; therefore the trusts were not tax dodges. The decision was final and Major J.J. Astor, and Lord Astor's four sons, were $5,000,000 richer.

Next came litigation over the trust that William Waldorf had established in 1919, amounting to $50,000,000 to be divided equally between the present Lord Astor and his brother. The case was fought on much the same ground, but this time, perhaps because William Waldorf had died the same year, juries and judges consistently supported the claims of the US government. The Astors won only once, in 1930. But in 1933 the Court of Appeal reversed the decision and found for the government; it found again in 1937, while in 1938 the Supreme Court refused to rehear the case. The original $11,000,000 demanded by the government amounted to nearly $20,000,000 by the late thirties because of the accumulation of interest.

However, the Astors were not plagued by a shortage of money. They could afford to devote themselves to 'public service', a term frequently used by millionaires to describe their altruism in entering Parliament – despite the fact that every safe Tory seat had several dozens of frantic applicants. Major J.J. had tried to follow the lead of his elder brother, Waldorf, when in January 1921 he fought a by-election at Dover as a coalition candidate in support of Lloyd George's government. Unfortunately Astor was opposed by an Independent Conservative, Colonel Sir Thomas Polson, who campaigned as an 'anti-waste' man, accusing the government of 'financial extravagance'. Polson was supported by Northcliffe's *Times* and Rothermere's *Daily Mail*, and when the votes were counted, 'anti-waste' had triumphed and Polson had a majority of 3130.

J.J. was very fond of Waldorf but unfortunately their two wives, Violet and Nancy, could not get on so the two families seldom met. J.J. lived at Hever Castle with his wife and three boys, Gavin, Hugh and John, and played an important part in country life. In 1922 J.J. made a second attempt to move into the political arena, but decided that first he would do as his father had done, and buy a newspaper – and why not the very paper that had been partly responsible for his defeat? Lord Northcliffe, the owner of *The Times*, had died a short while before and the trustees were rumoured to be anxious to sell in order to raise the death duties. Northcliffe had bought *The Times* when its circulation was only 40,000. Over the years he had dropped the price from threepence to a penny and raised the readership to 165,000. Even this did not make 'The Thunderer' a paying proposition, but at least it carried great prestige. Indeed, Major J.J. was fond of quoting his hero, Abraham Lincoln, who had once commented on the London *Times* saying, 'I don't know of anything that has more power except perhaps the Mississippi.'

The Major had competition from Lord Northcliffe's brother, Lord Rothermere. However, Northcliffe's Will stipulated that John Walter, a descendant of the founder of *The Times* must be offered first refusal if *The Times* shares were put on the market. Astor was able, therefore, to come to an arrangement with Walter who was not well off but who agreed to buy the paper for J.J. in exchange for a small percentage of shares. Rothermere hinted that he was willing to pay $5,000,000 and Astor hoped to get it for the same amount; but in the end it cost him $7,000,000, a fairly stiff price for a money-loser. In order to prevent the paper from ever again falling into such unsuitable hands as Lord Northcliffe's, Astor set up a Board of Trustees whose approval would be necessary before another sale could be made. The trustees included the Lord Chief Justice, the Warden of All Souls and the Governor of the Bank of England.

By this time *The Times* had an almost sacred glow about it and it was no surprise when Major Astor outlined his policy in equally pious terms. The function of *The Times*, he said, was not 'to enter into rivalry with the party in power but to lean as far as possible in support of the government of the day and especially so when the government is the spokesman of the nation in international affairs'. Astor reinstated Geoffrey Dawson,

Major Astor, now a Lieutenant-Colonel, discusses the change of editorship at The Times *in 1941. He took over the direction of the paper after Lord Northcliffe's death in 1922.*

who had edited *The Times* from 1914 to 1919. Dawson was a close friend of Philip Kerr and Lionel Curtis and a frequent visitor to Cliveden, which prompted Waldorf Astor to write his brother a warm letter of congratulation on choosing 'the best man for the job'.

Very soon after buying *The Times* Major Astor stood again for Dover, and this time was elected. However, he seemed to have a jinx as far as Parliament was concerned. In 1923 there was yet another general election at which he was unopposed. He did not feel it necessary to disturb his constituents so he passed the time by taking a trip to Egypt. When he came back he took his seat in the Commons, went into the lobby and voted for a protective tariff. But alas, alas, he had forgotten to get himself 'sworn in'. This heinous offence, termed 'a grave Constitutional lapse', automatically vacated his seat 'as thought he were dead' and compelled him to stand yet again for Parliament. Although J.J. was deeply embarrassed, his constituents probably were not put to any more bother than on the previous occasions, and at last Major Astor was installed in the Commons.   He did not develop much of a relationship with his talkative sister-in-law, but he saw and heard her on many occasions as she made a point of interrupting Opposition speeches. At times he was embarrassed by the irritation she provoked, but whatever the criticisms, one could not deny her courage. But it was sad that she never really knew what to direct her courage against.

However, Nancy won the admiration of the *Daily Express* reporter at the General Election of 1929 when she sailed into the roughest district in Plymouth to do battle.

She stood completely alone in the courtyard of the worst tenement of the worst street in Plymouth, a Communist stronghold, and glowered at balcony on balcony above her packed with more than a hundred shouting, shrieking, hostile women. 'So you are a pack of Bolshies, eh?' she challenged, waving the umbrella threateningly.

'Better get away, Lady Astor,' I warned, for a hefty woman with sacking over her head was reaching for a cabbage.

She spun round fiercely. 'Leave this to me.' A man caught her roughly by the shoulder, and she raised the umbrella. He ran like a hare and she faced the crowd.

'Too proud for the working woman, am I?' she laughed merrily and struck an attitude, nose perked comically. . . .

'They say I drink gin and bitters,' she cried. 'Hoy, you up there' – she pointed to a woman who had been shouting herself hoarse – 'How many gin and bitters have I had with you, Pleasant?'

A little dog flew snarling at the crowd. Someone threw a brick at him. Like an avenging angel with her umbrella Lady Astor dashed up, saved the little dog, and then, with arms akimbo, harangued the crowd. . . .

They cheered her – cheered her like mad, and as her car left the place, roared and roared again 'Good old Nancy!' She just made it, winning the seat by 211 votes.

The new deal and the Cliveden set

Previous page *Cliveden,
designed by Sir Charles Barry,
architect of the House of
Commons, had been given to
Nancy and Waldorf by the first
Viscount on the occasion of their
marriage. Before the war it was the
meeting-place of the 'Cliveden Set'
– a group of people who worked
for an understanding with
Hitler. During the war Cliveden
became a hospital for the
Canadians.*

The Waldorf-Astoria Hotel that opened on Park Avenue in the 1930s had nothing to do with the Astors. Nevertheless, Elsa Maxwell, the fat, ugly, energetic party organizer of the inter-war era, put the omission right by holding a subscription ball at the hotel entitled 'Mrs Astor's Horse' (an American slang expression of the 'thirties meaning everything but the kitchen sink).

Mrs Vincent Astor arrived in a white dress wearing the famous Astor pearls while Vincent's ex-brother-in-law, Prince Serge Obolensky, appeared resplendently arrayed as an officer in the Imperial Russian Guard. Beatrice Lillie was the hit of the evening. 'Mrs Astor's horse is a very cross horse today,' she trilled. 'He's quite indisposed; there's a goat in his stall.'

At the time the ball was given, in 1934, Vincent Astor was enjoying the prestige of being 'the President's friend'. He had known Franklin Roosevelt since boyhood as they lived within a few miles of each other in Dutchesse County, New York. And, of course, they were linked by marriage. Vincent's great-aunt, Laura Astor, married the Delano who was a brother of Franklin's mother; and Vincent's Aunt Helen had married James Roosevelt (Franklin's half-brother) and was buried in the Roosevelt family cemetery at Hyde Park. Apart from these connections the two men were drawn together by a love of the country and a love of the sea. In 1921 Astor was deeply shocked to learn that Franklin had been stricken with infantile paralysis and at once arranged for him to exercise every day at his large indoor pool at Rhinebeck.

In 1928 Vincent supported Roosevelt when he ran for the New York governorship, and in 1932, when the nation was in the grip of the worst depression in American history, he came out for Roosevelt for President. That was the year that Astor was reputed to be facing a million dollar deficit in the real estate business.

At the beginning of the presidential campaign in August 1932, Astor had lunch with Governor Roosevelt at Albany. Also present was John Rascob, Roosevelt's financial adviser. After discussing Democratic party funds Astor accepted an appointment on the Finance Committee and set about collecting subscriptions. He soon discovered that the most enthusiastic contributors were not the Wall Street millionaires but merchants and manufacturers. He was successful in raising money by making a thorough canvass of small capitalists, while Roosevelt was successful in winning the election.

Before his inauguration, the President-elect accepted an invitation to cruise aboard the *Nourmahal* but when the party landed at Miami the voyage nearly came to a grisly end. The presidential group took a triumphal motor ride through streets lined with a cheering populace. Roosevelt rode in the first car accompanied by Mayor Cernak of Chicago and a bodyguard, and Vincent followed in a car with Kermit Roosevelt, William Rhinelander Stewart and Raymond Moley, a professor of criminology who had become friend and adviser to F.D.R. As the first car made its way down the street, a lunatic named Zangara fired at Roosevelt, missing him, and wounding Cernak instead, who died before he reached the hospital.

*Vincent Astor in 1916 when he
was a lieutenant in the New
York Navy Militia. He had just
become a friend of his Hyde Park
neighbour, Franklin Roosevelt,
at that time assistant secretary of
the Navy.*

Now that Franklin Roosevelt was about to be installed in the White House, Vincent Astor turned his attention to public service. After a discussion with his friend, Averill Harriman, he decided that Roosevelt and his adviser, Raymond Moley, should have a newspaper or magazine that would reflect the ideas of 'the new regime'. Averill's sister, Mary Harriman Rumsey, scouted about and reported that the defunct *Washington Post* was on the auction block. They were not wholly enthusiastic about the idea of a daily newspaper and only offered a modest sum which was inadequate against a much larger bid from the Jewish millionaire, Eugene Meyer. After several profitless months Vincent decided to launch a new magazine. Both Roosevelt and Moley were enthusiastic, and the two Harrimans joined Vincent as shareholders. They named the magazine *Today* and the President took the first subscription. The circulation rose to 100,000, which was considered good at the time, and as the magazine was thought to reflect the President's views, it became the most widely quoted periodical in the country.

Although Astor announced with majestic impartiality that *Today* would oppose alike 'the predatory rich and the predatory poor' – whatever that was supposed to mean – his own life had its problems. In 1934 when La Guardia was elected Mayor of New York, he set up a Tenement House Department to investigate the city's slums. The *New York Post* talked about Vincent Astor's tenements whereupon the President's friend promptly replied that he would sell his tenement houses, and the land on which they stood, for whatever sum of money the city authorities deemed a fair price. Eventually the city named $189,181, a sum so small that many people said it did not even cover the minimum value of the land. But Astor did not quibble. He accepted the city valuation and wrote *finis* to this aspect of his estate business.

Even so, before long Vincent Astor began to see that he had bitten off more than he could chew – at least as far as the President was concerned. In 1935 when he invited Roosevelt on a cruise, the latter replied that he could not spare more than a week and it would not justify the expense of putting the huge yacht in commission. 'The *Nourmahal* is

Below right Vincent Astor's yacht the Nourmahal *as she left Jacksonville Harbour on a fishing trip with Franklin D. Roosevelt on board.*

Below Giuseppe Zangara (centre) who on 15 February 1933 attempted to assassinate Franklin D. Roosevelt shortly after the President-elect had docked at Miami in the Nourmahal. *The officer on the right is holding the pistol used in the attempt.*

always in commission,' replied Astor. 'Really?' quipped the President. 'In that case it looks as though we'll have to increase taxes on the rich.' This was no idle joke for on 19 June 1935, the President sent his 'soak-the-rich' tax programme to Congress, with a message 'on the disturbing effects upon our national life that come from great inheritances of wealth and power. . . . The transmission from generation to generation of vast fortunes by Will, inheritance, or gift is not consistent with the ideals and sentiments of the American people.' Shades of William Waldorf Astor! As long ago as June 1899, when he had informed the world that he was becoming a British subject, he had given as one of his reasons the fact that Americans believed 'that large fortunes were contrary to austere tenets of republican simplicity and made a point of passing laws against entails, primogeniture, and hereditary successions'.

It was not surprising that newspaper commentators were wondering if Roosevelt would go cruising on the *Nourmahal* again. 'Everyone says there has been no cooling off of the friendship between the two,' wrote one reporter. 'Nevertheless it will be interesting this spring [1936] to see whether President Roosevelt takes his next fishing trip on the *Nourmahal*.' Journalists did not have to wait long for an answer. That year the navy supplied the President with an improvised yacht and Vincent Astor cruised alone with his friends.

About the same time, Professor Raymond Moley fell out with the President and accepted a job working full time on Vincent's *Today*. However, Astor felt that the magazine should be doing better than it was, and eventually bought *Newsweek* and merged the two. Moley became editor and for many years was Vincent's most respected adviser. He enjoyed the distinction of being the only person permitted to telephone the proprietor during the breakfast hour.

Astor did not allow his interest in politics to distract him from the Astor Estate Office. Although his sister Alice had divorced Serge Obolensky and married again, Vincent remained loyal to his former brother-in-law, and during the depression employed him to renovate two brownstone houses on East End Avenue. Serge did the job superlatively well, introducing steam heating and modern plumbing and employing all the newest techniques and gadgets in rewiring the buildings. He named one of them Poverty Row, the other Busted Row, but they were in such immaculate condition they soon constituted one of the most fashionable addresses in Manhattan.

Vincent was so pleased with Serge's work that in 1935 he asked him to redecorate the St Regis. This hotel had been built by Vincent's father, sold, and reclaimed by the Astor Estate Office through default of the mortgage. Serge was astonished by the building, which he described as 'an architectural masterpiece of a sort'. He wrote:

When Colonel John Jacob Astor built it, he had wanted to make it the great luxury hotel of the New World. Colonel Astor was an inventor . . . extremely able. In the St Regis he had installed an air-conditioning system of his own design. On each floor there was a room in which sheets of dampened cheese-cloth were hung, and powerful fans drove the air through these sheets and into ducts that went to every room. And of course that kind of cooling system works quite well, as anyone who has ever placed a damp cloth before an electric fan well knows. Vincent put coils and compressors in these cooling rooms and, presto, thanks to his father's foresight he had the first fully air-conditioned hotel in the world.

Serge redid all the main rooms, bar, restaurant, roof and basement. The two most famous rooms were the *Maisonette Russe* and the Iridium Room which staged fully-fledged ice shows on a rink that rolled out and over the pinewood ballroom. With these sensational innovations it was not surprising that the St Regis became the talk of the town and the centre of a buoyant new social life where European visitors flocked to take a look at American expertise.

Everything that Vincent Astor touched seemed to turn into money. Indeed, the huge Astor fortune appeared to have the quality of self-perpetuation, for no matter how much money an Astor spent there was always more to be had. And as a result of the interest and speculation aroused by the family, the old fairy tale about the first John Jacob Astor stumbling fortuitously upon Captain Kidd's hidden strong-box of gold and precious jewels continued to be revived periodically and very often believed.

The only Astors who seemed to be at odds with the world and always in need of more money than they possessed were the young widow of John Jacob Astor and her son Jack. In 1931 Madeleine divorced Mr Dick

Madeleine Force, now Mrs William Dick, and her son, John Jacob Astor VI, who was born shortly after she was rescued from the Titanic.

to marry an Italian prize-fighter, Enzo Fiermonte, seventeen years her junior. The marriage was not a success and six years later poor Mrs Fiermonte found peace through an overdose of sleeping pills.

Her son, Jack, also paddled in troubled waters. When he came of age in 1933 he inherited $5,000,000, only a fraction of Vincent's fortune, but used it with 'breathtaking *panache*'. He bought a railway carriage and ten motor cars, one of which was a yellow Rolls Royce. In New York he equipped himself with a house at 7 East 91st Street which he staffed with twenty-five servants.

The following year he became engaged to Eileen Gillespie of Newport and gave her a fabulous ring which originally had belonged to the Empress Eugénie of France and was said to be worth $100,000. However, almost at once he quarrelled with Eileen, broke off the engagement and married one of her bridesmaids, Ellen French. Once again the wedding was arranged at Newport, this time the guests being infiltrated with a host of private detectives. 'There were four bodyguards', reported *Fortune Magazine*, 'besides a corps of uniformed police. When the Astors arrived in Providence to begin their honeymoon to the West Coast they were accompanied by six guards. During the trip, at each stop, bodyguards hovered near the Astor's private car and upon their return to New York 46 detectives were on hand to greet them.' Jack Astor's army of detectives, he later explained, was part and parcel of 'being an Astor'.

Jack Astor soon began to complain about not having enough money, but at least his wife obliged him by producing a son whom he named William Backhouse Astor. Vincent and Helen, on the other hand, had plenty of money but no children. Would Vincent be the last of the truly rich, truly spectacular, Astors? And what would become of the Astor Estate Office? 'How do you know there will be any estate to give away?' said Vincent. 'The inheritance and other taxes may wipe it out so that Uncle Sam gets it all.'

Back in 1931 when Vincent Astor was making plans to support Governor Franklin Roosevelt in his bid for the presidency, Lord and Lady Astor in far away England were also making plans – but their activities were pitched in a lower key and centred on a trip to Soviet Russia in the company of George Bernard Shaw. The English Astors received the most publicity. Americans were bored by political speeches, while the thought of sparkling anti-Bolshevik Nancy Astor travelling to Russia with the witty Irish playwright who openly boasted of being a Marxist Communist seemed to promise limitless entertainment.

Lady Astor loved celebrities and Bernard Shaw loved the luxury of Cliveden where he had been a frequent guest over the past four years. Nancy used Shaw shamelessly, often enticing him on to her political platform in order to draw a big audience. Notwithstanding this friendly badinage, what did these two – the virulent anti-Bolshevist and the vociferous millionaire Communist have in common? They were 'theatrical partners', Lady Astor's biographer, Christopher Sykes, explains, '...both actors, both specializing in comedy'. And as Bernard Shaw and Nancy Astor shared a liking for the limelight, and realized that the joint

Nancy Astor and G.B. Shaw on their trip to Russia, photographed with a group of intellectuals in Leningrad. As a long-standing critic of the Russian system, she provoked world-wide censure when she returned home and refused to contradict Shaw's lyrical descriptions of the Soviet Union despite the fact that millions had died in Stalin's purges.

trip to Russia would involve them in world-wide publicity, they were very much in favour of it.

At that time Shaw was greatly admired in Russia as a man violently opposed to democracy and universal suffrage, so the red carpet was ready for him. Indeed, he was able to announce quite casually that he was bringing a few travelling companions with him. The party consisted of Nancy and Waldorf Astor, their son David, Philip Kerr who was now Lord Lothian, and a Christian Science friend, Charles Tennant. At Warsaw the travellers were joined by Maxim Litvinoff and Maurice Hindus, an American of Russian origin who was a passionate admirer of the USSR.

The world press was deeply disappointed in the visit. The trip was a three-ring circus from which they hoped to get columns of amusing copy. Instead the Russians' propagandists took strict control of the party and discouraged interviews. The visitors were shepherded about, and taken on the usual round of schools, factories, juvenile prisons; on the usual tour of Leningrad, ballet, opera, museums; on the usual sorties to sports stadiums and gardens of culture and rest. The highlight of the trip was an interview with Stalin but even this might have been dull had not Lady Astor suddenly intervened and asked the dictator how long he intended to go on ruling by Tsarist methods. (Bernard Shaw's biographer, St John Ervine, declares that Lady Astor's question was 'Why have you slaughtered so many Russians?'; but Lady Astor's son, David, who accompanied his parents on the trip but was not present at the interview gives the version quoted above.) Apparently the interpreters were too frightened to translate until Stalin demanded to know what she had said. According to Waldorf's diary he did not turn a hair when the question was explained, and evaded answering by a non-sequitur in which he explained the necessity of firm action by citing the case of foreign engineers found guilty of attempted sabotage. He ended by hoping that the need for dealing drastically with political prisoners would soon cease.

Then he moved on to bigger things, asking the group when they thought that Winston Churchill would come back to power. The Astors and Lord Lothian shook their heads replying that Churchill was 'a spent force' and that no Tory government would have him as a minister. Stalin insisted, however, that a man of Churchill's ability was bound to reach a position of power in the end, and said that he hoped the latter would not try to launch a second anti-Soviet crusade.

When the party emerged from the Kremlin they were besieged by journalists and photographers but as they had agreed among themselves not to talk about the interview they refused to comment. It was not until the group reached Warsaw that George Bernard Shaw began to give a series of ecstatic interviews. 'It is torture to get back after being in Soviet land,' he told them. 'After you have seen Bolshevism on the spot there can be no doubt that Capitalism is doomed.' He went on to claim that 'Stalin is a giant and beside him Western statesmen are pygmies.' Later he expressed the regret that he was not young, in which case he would emigrate to Russia. 'I advise all young men to do just that.'

Astonishingly enough neither Nancy or Waldorf had any hard words for Joseph Stalin and his vast grey prison. In Warsaw Nancy told the *New York Times* reporter that Soviet Russia was 'the best run country on earth' and that she was enchanted with it. This infuriated the Princess Cantacuzene, a granddaughter of President Grant who had married a Russian émigré. The Princess told the Republican women of Pennsylvania that she was shocked that Lady Astor could visit the Soviet Union and 'find nothing to criticize there'. She said that she quite obviously was searching for sensationalism and that her actions were 'humiliating'.

What had happened to make the Astors so quiet? Lady Astor's biographer tells us that Waldorf was in touch with George (sic) Barnes of the *New York Herald Tribune* and therefore knew everything that was going on. However, in the thirties, Joseph (not George) Barnes was a fervent supporter of the Soviet Union and would have given the Astors nothing but glowing reports of the regime. One cannot escape the conclusion that both Nancy and Waldorf were brainwashed by the visit and, for a while at least, began to doubt their former views. After all, Waldorf did not make any corrections in his diaries after the trip, even allowing his impression of Stalin to remain as he had wrirten it. 'He had a clear, rather kindly eye,' he recorded, 'is a man of very few words, is supposed to owe his position to an iron will and to a close association with Lenin. He seemed shrewd rather than big mentally. He had quite a sense of humour and knew how to parry questions he did not wish to deal with. . . .'

It was all too much for Winston Churchill, who on 16 August wrote upon Russia in the *Sunday Pictorial*. He began:

Here we have a state three millions of whose citizens are languishing in foreign exile; whose intelligentsia have been methodically destroyed; a state nearly half a million of whose citizens, reduced to servitude for their political opinions are rotting and freezing through the Arctic night; toiled to death in forests, mines and quarries for indulging in that freedom of thought which has gradually raised man above beast. Is it not strange that decent British men and women can be so airily detached from realities that they have no word of honest indignation for all these agonies?

Churchill's most powerful guns were trained on Shaw whom he blew to pieces. Then he directed his lesser missiles at Nancy. He wrote in the *Sunday Pictorial* of 17 August 1931:

Similar though different conditions are to be observed in Lady Astor; and like Mr Bernard Shaw she successfully exploits the best of both worlds. She reigns in the Old World and the New, and on both sides of the Atlantic, at once as a leader of smart fashionable society and of advanced feminist democracy. She combines a kind heart with a sharp and wagging tongue. She embodies the historical portent of the first woman member of the House of Commons. She applauds the policies of the Government from the benches of the Opposition. She denounces the vice of gambling and keeps an almost unrivalled racing stable. She accepts Communist hospitality and flattery and remains the Conservative member for Plymouth. She does all those opposite things so well and so naturally that the public, tired of criticizing, can only gape.

Winston's attack was prophetic insofar as it gave an indication of the poor political judgment that was to make not only Nancy but most Astors sympathetic to Germany's territorial aims – despite the advent of Hitler – and later to give birth to 'Cliveden set' stories. It was sad that Lady Astor became a politician at all, as she was a born entertainer who would have made a great name for herself on the stage. As her knowledge of world affairs was limited, in the House of Commons she had the good sense to stick to subjects of especial interest to women. She talked untiringly on the dangers of alcohol, and in one speech inveighed against the great brewery fortunes. However, when she referred to the peerage as 'the Beerage' the Speaker called her to order pointing out that MPs were not allowed to make disparaging remarks about members of 'the other place'.

Her subjects were fairly repetitive: school milk, infant care, prostitution and the need for more women police. Her arguments were seldom based on logic but sprang from impulse and mischief. In the House of Commons she often kept up a running commentary when she disagreed with an Opposition speech, but as she was unusually insensitive she sometimes believed that she had made a contribution when, in fact, she not only had infuriated the speech-maker but galvanized his comrades into whole-hearted support. For years the staid *Morning Post* had complained about her heckling, once declaring that she had interrupted fifteen speeches including her own. 'It really is intolerable,' ejaculated Aneurin Bevan, 'when this old gas bag gets up and gabbles away.'

It is not surprising that Winston Churchill disliked her, as she offended his romantic notion of what a woman should be – 'the most unfeminine female I know,' he often said. 'Brash, noisy, ignorant,' and then, remembering her attacks on alcohol, he would purse his lips to deliver the final denunciation, 'and a prude'.

Once, before the war, when Churchill and the Astors were spending a weekend with the Duchess of Marlborough at Blenheim, Nancy attacked Winston angrily. 'If I were married to you I would put poison in your coffee,' she said. 'And if I were married to you,' retorted Churchill, 'I would drink it.'

Churchill's onslaught did not upset Nancy; on the contrary the public interest aroused by her trip to Russia undoubtedly encouraged her to play more of a part in world affairs. Unfortunately the years that presented themselves were not only perilous but perplexing. No one had ever seen anything quite like Hitler before. No sooner had he become Chancellor than he called for a revision of the Versailles Treaty; and no sonner had he impressed Britain with his demands than he took Germany out of the League of Nations.

What were Hitler's intentions? Were his grievances genuine or merely a camouflage for aggression? 'Whether Germany is soaring on a wave of moral regeneration,' commented Geoffrey Dawson in *The Times*, November 1933, 'or sinking (as others agree) into a trough of barbarism . . . the case for plain-dealing remains the same. . . . Now, if ever, is the time for the exposition of a strong and courageous British policy.' The paper did not outline the policy then, but a week later fired a shot across the bow of the Disarmament Conference. 'No substantial progress is likely to be made until the question of revision [in favour of Germany] is boldly faced and settled in one sense or another.'

The policy of appeasement that now began to emerge was the work of intellectuals and sprang from a guilty feeling that the Treaty of Versailles had been unjust; that there could be no real peace in Europe until Germany's sense of injury was removed. Furthermore, as the most appalling holocaust in history had ended only fifteen years earlier and the only alternative to a second confrontation seemed to be a willingness to negotiate, appeasement began to win wide support. 'There can be no doubt whatever,' Mr Mabane, a National Liberal, told the House of Commons, 'that the people of this country do not desire the Government to pursue a pro-French policy, but are definitely anxious that they should adopt a revisionist policy in Europe and that a clear lead should be given.'

The two Astors – Waldorf and J.J. – agreed with this analysis, and whole-heartedly backed Baldwin and Chamberlain in a policy of appeasement which won the support of MPs on both sides of the House. Hitler's huge rearmament programme was repeatedly brought to the attention of the Commons by Winston Churchill but the appeasers dismissed it as a diplomatic bluff. Even when Hitler reoccupied the demilitarized Rhineland in 1936, Geoffrey Dawson found the right excuses for him. Germany was entitled to strive for what she would accept as an 'agreed' peace, *The Times* leader declared, as opposed to Versailles' 'dictated' peace, and if Britain was prepared to accept the German terms there was no need 'for any war scares'. But by 1938 Hitler had grown far bolder. In the spring he invaded Austria and proclaimed an anschluss and in the summer he turned his attention towards Czechoslovakia.

Before these events took place – at the end of 1937 – Nancy and Waldorf Astor were receiving widespread notoriety as leaders of 'the Cliveden set'. This group, as everybody knew, was pro-German, pro-appeasement, and anti-French. But what the world was now asked to believe was that Nancy was head of a cabal that was determined to conduct its own foreign policy. One of its members, Lord Halifax, (so the story went) had visited Hitler on his own initiative in an attempt to come to an arrangement with the Fuhrer that would cut the ground from under the feet of pro-French Sir Robert Vansittart of the Foreign Office, and anti-Mussolini Anthony Eden, the Foreign Secretary.

There was not one grain of truth in this story, nor did its author, Claud Cockburn, think it was true. Cockburn was a young journalist who began life on *The Times*. In the 'thirties he became a Communist and left Printing House Square to propagate the party line. He spent most of 1937 in Spain helping his comrades to extend their influence over the flagging Republic. By a happy chance, when he returned to London at the end of the year, he hit upon the phrase 'the Cliveden Set' which his inventive mind soon managed to turn into a powerful conspiratorial group. This fantasy offered him endless amusement, as he could attack the pro-German appeasers and at the same time annoy the arch-capitalist Astors. He printed the story in *The Week*, his four-page mimeographed bulletin which was distributed by hand but travelled widely by word of mouth – a sort of *Private Eye* specializing in political devilry.

Although the sinister machinations directed by Nancy Astor were entirely invented by Cockburn, his attack was successful for the simple reason that there *was* a Cliveden set – if by this phrase one means a group of appeasement-minded people who frequently met each other at Cliveden. The most important single appeaser was Nancy's devoted admirer, Lord Lothian, who had been her friend since 1910. He had abandoned Catholicism and followed her into Christian Science, and later even became a teetotaller. He liked to put his thoughts on paper and corresponded regularly with her even when they were in the same city; in 1915 he sent her eighty letters. Some people say that he was in love with her but he dwelt so relentlessly on religion and morality that his carnal desires (if he had any) seem to have been smothered. 'The worst thing one can do is hate,' he was fond of saying and no doubt this attitude was what led him to 'appeasement'. Yet he was not all easy to fathom, as his 'anti-hate' crusade was of recent origin. For instance, when he served as Lloyd George's private secretary during the Versailles Peace Conference he himself drafted the bitter paragraphs that forced the Germans to accept 'sole guilt for the war' – an infliction that was more furiously resented by the German people than any other single humiliation imposed upon them. Not surprisingly, when Lothian moved to the opposite camp, Baldwin described him as 'a queer bird' and a 'rum cove'.

Lothian and the two Astors were delighted when their friend, Neville Chamberlain, became Prime Minister in 1937. Chamberlain was a fervent appeaser. Unlike Baldwin he did not seek good relations with European states, so that Britain could save money on armaments. He believed that Britain could make a genuine friend of Germany, particularly if she refused to allow France to dictate to her. Lothian made a point of gathering influential people under the Astors' hospitable roof: the Halifaxes, the new British Ambassador to Germany – Neville Henderson – MPs who sang the Prime Minister's praises; and once, at St James's Square for luncheon, the German Ambassador Herr von Ribbentrop. Lothian kept in touch with Geoffrey Dawson of *The Times*, and Dawson's assistant editor, the most ardent revisionist of all, Barrington-Ward. He was also on close terms with J.L. Garvin of the *Observer*; Tom Jones, secretary to the Cabinet; Lionel Curtis, a former member of the Round Table. Lothian saw Hitler in February 1935 and May 1937. 'I hope the British Government will go and have a real talk with Hitler,' he wrote to Nancy, 'as to how Europe is to be pacified. Hitler is a prophet – not a politician or an intriguer. Quite straight, full of queer ideas but quite honestly not wanting war.'

Nancy and Waldorf flung themselves into the revisionist camp with enthusiasm, but Nancy's tongue often led her into trouble. 'Oh Nancy, wait a minute!' Lothian once cried, 'If you'd just think two minutes you'd be the greatest woman in England.' Perhaps he made this comment when she visited New York in 1937, and, dismayed by the surge of anti-German feeling, blurted out: 'If the Jews are behind it, they are going too far and they need to take heed.'

Back in England she kept Lothian, who was ravelling in India, informed on current happenings. 'Edward Halifax came to luncheon the day after he returned from Germany,' she wrote in November 1937. 'He liked everyone he met in Berlin and particularly Goebbels....' Two weeks later she wrote again, this time making a passing reference to Cockburn's attacks: 'Neville Chamberlain is lunching with me on Thursday; and I hope Edward Halifax and Tom Inskip. A letter from Rebecca West will be coming to you from Waldorf. Apparently the Communist rag has been full of the Halifax-Lothian-Astor plot at Cliveden, and the *Time and Tide* have taken it up; people really seem to believe it.'

Far worse, the *New York Times* (mindful of Lady Astor's remarks about the Jews) took up the story and gave it a wholly fallacious

Right The portrait of Nancy Astor by John Singer Sargeant, which hangs in Cliveden.

Overleaf When Nancy moved into Cliveden she set about redecorating energetically, believing that William Waldorf would never return to his former home. In 1907, however, he decided to visit, but was 'charm personified' about the changes she had made.

interpretation: 'FRIENDS OF HITLER STRONG IN BRITAIN – Fear of Communism Impels Many Men Of Wealth And Of The Middle Class.' 'When men like Londonderry or Viscount Rothermere or Lord Astor have political nightmares,' the writer explained, 'the ogre of their imagination is Russia not Germany. Menace to their wealth, their social position, is the creed of communism and, in their minds, whatever endangers themselves endangers England.' The *Washington Post* swallowed the Cockburn story in its entirety and gave a whole page to the affair: 'ASTOR COUNTRY HOME BECOMING REAL CENTRE OF BRITAIN'S FOREIGN POLICY – Empire's New Leaders Friendly to Fascism.' Lady Astor was used to being the toast of America and did not like the tone of these allegations; so in the spring of 1938 Waldorf and she wrote letters to *The Times* and the *Daily Herald* scoffing at the whole idea and pointing out, quite accurately, that because people met at a country house to discuss politics did not mean that they were trying to set up a rival Foreign Office.

A policy of appeasement, for a short time at least, was inevitable. The First World War was still too painful a memory for any British government to ignore the possibility of negotiation, particularly when national security did not seem to be affected. 'We have to convince the world that for the sake of peace we are prepared to go to absurd lengths,' Tom Jones wrote in his diary. 'Our people will not fight unless they are satisfied that fair treatment of the potential enemy has been tried.'

This was a perfectly true statement, but for how long? Apparently the Astors and their friends were blinded by the gods. From 1936 to 1939 Hitler launched a whole series of outrages but it did not seem to matter what he did, the appeasers remained stolidly on his side. He could invade Austria; massacre his political opponents; tighten the restrictions on Jews; increase the number of concentration camps; inaugurate new methods of terror; and of course bury his enemies in an avalanche of lies. In the summer of 1938 he was accusing the Czech government of brutality toward the Sudetan Germans, when in fact his agents were infiltrating the territory and stirring up the local violence themselves. Yet the habitutés of Cliveden did not seem to notice. 'I don't think "scoundrel" describes Hitler,' Tom Jones wrote from Lothian's country house in March 1938, 'It applies more accurately to some of those around him.'

Meanwhile Geoffrey Dawson was much more concerned about Hitler's attitude to *The Times* than anything else. 'It would really interest me to know precisely what it is in *The Times* that has produced this antagonism in Germany,' he wrote rather plaintively to his German correspondent in May 1937. 'I did my utmost, night after night, to keep out of the paper anything that might hurt their susceptibilities. I can really think of nothing that has been printed now for many months past which they could possibly take exception to as "unfair comment".'

Lord Astor, on the other hand, refused to be diverted by personal criticism and continued to hammer the revisionist line. In September 1937 he wrote a letter to his brother's prestigious paper saying that all powers (including Britain) were predatory but that some powers (including

Bill, later third Viscount Astor, with Mrs Cornelius Vanderbilt Whitney at the Races at Belmont Park. Bill was elected to Parliament for East Fulham in 1935, making history as this was the first occasion that a mother and son had sat in Parliament together.

Germany) were more predatory than others. Britain would be split in two and her Empire shattered, he insisted, if she went to war to defend the *status quo* of Europe. 'While there is yet time,' he urged, 'let us repair some of the mistakes of the dictated Peace Treaties and reverse our post-war attitude.'

Meanwhile Major J. J. Astor was living quietly at Hever Castle with his wife and three boys, all of whom were at Eton. He and Waldorf frequently met in London, sometimes at the Palace of Westminster where one was in the House of Commons, the other in the Lords.

J.J. was a painfully shy man who forced himself to devote most of his time to public service. He not only played a leading part in the country but served as the head of innumerable charities. His engagements have an almost royal flavour of worthiness and tedium. In 1938 you find that he donated and opened an extension at Dover College; presided over a Cricket Dinner at the Café Royal; took the chair at the Newspaper Press Fund Dinner at the Connaught Rooms; took another chair at the Empire Press Union; made a speech at the Guildhall on Girls Clubs; another speech at the Mansion House on Boy Scouts.

Every year huge tents were put on the lawns at Hever for the Major's annual buffet luncheon for the employees of *The Times*. The editorial staff arrived in black coats and pin-striped trousers while the linotype-setters and copy-readers were more suitably dressed in grey flannels and made a beeline for the bar. J.J.'s contribution to foreign affairs seems to have been mainly concerned with publishing Waldorf's letters. Indeed people said that although Major Astor owned *The Times* he never read it. The truth was that he had no authority to interfere in the policy of his newspaper as his contract with Geoffrey Dawson gave the latter complete editorial freedom. His one and only sanction was his power to dismiss his editor.

The Major often saw his nephew Bill, Waldorf's eldest son, who was elected to Parliament for East Fulham in 1935. (None of the Astors had any trouble getting parliamentary seats as the Conservative party made a point of choosing rich young men as candidates who would contribute generously to their constituencies.) Bill followed the family lead on foreign affairs by becoming a fervent appeaser, asking the public to forgive Mussolini for invading Ethiopia. After all, he argued, Britain had done the same sort of thing in the distant past, and as the League of Nations seemed to be fizzling out, collective security was no longer an obligation.

Then came the Munich crisis of 1938, when the world hung between peace and war. Chamberlain made three trips to Germany to see Hitler, who was threatening to march into Czechoslovakia. In London people began to construct air-raid shelters; J.J.'s *The Times* ran a leader suggesting the Czechs would be better off without the Sudetan Germans; and Waldorf's *The Observer* printed an article by J.L. Garvin saying that the time had come when 'the stinking Czech sausage should be crushed'. Czechoslovakia finally bowed to the pressure of Britain and France (who told her that she would have to fight alone) and capitulated. Neville Chamberlain came home crying 'Peace with Honour'; Duff Cooper resigned from the government; and Lady Astor's nephew, Anthony Winn, resigned from *The Times*.

A wildly enthusiastic House of Commons assembled to greet their gallant Prime Minister. But Winston Churchill spoiled the atmosphere by striking an unpleasant note of criticism, and Lady Astor made interjections that have since become a symbol of fatuity. Winston replied very politely: 'I will begin by saying the most unpopular and the most unwelcome thing. I will begin by saying what everyone would like to ignore or forget but which must nevertheless be stated; namely that we have sustained a total, unmitigated defeat, and that France has suffered even more than we have.' At this point Nancy was unable to control herself and shouted 'Nonsense!'

'When the noble lady cried "Nonsense",' Churchill continued serenely, 'She could not have heard the Chancellor of the Exchequer admit in his illuminating and comprehensive speech just now that Herr Hitler had gained in this particular leap forward, in substance all he set out to gain. The utmost my Right Honourable friend, the Prime Minister, has been able to secure by all his immense exertions, by all the great efforts and mobilisation which took place in this country, and by all the anguish and strain through which we have passed in this country – the utmost he has been able to gain – '

'Is peace!' shouted Nancy.

Churchill paused to let the commotion die. 'I thought,' he said quietly, 'that I might be able to make that point in its due place and I propose to deal with it. The utmost that the Prime Minister has been able to gain for Czechoslovakia and in the matters which were in dispute has been that the German dictator, instead of snatching his victuals from the table, has been content to have them served to him course by course.'

A few minutes later the orator's tone changed. 'All is over. Silent, mournful, abandoned Czechoslovakia recedes into the darkness. She has suffered in every respect by her association with the Western democracies and the League of Nations of which she has always been an obedient servant.' He went on to point out that this was the end of the French alliances in Eastern Europe 'of countries which are a long way off and of which, as the Prime Minister might say, we know nothing....'

Nancy shouted, 'Don't be rude about the Prime Minister.'

Mr Churchill: 'The noble lady says that that very harmless allusion is ...'

Lady Astor: 'Rude.'

Mr Churchill: 'She must very recently have been receiving her finishing course in manners. What will be the position of France and

Nancy Astor at Cliveden with some of her celebrated guests, Amy Johnson the famous flier, Charlie Chaplin, and G.B. Shaw.

England next year and the year afterwards? If the Nazi dictator should choose to look westward as he may, bitterly will France and England regret the loss of that farm army of ancient Bohemia, which was estimated last week to require not fewer than thirty German divisions for its destruction. . . .'

The Munich crisis and the Astors' hostility toward Winston Churchill created a new wave of publicity, particularly in the United States, about the Cliveden set. This was further enhanced by Charles Lindbergh who told the world that the German air force was unbeatable and received a decoration from Hitler; he then visited London and was entertained by the Astors.

These events prompted *Liberty magazine* to run an article (by a Mr Collins) describing Lindbergh as a member of the Cliveden set, and describing the Cliveden set as a disgrace to Britain. Amazingly, Lady Astor turned to her celebrated friend, Bernard Shaw, the avowed Communist and political clown of the 'thirties, to defend her. He wrote in *Liberty*:

Cliveden is like no other country house on earth. Mr Collins' list of noble conspirators is authentic; but you meet these aristocrats at Cliveden because you meet everybody worth meeting, rich or poor, at Cliveden. You meet the Duchess of Athol; but then you meet also Ellen Wilkinson, the leftist member of the Labour Party in Parliament. You meet Colonel Lindbergh, the friend of Herr Hitler's Chief of Staff; but you meet also Mr Charles Chaplin whose dislike of Nazi rule is outspoken to a degree which must seriously threaten his interests in Germany. You meet the Marquess of Londonderry, descendant of Castlereagh and so far to the right that he was too much for even the existing Nationalist Cabinet with his famous majestically beautiful wife; but then you meet also ME, an implacable and vociferous Marxist Communist of nearly sixty years standing with MY beautiful wife. . . .

Shaw's defence of the Astors consisted of praising Hitler for the 'socialization of property unparalleled anywhere except in Russia' and scoffing at the idea that the 'British aristocracy' could ever back such an egalitarian ruler.

However, talk about the Cliveden set came to an end in March 1939 when the German army marched into Prague. At the time of Munich Hitler had solemnly declared that he had 'no more territorial ambitions in Europe'. This latest violation shattered appeasement and silenced the revisionists. Indeed, two days later Nancy Astor rose at Question Time to ask: 'Will the Prime Minister lose no time in letting the German Government know with what horror this country regards Germany's action?' At which, a fellow Conservative, Vyvyan Adam, interjected: 'You caused it yourself.'

In August 1939 Lord Lothian was sent to America by Neville Chamberlain as the new British Ambassador. Two weeks later war was declared. After Germany and Russia had smashed Poland Hitler appealed for an end to hostilities hinting at favourable peace terms, particularly for Britain. Lord Lothian never seemed able to learn. He telephoned wildly from Washington, Harold Nicolson wrote in his diary, 'begging Halifax not to say anything in his broadcast tonight which might close the door to peace. Lothian claims that he knows the German terms and that they are most satisfactory. I am glad to say that Halifax pays no attention to this. . . .' A year later, in December 1940, poor, disastrous Philip Lothian had a heart attack and died. For Lady Astor the loss was irreparable.

In New York, that same year, Helen and Vincent Astor got one of those friendly American divorces and Vincent married thirty-four-year-old Mary ('Minnie') Cushing, a sister of Mrs Jock Whitney and Mrs William Paley.

All Astors of a military age – and some, like Vincent Astor, well over the age – served in the armed forces throughout the war. Lord Astor's youngest son, Jakie, and Colonel J. J. Astor's eldest son, Gavin, were both officers in the Life Guards. Lord Astor's heir, Bill, served in the Royal Navy in the Middle East; Bill's brother, Michael, was a member of a Reconnaissance Unit attached to General Patton's army, while another brother, David, was a liaison officer with Combined Operations. Gavin's brother, Hugh, who was only nineteen when war broke out, worked in military intelligence in Europe and South East Asia, rising to the rank of Lt Colonel. His brother John, three years younger, also managed to join the armed services as a member of Coastal Command.

Across the sea, fifty-four-year-old Vincent Astor was in naval uniform the day after Pearl Harbour. He was immediately assigned to a hush-hush job with the Eastern Sea Frontier. His task was to collect and organize fishing boats to report the movements of suspicious craft. Commander Vincent Astor was despatched to Block Island where he rounded up 'about twenty operators of small fishing vessels . . . ideally situated in every way except that none have radios'. He reported:

The loyalty of the men is unquestionable and I am inclined to think that they have a good fighting spirit too. Some of them come from families who have lived on the Island for generations. One of the leading ones with whom I had a long talk told me that he not only would report an enemy submarine, but would trail and chase it until he had been shot full of holes and sunk.

These men go after swordfish which, as you know, have to be harpooned and not caught, which requires that a very alert look-out be kept, for the fish can only be spotted by the fin which just breaks the surface. These boats operate about twenty miles southeast and southwest of Block Island and No Man's Land, and therefore could be expected to be in those areas of approach to Vineyard Haven Sound, Buzzard's Bay, Black Island Sound, Narrangansett Bay and the entrance to Long Island Sound from the east. I may be over-optimistic but it may well be that eventually I can dispose of one hundred [radio] sets.

Astor's work in organizing and equipping the 'Fishermen Observers Plan' was hugely successful. In 1943 he was promoted to the rank of Captain and at the end of the war was awarded the Victory Medal.

9 From billionaires to millionaires

Previous page Vincent Astor at the Newsweek *office. When he began to liquidate his real estate holdings and invest in the Stock Market, he was careful to keep* Newsweek *which Raymond Moley ran for him.*

After the war everything changed, not at once, but gradually; and before long Astors on both sides of the Atlantic were sliding down from the peaks of superabundance to the mundane valleys of mere affluence. The war, of course, was responsible. Whereas the First World War had been fought – or so people thought – to make the world safe for democracy, the Second World War resounded to the cry of egalitarianism, inspired by the Soviet Union and heartily supported by the Americans who love to have the best of all ideologies. In Europe socialist governments and high taxation cast shadows that thoughtful millionaires across the Atlantic could heed; and although some people still liked to describe Captain Vincent Astor of the United States Navy as 'backward', he was the first of all the Astors to see the shape of things to come and to adapt himself accordingly.

In 1945 such understanding required considerable imagination, particularly for a man whose grandmother had ruled feudal New York society only forty years earlier. Astor was still an awkward customer, rude, temperamental, with the fitful arrogance bequeathed to him by a mother who firmly believed herself descended from royalty. He was very unpredictable; for instance he was tremendously proud of possessing the naval rank of captain, and once, when a sycophantic doorman got his fighting services mixed and addressed him as a mere colonel, he flew into such a rage that he nearly struck him.

However, when it came to reorganizing his finances Astor kept his head. During the war he had allowed his business managers to sell the Astor Estate Office on West 26th Street; and now these same experts advised him to relinquish the fading title 'Landlord of New York' and get rid of his property. Vincent Astor was fifty-four years old in 1945; he had no children and detested his half-brother, Jack. These considerations encouraged him to earmark the bulk of his fortune for the benefit of posterity. In 1948 he took the first step by creating the Vincent Astor Foundation devoted to 'the alleviation of human misery'.

Then he began to follow the advice of his brilliant manager, Alan Betts, to liquidate his real estate holdings and invest his profits on the stock market. The result was that in five years between 1953 and 1958 he nearly doubled the original stake of $69,000,000 inherited from his father. On a few things, however, he put his foot down. Although Betts described the St Regis Hotel as 'lustreless' he refused to sell it, insisting that he liked 'to lunch there'; and, of course, no one dared suggest that he part with his prodigy, *Newsweek*, which was still run by Raymond Moley.

Nevertheless even Betts failed to persuade Astor to invest in real estate in Venezuela which was enjoying an impressive oil boom. When the place was mentioned Vincent shuddered and shook his head. Apparently when he had been cruising in Latin-American waters before the war Venezuela's dictator had invited him to try his hand at shark-fishing. To Astor's surprise, arrangements were made to conduct the sport aboard the *Nourmahal*. After the dictator and his party had boarded, and just as the yacht was getting ready to leave, two soldiers appeared and led a horse up the gangway. Vincent was puzzled but said nothing. All became clear when the yacht entered shark-infested waters. The dictator and his minister ordered the soldiers to throw the horse overboard, then riddled the animal with machine-gun bullets. When the water was red with blood a posse of sharks appeared. Everyone shot into the crimson sea but no one managed to kill or capture any of the man-eaters. However there was excitement on the way home for the dictator got drunk and ordered his minister to jump overboard and swim for shore. As the unfortunate man struggled in the water the dictator amused himself by firing shots around him. Luckily no sharks appeared and the minister arrived safely on land. 'What better example do you need of lunacy?' Vincent demanded of Alan Betts, resolutely refusing to put a penny into the new venture.

During the post-war years Vincent's personal life went through the same dramatic upheavals as his business ventures. Although he had been deeply in love with Minnie Cushing when he married her in 1940, she found Vincent's complicated personality more than she could contend with. When she asked him for a divorce in 1952 he could not believe his ears as he was convinced that every woman would like to be Mrs Astor. 'She must be mad,' he confided to a friend. However, he gave her the divorce and a few months later she married a painter, James Fosburgh.

Vincent also remarried. His third wife was a charming fifty-year-old widow, Mrs Brooke Russell Marshall, who had worked for eight years as features editor of *House and Garden* magazine, and was one of the best-liked women in New York society. She had been married to 'Buddy' Marshall, who was president of the Brook Club and a close friend of Vincent until his death. Indeed, they had been related in a vague way, for Buddy's first wife, Alice Huntington, was a sister of Vincent's first wife, Helen.

Vincent's third marriage was extremely successful. His new wife liked to dine alone with her husband and for the first time Vincent found himself with a cosy home life. Furthermore Brooke did not have to cope with the lengthy annual cruises that had absorbed so much of Vincent's attention in the pre-war era to the dismay of both wives. He made no plans to replace the *Nourmahal*, which he had lent to the navy in 1941 and at the end of the war had sold to the government, probably because of his failing health. After his sixtieth birthday in 1951 he began to suffer from respiratory trouble and found it increasingly difficult to move about.

Vincent spent most of his weekends at Rhinebeck where his sister Alice also had a house. Alice was a beautiful, spoiled, unhappy woman who not only took an interest in the arts and for many years supported the Sadlers Wells Ballet in London, but who dabbled in the occult and became convinced that she was the reincarnation of an Egyptian princess. Perhaps this was what made her so restless, for she found it impossible to settle down. She divorced Serge Obolensky in the 'thirties and married Raimond von Hofmanstahl; she divorced Raimond in the 'forties and married Philip Harding; then she divorced Philip and married David Pleydell-Bouverie. After the war she moved to New York but nothing seemed to gratify poor rich Alice of the discontented mouth. In the end she left David, like all the others, and in 1956 brought her troubled existence to a close by taking an overdose of sleeping pills. She was survived by her eighty-six-year-old mother, the one-time dazzling Ava, who clung to life as insistently as Alice decried it and managed to survive her daughter by two years. (Indeed she only missed surviving her son Vincent by eight months.)

Meanwhile Vincent was both active and happy, and in the mid-'fifties made one, final incursion into the Manhattan real estate world. He wanted to create an 'Astor Plaza' that would compete with 'Rockefeller Center' as a world-famous landmark. He selected Park Avenue and 53rd Street as the site for his new colossus and announced plans to put up a forty-six-storey office building with a helicopter pad on the roof. The cost was to be $75,000,000, and even an Astor needed help in raising this sort of money. But Vincent soon ran into trouble. He asked for a mortgage on the land to provide him with some of the necessary cash but to his chagrin it was pointed out that it was the English Astors who owned the land, and that it was not customary to give mortgages on ground scheduled for office building. The English Astors would like to help but their advisers felt it would be wrong to ignore established practice. Vincent set about trying to persuade a host of other institutions – mainly banks – to grant him a loan but the depression of 1957–8 cast a blight over his project. Astor Plaza was nicknamed 'Disaster Plaza' and before the end of 1958 he sold the site, on which he had a long lease, to the First National Bank, now known as Citibank, which eventually erected a building of its own.

Although 1958 marked the end of Vincent's role as a landlord, he had done extremely well financially over the years. An article published in *Fortune Magazine* in 1957 showed that 175 years after the first John Jacob Astor had appeared in New York his great-great-grandson was still among the nation's richest men. Although he was outstripped by over fifty Americans, most of whom had oil fortunes, he was still in a very impressive category. Paul Getty was at the top of the list with a bank balance somewhere between $700,000,000 and $1,000,000,000. Then came the $500,000,000 to $700,000,000 category consisting of seven men including Bunker Hunt, Paul Mellon and J.D. Rockefeller; after that the $200,000,000 to $400,000,000 bracket with eight names including Joseph Kennedy, Howard Hughes, Irenée and William du Pont; and finally the $100,000,000 to $200,000,000 group headed by Vincent Astor and including Doris Duke, Nelson Rockefeller and Mrs Edsel Ford.

As far as Vincent Astor was concerned *Fortune Magazine* had made an accurate assessment. When he died two years later and his Will was published he had left $129,000,000, nearly twice the sum that he had received in 1912. Half the fortune had been given to the Vincent Astor Foundation and the other half went to his wife, Brooke, to dispose of as she liked.

Vincent's half-brother, forty-seven-year-old Jack Astor, could not believe that both he and his son, William Backhouse Astor, had been cut off without a penny. Although Jack Astor had received $5,000,000 when he came of age, and although he was well aware that Vincent both disliked and disapproved of him, his imagination had refused to accept the possibility that the Founder's sacred accumulation of gold could go to people with no Astor blood and eventually be scattered to the four winds.

Of course, if Jack Astor had managed to win Vincent's friendship things might have been different, but everything about Jack's life, beginning with his choice of a mother, infuriated Vincent. Nevertheless he tried to help and did everything he could to persuade his half-brother to settle down and do some serious work. He found him a job with the International Mercantile Marine Company for $25 a week which Jack accepted manfully, carrying out his duties for a year and a half. Although Vincent arranged that Jack should be moved from department to department to learn the business and to escape boredom, Jack finally left. 'I felt I wasn't getting anywhere,' he told the press. 'Furthermore I sometimes didn't get through until five o'clock. It would be six o'clock before I reached home and I would have to get up very early next morning.' This remark delighted sophisticated Americans and made Jack famous but in quite the wrong way. Once more Jack was seen at all the nightclubs and Vincent turned away in anger. The war caused the final breach; Vincent felt that all able-bodied men should volunteer for the armed forces, and the fact that Jack only served in the army for a few weeks before being pronounced medically unfit aroused Vincent's suspicions about his enthusiasm, and caused a rift that was never healed.

Gertrude Gretsch, Jack Astor's second wife, who was divorced in Mexico by Jack so that he might marry Dolores Fullman. Both women sued Jack for alimony and it was never fully decided to which woman he was married.

During the war Jack divorced 'Tucky', the mother of his son William Backhouse Astor, and in 1946 married Gertrude Gretsch, with whom he had a daughter. Unfortunately in 1954 he fell madly in love with a budding starlet, Dolores Fullman. He got a Mexican divorce from Gertrude and married 'Dolly' in Virginia. The couple parted after only six weeks and then the trouble began. Both women sued for alimony; Florida declared that Dolly was Jack's legal wife; New York that he was still married to Gertrude. Lawyers fees cost him hundreds of thousands of dollars and the muddle was never sorted out. However, it was made clear to him that he had better not chance the matrimonial field again. He now lives in Florida as a bachelor.

It is not surprising that Vincent left his half-brother no money since Jack had already inherited a large sum of his own. However, although Jack was well aware of his half-brother's antagonism, he could not believe that Vincent would overlook his son William, and immediately announced his intention of fighting the Will. First, he hired an expert to study the twenty-page document for erasures or insertions. When none was discovered he tried to break the Will on two charges: undue influence on the part of the executors, and Vincent's mental incompetence at the time of signing. The hearing dragged on for months but it was plain that all Jack Astor was doing was accumulating a lawyer's bill and that his chances of winning the case were naught.

He finally settled out of court for $250,000 which Brooke Astor volunteered and willingly paid to bring the proceedings to an end. 'There have been three important Astors,' Jack said bitterly. 'John

Jacob I, who made the fortune; William Backhouse Astor who doubled it; and Vincent Astor who gave it away.'

In wartime England Lord Astor did not have much time to ponder about the future. In 1940 many people were disappointed that he did not feel able to accept the offer of the new Prime Minister – Winston Churchill – to serve in the government as Under-secretary of Agriculture. Churchill was anxious to heal the breach between the various political groups and was aware of Astor's expertise not only as a farmer but as the author of several important books on the science of growing food. Indeed, if Waldorf Astor had shown the same magnanimity in accepting the job that Winston showed in offering it he might have made an invaluable contribution to the war effort. However, he excused himself on the grounds that he did not approve of the policy of the Agricultural Minister, Mr Hudson; furthermore, he had already agreed to serve as Lord Mayor of Plymouth. He did not mention an even more important consideration: Plymouth was Nancy's constituency and he was determined to share her anxieties and help her as he had always done.

As things turned out, a monumental year lay in front of The Astors, for strategically-placed Plymouth proved to be one of the enemy's most important targets. The city not only boasted a large naval base, but served as headquarters for operational groups ranging from a Combined Operation Intelligence section to an RAF Flying Boat Unit whose mission was to scour the Atlantic searching for U-boats. Nancy travelled from London to Plymouth almost every weekend on the night-sleeper and the Astor house at 3 Elliot Terrace soon became a rendezvous for a stream of important visitors ranging from Robert Menzies, the Australian Prime Minister, to General McNaughton, Commander of the Canadian First Division.

On 20 March 1941, the King and Queen arrived in Plymouth for a brief daylight tour which ended with tea at Elliot Terrace. While the guests were munching their unappetizing utility biscuits the air-raid sirens wailed but no one paid any attention; enemy aeroplanes on their way back from Altlantic shipping targets often skirted the city. However, two hours after the royal train had moved out of the station on its return to London, Plymouth was subjected to one of the worst attacks of the war. Ben Robertson, an American journalist who was staying with the Astors later gave an account of the raid.

After the departure of the King and Queen, while we were eating some chicken and stewed rhubarb and the cakes left over from the royal tea party ... guns began to thunder. From the very start there was something about the intensity of the whole which made us think that this was it. We had all the tubs in the house filled with water and saw that the spades were handy. Lady Astor's maid, Rose Harrison, said, 'Lady Astor, I must tell you, I have a sailor visiting me.' 'Tell him to stay,' said Lady Astor. ... We heard a stick of bombs coming nearer and nearer and fell flat on our faces by the hall door.

The blast from one of the bombs smashed all the windows on the Hoe side of the house and an air-raid warden came running in and ordered everyone to go down to the basement. Lord Astor sat there, chafing to be out on the streets helping; and Lady Astor talked about her child-hood in Virginia while her maid occupied herself by picking bits of glass out of her ladyship's hair.

The house was struck by one of the hundreds of incendiary bombs that the Germans were scattering over the city.

'Come on,' called Lady Astor, 'get the sand-bags. Where in hell are the buckets?' Everyone raced up and down the stairs; and once, when Lady Astor stopped by a bombed window to look at blazing Plymouth her eyes filled with tears and she said: 'There goes thirty years of our lives, but we'll build it again.'

Early the next morning Lord and Lady Astor walked about the city assessing the damage and reviewing the efficiency of the services. They took charge of rehousing, feeding, clothing and comforting. 'It seemed an impossible task,' wrote Lady Astor's maid, Rose, 'but there were no theatricals from my lady, just confidence and strength. His Lordship was authoritative and efficient, a great organizer.'

That night there was a second air-raid, even worse. This time the Astors were out among the people and Rose was desperately worried for fear they would not survive the bombing. When the raid stopped she went on the roof to take a look at Plymouth. 'It was a horrifying yet magnificent sight, like a gigantic volcano crater, a city on the boil. All immediately around us had been destroyed. Later I looked inside my lady's room and saw windows shattered, walls cracked, part of the ceiling down, glass splinters everywhere....'

Suddenly master and mistress walked in from the world of shambles. 'My lady was completely exhausted,' continued Rose. 'She and Lord Astor had been on duty all day and had been out with the services during the raid. His lordship was little better, but having delivered Lady Astor into my hands, he set off walking the ruined streets. We tried to stop him. We told him it was foolishness, but he wouldn't listen.' Rose went out at day break. 'Somehow it looked worse in the light: skeletons of houses, twisted girders, wrecks of cars, the rubble that was once a house and possessions strewn across the streets.'

The Astors were now well into their stride: whatever political mis-takes they had made before the war were now expunged by their courage and energy. The wail of the air-raid sirens, repeated many times in April and with relentless regularity until the end of the year, were a signal for the Astors to visit the shelters and laugh and talk with the people. Nancy used all the arts that had won her so many elections – joking, comforting, fortifying. She nursed babies and made comical references to men fortifying themselves with strong drinks: 'That man will tuck away a couple of bottles while his friend is looking for a cork-screw!'

Waldorf and Nancy rallied the citizens of Plymouth by their complete absence of fear. They never waited for a lull in the bombing to walk from one shelter to another; and on one occasion when the indomitable Lady Astor decided to divert the inmates of a shelter whose morale seemed rather low, she turned cartwheels the length of the room and at the end cried: 'Are we downhearted?' The roar of approval and the shouts of 'No! Never!' were all that she could desire. Later she wrote to a friend: 'Only I and the Prime Minister enjoy the war, but only I say so.'

In the House of Commons Nancy begged that Plymouth should be designated an evacuation area and that the government should sponsor a national fire-fighting organization. The Ministry of Health responded by ordering the evacuation of 10,000 school-children from Plymouth; but on 2 May, long before the fire-fighting problem had been resolved, Winston Churchill, accompanied by his wife, Clemmie, and by President Roosevelt's special envoy, Averill Harriman, visited Plymouth. Although no love was lost between the Astors and Churchills the party gathered at 3 Elliot Terrace. Nancy was determined to impress her constituents by holding a meeting with Clemmie at her side on the platform; and Clemmie was determined to accompany Winston and no one else. Therefore, when Winston read Nancy's proposed programme he shook his head and said 'Impossible'. Nancy insisted that it was too late to alter the schedule whereupon Churchill strode to the window and gazed at the sea. Then he turned back to the room gravely (no doubt mindful of Clemmie's intractability): 'In time of war the supreme decisions must rest with the Prime Minister and with him alone.... Mrs Churchill will

Winston Churchill and his wife Clemmie with Nancy Astor as they toured the blitzed areas of Plymouth on 2 May 1941. After the tour, Churchill said of the people of Plymouth: 'Their houses may be low but their hearts are high.'

come with me.' As he made his way to the car he gave Averill Harriman a wink. Later, Nancy drove around the city with Churchill but she was not in a forgiving mood. The devastation was worse than Churchill had imagined but when the gallant crowds burst into a frenzy of cheering, raising their hands in the Victory sign, he could not hold back the tears. 'It's all very well to cry, Winston,' said Nancy coldly, 'but you've got to do something.' Three weeks later the Home Secretary did just that by bringing in a bill to establish a national fire-fighting service. 'I welcome the Bill,' said Nancy in the House of Commons 'but it horrifies me that we have waited six months to bring it in.'

Lady Astor's maid Rose had always been devoted to her mistress but now, in the war, she began to look upon her as a goddess. She wrote:

In battle her qualities were shown. Her courage, not the 'backs to the wall' stoic kind of British courage but the flashing, tempestuous rousing roistering courage of the Virginian exemplified by the way she would turn cartwheels in air raid shelters to cause a diversion when things were at their worst. Not your sixty-one-year-old Nancy Astor, Lady of Cliveden, hostess to the aristocracy and Member of Parliament, but Nannie the wild-eyed girl who rode unbroken horses. And along with this went the softer, compassionate creature; the voice behind the sad Virginian songs, that would comfort a mother whose child had been killed while her own heart was grieving for the mother, yet hardening against Whitehall officials who in their short-sightedness had not declared Plymouth an area for the evacuation of children. Then catching the night train to London and the next day telling Parliament what should be done and being accused that by saying what she had, she'd given information and help to the enemy. Yet still not giving a tinker's cuss. This was a woman I could idolize.

Lord and Lady Astor did not believe in allowing the war to curtail social activity. The best way for people to keep up their morale, they insisted, was to mix with others. Pursuing this theme, Lady Astor persuaded the Plymouth Council to organize dances on the Hoe. Every evening a band played and the locals gathered to laugh and talk as though they were living in another epoch. 'Things were cruel,' said a Plymouth woman, 'but the Astors made them bearable.'

During the war Lord Astor had a mild stroke and recovered; but his illness reminded him that life was not permanent and he began to put his affairs in order. He did not believe that England would ever regain the pre-war rhythm of life and after consulting his family, he endowed Cliveden with a large sum of money and presented it to the National Trust. This did not mean that Waldorf or his heir, Bill, could not live there; the house remained strictly private except for the main living rooms which were opened to the public twice a week.

Next came the decision about *The Observer*, the Sunday newspaper that old William Waldorf had bought in 1910. Waldorf's second boy, David, was closer to him than his other sons as they both shared an uneasy feeling about the large fortunes that had come their way through no effort of their own. Although Lord Astor was a brilliant organizer, he was not an astute political thinker and never seemed able to understand the outcome of the ideas he advocated. He pressed for an understanding with Hitler; he felt that Stalin had 'a rather kindly eye'; and even when the burden of the war was at its heaviest he did not hesitate to reprove Churchill in a letter to *The Times* for undertaking too many responsibilities. David did not agree with his father about either Hitler or Stalin and he was far more to the left than any other member of the family, almost a natural consequence of his disapproval of the English class system and his dislike of his mother's social life. Lord Astor was sympathetic, and after considerable thought, overlooked the rights of his eldest son, Bill, and appointed David editor-in-chief of *The Observer*, a position which carried with it virtual ownership.

Perhaps the worst mistake that Lord Astor made, as far as his personal life was concerned, was to persuade his wife Nancy not to stand again for Parliament. The stroke he had suffered earlier in the war seemed, in some strange way, to have changed his personality, and instead of being a devoted admirer of his wife he suddenly began to be critical of her. In 1944 when it was possible to see the end of the war, the Plymouth Conservative Association rather ungallantly hinted that as the country would face new problems when peace came, new ideas would be needed. Nancy Astor was sixty-five years old and had represented Plymouth for twenty-five years; could her husband not persuade her to retire? If Astor had been a more sensitive man he would have refused to become involved. Instead he decided that he must spare Nancy the humiliation of being turned down as a prospective candidate; or did he secretly agree with the arguments of the Plymouth Committee? Whatever the reasons, he suddenly told Nancy that he, Waldorf, was getting too old to support her in another election and that he hoped for his sake she would resign. In a weak moment she complied, but she soon bitterly regretted it and never forgave his interference. Later, one of Waldorf's sons explained that even if Nancy had been adopted as the candidate, Waldorf felt that she might be defeated at the polls and wanted to spare her this final rebuff. However, as her rejection would have been part of an avalanche of Tory defeats, she might have found it easier to accept than Waldorf's opposition.

But there was no way to retrieve the situation. What she had done was irrevocable and when the new Parliament met in 1945 she was no longer a member. As the days passed she longed for the House of Commons as a child might pine for a circus. Without the cut and thrust of parliamentary debate, life suddenly seemed empty, even pointless. While Waldorf's ill-health made him increasingly critical, Nancy's resentment of Waldorf grew to pathological proportions. She could not contain her fury, so much so that she hated to be in the room with him. Indeed, in the seven years between 1945 and 1952, they spent very few nights under the same roof. Waldorf lived at Cliveden and Nancy at Sandwich. When Waldorf sold the St James's Square house in London he bought her another house on Hill Street. He begged her to come back to Cliveden but she could not overcome her anger; and this anger was accentuated when Waldorf turned over *The Observer* to David and he refused to censure him for supporting the Labour Party. After all, when

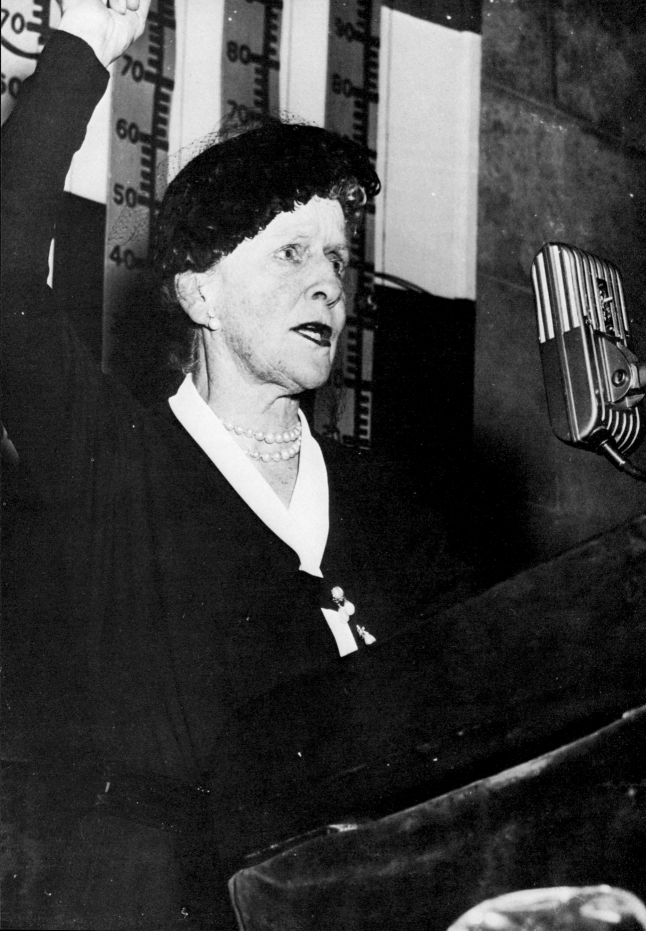

Waldorf's father had made up his mind to sell *The Observer* in 1910 Nancy had been instrumental in persuading him to give the paper to his son. And now she had to tolerate *The Observer's* attacks on the Tory party and its praise of 'the common man', when what she valued – as she often pointed out – was the 'uncommon man'. However, she derived some satisfaction from the fact that all three of her other sons were at one time or another Tory MPs.

During this period Waldorf had another stroke which had the effect of detaching him from his immediate surroundings. When he became critically ill in 1952 Nancy's resentment suddenly melted away. She moved into Cliveden to look after him and for a while her presence seemed to renew his zest for life and to restore their old relationship. He died in September. She wrote to Tom Jones:

I am down here by myself, trying to get over the shock, and am simply in-undated with hundreds of letters or I would write you more, only there's so little to say. We had forty happy years together. No two people ever worked happier than we did – the last seven years have been heart-breaking – but thank God he was like his old self the last ten days and oh how it makes me grieve for the years wasted! . . . I wish I had never saved *The Observer*. You can see why it has caused me more misery than I would have thought possible. But I don't want to look back but forward and thank God I have had such a long happy life and that Waldorf is now safe. . . .

In 1952 things seemed to be running in threes for forty-five-year-old Bill Astor. He was now the third viscount and three years later he married for the third time. His new wife was Bronwen Pugh, twenty years younger than himself, the daughter of Sir Alan Pugh, a judge.

Bill Astor married Bronwen Pugh in 1955, and they are pictured here with their daughter, Janet Elizabeth.

Bronwen was a tall, slender, beautiful girl who worked as a model, and who that very year had been voted 'woman of the year' by a London fashion group.

Bill was happy with Bronwen but like many other men found it difficult to ignore a pretty face. Unfortunately he became acquainted with Mr Stephen Ward, a capable osteopath who shared Bill's penchant for attractive girls. However, Ward's female companions did not come from respectable circles but consisted of an alluring selection of call-girls. Ward liked to entertain at the weekend and Bill offered him a cottage on the Cliveden estate. Later it was revealed in court that Ward frequently staged orgies in his flat in rooms fitted with two-way mirrors.

Bronwen did not seem to know much about Bill's new friends and Ward, who often came to dinner, sometimes brought one or two of the girls with him. One weekend when Jack Profumo, the Minister of War, and his wife Valerie, were spending the weekend with Lord Astor, Jack took pictures of Christine Keeler and some of the other girls around the swimming pool and underneath wrote: 'The New Cliveden Set'.

The world knows that one of the attachés at the Russian Embassy, Captain Eugene Ivanov, occasionally visited Ward's cottage and also met Christine Keeler, and that before long Jack Profumo was being told that Miss Keeler had slept with the Russian; and was being asked (on security grounds) if he had also shared her favours.

Meanwhile Ward was charged with living on the immoral earnings of women. The trial opened on 22 July 1963 and lasted for eight days. Newspapermen from all over the world reported the titillating details of perversion, voyeurism, prostitution and drugs. One blonde prostitute told how she had been paid a pound a stroke for whipping her customers with a cane, which she did arrayed in flame-coloured panties and high-heeled shoes. Ward was found guilty but he escaped from the law by committing suicide. Lord Denning investigated the matter and in September published a report declaring that British security had not been breached.

For a few weeks Cliveden was on the front page of every newspaper every day. Although Bill Astor was only involved because he had made the mistake of letting his cottage to Ward, the friends and relations surrounding eighty-two-year-old Lady Astor went to ingenious lengths to keep the newspapers from her. They arranged for people to telephone her every day just before the one o'clock and the six o'clock radio news. It worked wonderfully well until she went to stay with her son, David, at Sutton Courtenay. Here she rose early one morning and took in the papers herself. She read the whole story and when the others appeared for breakfast announced that she was going to Cliveden. 'I want to be seen at Bill's side,' she said. But Nancy was old and her memory was spasmodic. On the way she asked her maid Rose 'Why are we going to Cliveden?' 'To see Bill.' 'Why am I going to see Bill today?' Rose realized that all knowledge of Bill's troubled life had passed from her mind, so she let the matter drop and never referred to it again. Lady Astor did not die for another six years but she was still mercifully unaware of the notoriety that had gripped her beloved Cliveden.

Christine Keeler, the call-girl who visited Stephen Ward's house at Cliveden, which he rented from Bill Astor.

One story, probably apocryphal, that persistently went the rounds told how Lady Astor had informed Bill that she was entertaining a group of senators for Sunday lunch at Cliveden. Bill protested that he, too, was giving a lunch party that day. He did not explain, of course, that his guests were Stephen Ward and eight glorious young ladies. Lady Astor refused to be put off and finally suggested entertaining jointly. And so they did. And the Senate's Foreign Relations Committee went back to America declaring that they had never attended a more agreeable party.

The scandal of 'the new Cliveden set' took place in 1963. Three years later (still another three) Bill Astor died of cancer and his fourteen-year-old-son, William Waldorf Astor, became the fourth viscount.

The variation on the first Astor family crest which was adopted by Colonel John Jacob Astor when he was made Baron Astor of Hever in 1956.

In 1956 the name of Waldorf Astor's younger brother, Colonel the Honourable J.J. Astor, appeared in the New Year's Honours List as Baron Astor of Hever, of Hever Castle in the County of Kent. Six years later the new Finance Act passed by a Tory government declared that overseas property belonging to British subjects would now be liable for taxation. This meant that when Baron Astor of Hever died, his New York property would be taxed at the highest rate, in the area of eighty per cent. Lord Astor made a public statement saying that unless he gave up his British residence and moved abroad, his heirs would not be able to continue to live at Hever. So the quiet American, now an impeccable Englishman, turned over The Times newspaper to his two sons, Gavin and Hugh, and departed to a charming estate near Cannes in the south of France. Undoubtedly the Colonel enjoyed his life abroad. His yacht was anchored in the harbour and in the spring and summer he took his friends on Mediterranean sorties. J.J. was a man of great generosity. Once, after a superb cruise he sent each of his guests gifts of £100 saying that they had made the trip so agreeable for him he hoped they would each buy a little memento to remember him by.

Lord Astor's wife, Violet, died three years after leaving England and J.J. followed her to the grave in 1971. His fifty-three-year-old son Gavin inherited the title but not The Times which had been sold five years earlier. The Astors were no longer rich enough to cope with papers that were not making money. Although The Times had great prestige, its circulation in 1966 was not much more than a quarter of a million and falling. Gavin was relieved to find a buyer in the form of Roy Thomson, a Canadian newspaper-man who had made a great deal of money from a Scottish television station. Thomson judged correctly that the acquisition of The Times would win a peerage for him, and before long Lord Thomson of Fleet was trying to shore up his coffers to prevent his money from escaping. But first he had to spend large sums. He introduced a new layout, new pictures, new writers, but the circulation rose by only 16,000 and he finally was forced to accept the fact that The Times was destined to run in the red. Fortunately he owned a string of successful Canadian papers, as well as his Scottish TV station, which more than counterbalanced his loss.

David Astor hung on to The Observer for ten years after Gavin had sold *The Times*. But newspapers clearly were not made for men without a good many profitable strings to their bows. David was fortunate to find a rich California company – The Atlantic Richfield Oil Co. – which felt (surprisingly) that an internationally renowned newspaper would create 'a good image' for the humdrum and rather despised occupation of providing the world with fuel.

Today the wealth and power of the American Astors has devolved upon the unlikely shoulders of a seventy-five-year-old widow, Brooke Astor, who married into the family only seven years before her husband Vincent died. As Vincent never had any children, the fortune that he bestowed eventually will pass from the Astor possession. Brooke was left $60,000,000 'to dispose of as she saw fit'. She was also given full control of the $70,000,000 Astor Foundation 'to alleviate human misery'. She has proved herself a capable and imaginative administrator, making gifts of breathtaking generosity to institutions ranging from the Metropolitan Opera Association to the New York Botanical Gardens; from the Pierpont Morgan Library to the East Harlem Tutorial Program; from the Bronx Zoo to the Navy Yard Boys' Club; the Natural History Museum to the Greater New York Ice Hockey League. Perhaps the greatest of all the Foundation's gifts was a recent pledge of $5,000,000 to the New York Public Library if the Library could raise $10,000,000 on its own – a goal that its new fund-raiser, Richard Salomon, is confident of achieving. The Foundation has already donated $3,000,000 for, after all, the Library sprang into being as a result of the original bequest from the family Founder, the first John Jacob.

The only other members of the Astor family are Vincent Astor's half-brother, Jack, and Jack's son William Backhouse who also has a child. Once upon a time everything Jack Astor did made front-page news, particularly his rapid dispersal of the $5,000,000 trust he received at the age of twenty-one. He now lives unobtrusively in Miami, Florida, but whenever he makes a statement it still provides food for thought. Recently he talked to a friend, inveighing against 'more books on the Astors'. 'Why can't people let the Astors die?' he fumed. 'No one ever would have heard about them if it hadn't been for those two lunatic women who married Astors – the governess who tried to dragoon New York society and the chatterbox who became a British MP. It was too unlucky that they managed to attach themselves to our family!' Jack Astor's only son, William Backhouse, lives in New Jersey where he has established a small business consultancy, and where his wife does her own housework. His son, yet another William Backhouse, is not quite twenty-one. 'People who refer to the British Astors as a branch of the family don't know what they're talking about,' pronounced Jack. 'Today they are the trunk and we are the branch.'

While the American Astors are dwindling from branch to twig the English Astors are a flourishing green bay tree. The brothers, the second Lord Astor (of Cliveden) and the first Lord Astor of Hever produced a total of seven sons; the seven sons produced fourteen male Astors.

A picture of David Astor taken in 1975. As editor of The Observer *he took the paper to new heights, inviting writers such as George Orwell, Arthur Koestler and Cyril Connolly to contribute to its columns.*

Today the seven sons are only six, as Bill Astor, the third viscount, died twelve years ago. These men are very different from the haughty, purse-proud Astors of a century ago. Indeed, it would be difficult to find six members of any family anywhere who are more charming and likeable than these cousins. They are all in their fifties or early sixties; they all have country estates and most of them like to shoot and fish. They are not rich by present-day standards (oil or ships or electronics) and no longer have impressive yachts or racing stables or enormous houses. But they still draw an income from Manhattan real estate and all of them are, as the English say, 'comfortably off'. For the most part they are glad to be country squires and from time to time take on the responsibilities of Lord Lieutenant or High Sheriff or perhaps serve as magistrates. Of course, like other squires, they have the usual connections with the business world in London, which means directorships in banks or insurance companies.

The exception that proves the rule came out of the Cliveden stable – sixty-year-old David, who edited *The Observer* for many years. Despite his good looks and his bland smile he is anything but a country squire. He is complicated and inhibited and so secretive that his brothers often joke that if he could enter a room by coming down the chimney instead of using the door he would gladly do so. When David joined *The Observer* he began as foreign editor and eventually replaced the elderly and highly-respected Ivor Brown as editor. He offered a striking contrast to his predecessor. Whereas Brown had a direct, open personality David not only was hesitant and diffident but so tortuous that his colleagues did not know what to make of him.

Nevertheless his preferences were clear. He was not interested in public school Englishmen but in the ideas of intellectual refugees who had made their way from beleaguered and subjugated countries to Britain. David had a natural affinity for men against the odds and in the pre-war years had struck up friendships with several Germans who were conspiring against Hitler: Rix Loewenthal, a one-time socialist member of the German parliament, and Adam von Trott zu Solz who became involved in the plot to kill Hitler on 20 July 1944. When von Trott was executed by the Nazis, David gave generous financial help to his family.

Although none of David's brothers shared his political views, they admired the panache with which he ran his paper. Indeed, he carried *The Observer* to new heights; at one and the same time it was intellectual, sophisticated and witty. It not only became a Bible for moderate Labour supporters but won international acclaim for its *avant garde* ideas. This was largely due to David's patience and skill in gathering and garnering a group of outstanding contributors. Needless to say, his first two 'discoveries' were exiles: Sebastian Haffner who wrote a political column under the pseudonym *Student of Europe*, and Isaac Dautcher, an ex-communist Polish Jew who supplied regular articles and later wrote the standard life on Trotsky. However, his most brilliant writers were Arthur Koestler, George Orwell and Cyril Connolly, who formed the 'cabinet of talent' that guided the paper to pre-eminence. Although David could be stubborn and inflexible, sometimes punctuating his editorship with feuds as well as friendships, he managed to exercise enough control over his temperamental team to keep them on their golden peak.

In the late 1960s Britain's industrial and economic troubles brought most of the papers of Fleet Street face to face with the stark problem of survival, and *The Observer* was no exception. For ten years David struggled aginst the tide, but with no collateral activities and no outside business ventures to cushion *The Observer* against mounting financial pressure, in 1976 he had no alternative but to sell. Luckily there was no shortage of rich men and rich companies in search of prestige. For several weeks David and his board of directors discussed the bids behind closed doors. Rupert Murdoch was regarded as the favourite but the race had an entirely unexpected photo-finish ending, with the paper being sold to the American oil magnate, Robert Anderson, the status-minded chairman of Atlantic Richfield.

Although David has no direct power he still exerts some influence as he sits on the new board set up by Anderson; and he has the satisfaction of knowing that the oil company has to meet the paper's impressive losses, not himself. David has been married twice and has three children. He still supports the political left and still concerns himself with the under-privileged. At present his chief interest is 'battered wives'.

Perhaps the relation most unlike David in outlook and temperament is his younger brother, Jakie, a sportsman with a piquant sense of humour that delights his friends. In the last war his regiment served in Norway, Italy, France and Germany and he won both the Croix de Guerre and the Legion d'Honneur. When peace came he married the daughter of the Argentine Ambassador, Ana Carcano, and from 1951 to 1959 sat in Parliament for his mother's former seat, the Sutton Division of Plymouth.

After that he retired to his house in Bedfordshire and devoted himself to farming and racing. He had inherited half his father's racing stable (Bill got the other half) and now he began to operate his own stud farm. In 1962 he was made president of the Thoroughbred Breeders Association, and served at various times on the Horserace Totalisator Board and the Betting Levy.

As the Astor racing colours, light blue with a pink sash, were always at the fore of every big event, Jakie's announcement in September 1975 that he was selling his Newmarket stud hit the racing world like a clap of thunder. 'One of the great turf eras ends next month,' declared the *Daily Mail*. 'The names of the Astor horses in the last sixty years are like a roll-call of turf history: Court Martial, Pay Up, Buchan, Pennycomequick, Craig an Eran, and Brooklaw were among the earlier winners. More recently, Provoke, Remand, Sharp Edge, Persian War and Trelawney have carried on the line.' The writer goes on to say that Jakie's horses are direct descendants of his father's mares and that 'the family has had a total of eleven Classic winners but the Derby has always eluded them although they have come second five times.'

Jakie still follows the sport of queens as a member of the Jockey Club. He has a son and daughter and has recently married for the second time. His wife was Mrs Susan Sheppard, a daughter of Major Eveleigh. She brings the number of present-day Lady Astors to three, as in the summer of 1978 Jakie was awarded a knighthood for his work as chairman of the Agricultural Research Council. Jakie's son, thirty-two-year-old 'Mickie' followed in his father's footsteps by himself marrying in March 1979. His bride is a clever American girl, Daphne Warburg of New York, a member of the famous banking family and a professional photographer of distinction.

Perhaps the most interesting, and certainly the most talented Astor, is Michael, who comes between David and Jakie. Like his younger brother he has a vivid sense of humour and his accomplishments as a raconteur make him a delightful companion. After serving in the war he entered Parliament and remained there for six years. Later he became interested in television and formed Television Reporters International for which such stars as Robert Kee, Ludovic Kennedy and James Mossman made documentary films. Unfortunately the rivalry between the British television companies prevented a major group from networking the programmes and the enterprise eventually collapsed.

However, Michael's real interests have always been artistic. When he was twenty-one he left the family fold, took his own flat in London and enrolled himself as a student in the Royal College of Art. As a child he always wanted to be a painter but his father considered such a vocation 'unsuitable'. Unfortunately Michael's studies were interrupted by the war and afterwards he only painted as a hobby. Nevertheless painting still remains his chief interest and he has reached a degree of proficiency, both in traditional and modern work, well above the ordinary run. He has had two exhibitions which have won praise from the critics and financial support from the public.

Michael is also a gifted writer but his books are a rarity. Although he published a novel in 1969, his most important contribution was written before that, in 1961, – *Tribal Feeling*, an account of his childhood and the tumultuous life of Cliveden under his mother's auspices. Yet the slim little biography was a *tour de force*, almost impossibly well written for an amateur, amusing, sad and rather profound. Although

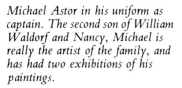

Michael Astor in his uniform as captain. The second son of William Waldorf and Nancy, Michael is really the artist of the family, and has had two exhibitions of his paintings.

the public pictured his mother, Lady Astor, as a woman who loved to provoke a laugh but whose aggressive nature often prompted her to make blatantly rude observations, apparently Lady Astor had never seen herself in this light. When extracts of Michael's book were serialized in *Encounter* magazine, and the *Daily Mail* rang her and asked what she thought of her son's statement that 'her prodigious tactlessness was the bain of her social life ... her overbearing desire to get her own way,' she was almost speechless. 'Michael was always unpredictable,' she countered. '... Perhaps I have been a little tough, but I don't think I have ever been tactless or ruthless or overbearing.'

Michael lives in a lovely old house at Shipton-under-Wychwood in Oxfordshire. He has been married three times and has five children. His present wife is Judy Innes, a former journalist. They farm and play tennis and entertain Oxford dons, and when they travel, which they do frequently, they often visit places where Michael can paint.

Michael is the chief link between the Cliveden Astors and the Hever Astors as he has always been a close friend of sixty-year-old Gavin, the present Lord Astor of Hever. Gavin is an attractive, good-natured, ruddy-faced man who married Irene, one of the daughters of Field Marshal Earl Haig who commanded the British Army in the First World War. They live at Hever Castle, where they brought up five children; and although the estate is now open to the public they occupy a private wing and still consider it their home. Gavin is almost an institution in Kent. He not only is Lord Lieutenant of the county but *Custos Rotulorum*, a medieval term meaning 'principal justice of the peace'.

He farms three and half thousand acres, has a herd of Jerseys and Fresians and a stud of Welsh ponies. After the war he became a director of Reuters and Chairman of the Times Publishing Company, but relinquished these jobs when he sold the newspaper. Like his father before him he is a man of good works and good humour. 'No one has ever called me melancholy' he once told a reporter. No doubt his affable nature has added to the demand for his services, for he has served in innumerable capacities from High Sheriff to Seneschal of Canterbury Cathedral; from a member of the Executive Committee of the Pilgrim's Society to the Central Council of the Royal Commonwealth Society. Gavin's chief sport is shooting. He has a large estate at Aberdeenshire in Scotland, where he frequently entertains the Duke of Edinburgh and the younger princes. Indeed, Prince Philip is godfather to Gavin's second son, Philip.

Gavin's youngest brother John, is a quiet, retiring person who farms a thousand acres at Inkpen in Berkshire and who fulfilled the family sense of duty by serving as a Member of Parliament from 1964 to 1974. He is married, has three children and like all Astors likes to shoot and fish. He is not devoid of originality for in 1971 he embarked on the speculative venture of making English wine. He planted a vineyard on his Berkshire farm and within a few years was marketing between five and six thousand bottles yearly of white wine and rosé under the Astor label. And although it may fall short of the product across the Channel it has the advantage of being cheaper.

Gavin's middle brother, Hugh, is probably the most adventurous of all the Astors and certainly the most travel-minded. Highly intelligent, modest and kind, he has always been very close to Gavin and worked as his chief assistant when they owned *The Times*. Like his two brothers he has married only once and enjoys a happy if noisy home life surrounded by five children. His vivacious blue-eyed wife, Emily Lucy, is the daughter of a Scottish baronet, Sir Alexander Kinloch.

Hugh's business interests are fairly routine – Hambros Bank and Phoenix Assurance – but his hobbies are not. He loves flying and has always had his own aircraft; originally a four-seater Cessna but now a two-engined Beechcraft in which he flies Emily Lou and the children around. Some years ago he took part in an air race from London to Sydney and although he was not among the first arrivals he at least had the satisfaction of completing the course.

However, more exciting than flying was his incursion into the world of ocean racing. In 1950 his 80-ton Norwind won the 235-mile race from Santander in Spain to Belle Isle near Brest. However his most exciting race took place in 1960 from Oslo in Norway to Ostend in Belgium. Hugh's strong social conscience led him to take, as part of his crew, seventeen novices from the East End of London – boys who had scarcely seen a blade of grass, much less an ocean wave. This was the first of the 'Tall Ship' races and most of Hugh's competitors (Belgians, Danes, Norwegians) were sailing three-masted, full-rigged clippers which should have won, but the good lord smiled on Hugh and sent him a head wind of which only his Class II yawl, *Nordwind*, could take advantage. And thus he became the overall winner completing the course in 122 hours and 7 minutes. The London novices were thrilled by the unexpected victory. 'Their parents wouldn't have known them,' said Hugh. 'They paraded through Ostend, chests out, heads up, cock-a-hoop, like the champion tars they were.'

Hugh and his brothers and cousins have added fourteen more male Astors to the world's population, among whom are Hugh's two sons, Robert, who is studying at London University and James, who is at Eton. Most of these young people are in their twenties although some have spilled into the thirties, and others are still at school. A few pursue traditional careers in army and city but most have branched out into a wide variety of occupations from the civil service to engineering, from property development to teaching, social work to diplomacy, diplomacy to swing music.

The richest member of the younger generation is twenty-six-year-old William, the fourth viscount, whose father, Bill, died prematurely. William is married to Annabelle Sheffield, an attractive lady several years older than himself who was married once before. He lives in modest houses in London and Berkshire, but what he really likes is the estate which he inherited in Jura, a wild remote island off the coast of Scotland. Here he spends several months every year surrounded by his dogs, stalking and shooting and fishing. He loves the open spaces and country life and if he had been a poor man probably would have been quite happy as a ghillie or crofter.

The old and new generations. William Astor, now twenty-six and the fourth Viscount, with his grandmother, Nancy, pictured at the wedding of his father to Bronwen Pugh.

Instead he has to attend (fairly briefly) to the Manhattan real estate which he inherited from father and grandfather. He also acquired a certain amount of jewellery, once the property of his grandmother, Lady Astor, which he is in the process of selling. Nancy's most famous gem was the Sancy diamond which had the place of honour in her tiara. This jewel was bought by a Frenchman, Nicholas de Sancy, in Constantinople in 1580. For many years it changed hands regularly and at one time belonging to Charles I of England who pawned it to raise money for the Civil War. It was bought by William Waldorf in 1906 and given to his daughter-in-law as a wedding present. Last year, in February 1978, young William Astor sold it to a consortium formed by the Bank of France for $1,000,000.

In June 1978 Gavin Astor celebrated his sixtieth birthday by giving a dinner party at the Goldsmiths' Hall in the City of London. He chose this place because of a long association with the Goldsmiths' Company of which he is fourth Warden. Sixty-four guests attended the dinner of which nearly a third were Astors. Mrs Brooke Astor flew from America for the occasion, but Vincent Astor's half-brother, Jack, and Jack's daughter, Mary Jaqueline, had visited Hever a few months earlier and were unable to make a second visit. Of the six English Astors of the older generation, the guests included two of the Cliveden Astors (not David who shies away from all social occasions) and the three Hever Astors. The large cocktail party that preceded the dinner was attended by sixteen young Astors out of a total of thirty-one – fourteen sons and seventeen daughters. Others could not come because of school and university demands.

At the dinner the guests of honour were the Queen and Prince Philip. The Queen, of course, sat at Gavin's right, and after dinner when Gavin's eldest son, the eighth John Jacob Astor, played the bagpipes, she said to Gavin: 'I thought I had the best piper in the British Isles but John is every bit as good.'

If the family founder, the first John Jacob Astor, could look down on his descendants two hundred years after his departure, he would be deeply content. Not only has the family managed to maintain the affluence with which he endowed it but Astors on both sides of the Atlantic still move in the influential circles so dear to his heart. 'Furlongs away from furs', as a wag put it. A monument to the perpetually escalating value of Manhattan real estate? Or a tribute to the civilizing propensities of that fast-disappearing commodity – inherited wealth?

Appendix: A notable law suit
(written in 1896)

The suit commenced some three years since by Mr Frederick Law Olmsted against the various members of the Astor family in the New York Superior Court, attracted considerable attention at the time, both from the prominence of the parties to the litigation, and the large amount claimed by Mr Olmsted, something over $5,000,000. As the case has not yet come to a hearing owing to the delays in the proceedings at law, the matter has, in a measure, passed from notice, scarcely anything connected with it having appeared in the public print since the commencement of the action.

Through the courtesy of Mr Olmsted, I spent several days during the summer of 1895 as a guest at his summer residence on Deer Isle, which lies on the Penobscot Bay, off the mouth of the Penobscot River on the coast of Maine; and having read quite in detail the history of the cause of action, which seemed to me a most forcible illustration of the maxim that truth is stranger than fiction, I take pleasure in giving the story as told to me by Mr Olmsted and the members of his family.

An ancestor, seven generations back, of Mr Olmsted, whose name was Cotton Mather Olmsted, was an Indian trader and spent a part of each year from 1696 to 1705 in what is now the State of Maine. His treatment of the Indians was always fair and honourable, whereby he won their confidence and esteem.

Winnepeasaukee, then the head sachem of the Penobscot tribe, was at one time severely wounded by a bear, and Mr Olmsted having cared for him, dressed his wounds and aided greatly his recovery, the chief, as a token of gratitude presented to him the Deer Isle before named, a portion of which has ever since remained the possession of his descendants and is now the property and summer home of Mr Frederick Law Olmsted.

The original deed of gift, written on a piece of birch bark, and bearing date of 24 January, 1699, is still in the possession of Mr Olmsted, and, after the independence of the United States was acknowledged, the validity of the transfer was recognized and affirmed, and a formal patent was issued by the Secretary of the Treasury during the second term of President Washington's administration.

Upon the rocky shore near the residence of Mr Olmsted, and at the extreme end of the island, is a cave, the opening of which is upon the sea. The cave is about ten feet wide and high, of irregular shape, and extends back into the rock formation some twenty-five feet. It had evidently been excavated by the ceaseless action of the waves upon a portion of the rock somewhat softer than its surroundings. At high tide, the entire cave is under water, but at low tide, it can be entered dry shod, being entirely above sea level. This was visited by the family of Mr Olmsted and other residents of the island.

In 1892 Mr Olmsted observed upon the rock at the inner end of the cave some marks of indentation, something in the form of a rude cross, which seemed to him possibly of artificial origin. If so, it was of ancient date, as its edges were not well defined – were rounded and worn as by the action of the waves and ice. Still, it was upon the walls of the cave; and Mr Olmsted one day suggested to his family, when in the cave, that as stories of Captain Kidd's buried treasures had sometimes located such treasures upon the Maine coast, they should dig at the place below the cross for such hidden wealth.

Purely as a matter of sport, the excavation was commenced, the sand was cleared away, and to their surprise a rectangular hole in the hard clay was discovered, about two inches by thirty inches on the surface, and about twenty inches deep. This was filled with sand, and upon the sand being carefully removed, there was plainly to be seen upon the bottom of the hole the marks of a row of bolt heads some three or four inches apart, and extending around the bottom for about one inch from its edge.

The appearance was precisely as if an iron box, heavily bolted at its joints, had been buried in the compact clay for a period long enough to have left a perfect impress of itself in the clay, and after its removal, the excavation having been filled with sand, the impression had been perfectly preserved. After a perfect facsimile of the bottom of the hole had been taken in plaster of paris, the excavation was again filled with sand. The clay was so hard that the taking of the cast did not in the least mar its surface.

The bottom of the hole and such portions of the sides as had not been marred by the removal of the box were heavily coated with iron rust, so that everything indicated the former presence of an iron box which had remained buried in the clay long enough to become at least thoroughly rusted on its surface and firmly imbedded in the clay matrix. As there were various legends relative to the presence of Captain Kidd upon the Maine coast, the discovery of the excavation was sufficient to awaken eager interest in the question of the iron box and the person who carried it away.

At about the year 1801, a French Canadian named Jacques Cartier, who was one of the employees of John Jacob Astor in his fur trade, and who had for several winters traded with the Indians and hunters along the upper waters of the Penobscot River, returned from New York, where he had been to deliver the season's collection of furs, and he then expressed a desire to purchase from Oliver Cromwell Olmsted, who was then the owner by inheritance of Deer Isle, either the whole island or the south end, where the case or box before described was located.

Mr Olmsted refused both requests, but finally sold him a few acres near the centre of the island, where he built a log house and lived for many years with an Indian wife, hunting and fishing occasionally as a diversion, but giving up his former method of gaining a livelihood.

This trader had had for several years previous to 1801 camped upon the south end of Deer Isle when collecting his furs, passing up the Penobscot River and its tributaries in a small canoe, and storing his furs in a hut at his camping place until the end of his season, when he sailed with his little cargo for New York.

He had always remained extremely poor, having but a meagre salary from Mr Astor, but when he purchased a portion of the island, he seemed to have an abundance of money, sufficient in fact to meet his wants for many years. Occasionally when under the influence of whiskey he would speak vaguely of some sudden good fortune which had befallen him, but when sober he always denied ever having made the statement and seemed much disturbed when asked about the source of his wealth, which led to various suspicions among the few inhabitants of the island as to the honesty of his methods of acquiring it.

These suspicions ultimately became so pointed that he disappeared from the island and never returned. On searching his cabin, some fragments of papers were found, torn and partially burned, so that no connected meaning could be determined from them. On one fragment was the signature of John Jacob Astor, and on another, in the same handwriting, the words 'absolute secrecy must be observed because . . .'.

These fragments were preserved, however, and are now in the possession of Mr Frederick Law Olmsted. From the story of the trader and from the fragmentary papers, Mr Olmsted fancied that there might be some connection between the mysterious box and the newly acquired wealth of the trader, and that the secret, if there was, was shared by Mr Astor.

As the trader for many years previous to his good fortune had camped upon the end of the island immediately adjoining the cave, it might readily be conceived that a heavy storm had washed the sand away so as to make the top of the box visible, and that he had found it and taken it to New York with him to Mr Astor with his boatload of furs. His desire to purchase this particular location in the island harmonized with this suggestion.

Various questions presented themselves regarding this theory. Had the box contained the long lost treasures of Captain Kidd? If so, to whom did the box and its contents belong? Mr Wm M. Evarts, to whom Mr Olmsted applied for an option as to the legal phase of this question, after careful examination of the evidence, gave his view in substance as follows:

1 That Captain Kidd, in the year 1700 had acquired by pillage vast treasures of gold and gems, which he had somewhere concealed prior to his execution in 1701.

2 That if such treasures were concealed upon Deer Island that island at the time was the absolute property of Cotton Mather Olmsted. For a while, the record title of the island bore date of a patent in President Washington's administration in 1794, yet this, as appeared by its tenor, was in affirmance of the title made in 1699, when the island was given to Cotton Mather Olmsted by the Indian chief, Winnepeasaukee, and

established the ownership of the island in Mr Olmsted, when the box, if concealed by Capt. Kidd, was buried and that Frederick Law Olmsted by inheritance and purchase, had acquired all the rights originally held by his ancestor in that part of the island where the treasure was concealed.

3 That, as the owner of such real estate, the treasure would belong to him as affixed to the land, as against the world, except possibly the lineal descendants of Capt. Kidd, if any there were.

Mr Olmsted learned that in his early life, Mr Astor kept for many years his first and only bank account with the Manhattan Bank, and as the books of the bank are all preserved, he was enabled by a plausible pretext, to secure an examination of Mr Astor's financial transactions from the beginning. His idea in this search was to learn if Mr Astor's fortune had increased at the same time as that of the French Canadian.

The business of both Mr Astor and the bank was small in those early days, and the entries of the customers' accounts were much more in detail than in our time, when, as a rule, only amounts are recorded. The account commenced in 1798, being one of the first accounts opened after the picturesque organization of the bank by Aaron Burr, and for several years the total deposits for an entire year did not exceed $4000.

He shipped some of his furs abroad and others were sold to dealers and manufacturers, and wherever he drew on a customer with a bill of lading, the books of the bank showed virtually the whole transaction. Entries like the following are of frequent occurence: 'Cr. J.J. Astor $33.00 – proceeds draft for sale of 40 musk-rat, 4 bear, 3 deer and 12 mink skins' or 'Cr. John Jacob Astor $131.00 – proceeds of draft on London for $126.10 for sale of 87 otter skins, 46 mink and 30 beaver pelts.'

Each year showed a modest increase in the volume of business of the thrifty furrier but the aggregates were only moderate until the year 1801 being the same year the Canadian trader bought of Mr Olmsted a portion of Deer Isle, when the volume of bank transactions reached, for the time, enormous dimensions, springing from an aggregate for the year 1799 of $4011 to over $500,000 for the year 1801.

Among the entries in the latter year are two of the same date for checks to Jacques Cartier, the French Canadian; one of $133.50 drawn 'in settlement to date'. Inasmuch as, in each year previous, the aggregate fur transactions with Mr Cartier had never exceeded $500, the entry of a check also for $5000 seemed inexplicable on any ordinary grounds.

The enormous growth of Mr Astor's own transactions also seemed equally mysterious. Mr Astor had evidently visited England in the year 1801, as the bank entries are filled with credits to him of drafts remitted by him from Roderick Streeter, varying from $10,000 to $40,000 and aggregating, during the year, nearly $495,000. Credits of the same Streeter drafts are made also during the two following years to the amount of over $800,000 more, or a total of over $1,300,000 when the Streeter remittances abruptly ceased.

Edwin W. Streeter, of London, is at the present time one of the largest dealers in precious stones in the world, and, as in England the same business is often continued in a family for many generations, it occurred to

Mr Frederick Law Olmsted who, from the facts already given, had become greatly interested in following the matter to a conclusion, that the Streeter who had made the vast remittances to Mr Astor might be an ancestor of the present London merchant.

An inquiry by mail developed the fact that the present Mr Streeter was a great grandson of Roderick Streeter and the business had been continued in the family for five generations.

Mr Olmsted thereupon sent a confidential agent to London, who succeeded in getting access to the books of the Streeter firm for the years 1798 to 1802 inclusive. Here was found a detailed statement of the transactions with Mr Astor.

The first item of $40,000 entered as 'advances on ancient French and Spanish gold coins', deposited by Mr Astor, and later another $14,213.8 for 'balances due for French and Spanish gold coins'.

All other entries were for the sale of precious stones, mostly diamonds, rubies and pearls, which in all, with the sums paid for the French and Spanish gold, reached the enormous aggregate heretofore given.

Certain of the gems were purchased outright by Mr Streeter and the others were sold by him, as a broker, for the account of Mr Astor, and the proceeds duly remitted during the years 1801–2. The whole account corresponded exactly, item for item, with the various entries of Streeter remittances shown on the books of the Manhattan Bank.

The facts gathered thus far enabled Mr Olmsted to formulate a theory in substance as follows: that Jacques Cartier had found the box containing the buried treasures of Capt. Kidd; that he had taken it to New York and delivered it to Mr Astor; that Mr Astor had bought the contents of the box, or Cartier's interest in them, for the check of $5000; that he had taken the contents to England, and had, from their sale, realized the vast sums paid by Mr Streeter. Many links of the chain of evidence, however, were still missing and a great point would be gained if the mysterious box could be traced to the custody of Mr Astor. It seemed reasonable that this box, if ever in the possession of Mr Astor, and if its contents were of great value, would be retained by him with scrupulous care, and that, if he had imparted the secret to his children, it would still be in their possession. If not, it might have been sold and lost sight of, as a piece of worthless scrap iron, after the death of the first Mr Astor.

Mr Olmsted learned that the last house in which the original Mr Astor had lived had been torn down in the year of 1893, to be replaced by a superb modern building (the old Waldorf-Astoria), and that the old building had been sold to a well-known house-wrecking firm, for an insignificant sum, as the material was worth but little above the cost of tearing down and removal. In the hope that the rusty box had been sold with the other rubbish about the premises, Mr Olmsted inserted the following advertisement in the *New York Tribune*:

A rusty iron box, strongly made and bolted, was by mistake sold in 1893 to a dealer in junk, supposedly in New York or Brooklyn. The dimensions were 15 × 30 × 15 inches. A person, for sentimental reasons, wishes to reclaim this box, and will pay to its present owner, for the same, several times its value as scrap iron. Address F.L., Box 74, New York Tribune.

Within a few days Mr Olmsted received a letter from Mr Bronson H. Tuttle of Naugatuck, Connecticut, an iron manufacturer, stating that in a car of scrap iron bought by him from Mr Melechidescec Jacobs of Brooklyn, was an iron box answering the description given in the *Tribune*; and that if it was of any value to the advertiser it would be forwarded on receipt of eighty cents, which was its cost to him at $11 per ton, the price paid for the carload of scrap.

Mr Olmsted at once procured the box and shipped it to Deer Isle, where the bolts upon its bottom and the box itself were found to fit perfectly the print on the clay bottom of the cave. The plaster cast of the bottom of the cavity taken when it was first discovered, matched the bottom of the box as perfectly as ever a casting fitted the mould in which it was made.

Every peculiarity of the shape of a bolt head, every hammer mark made in rivetting the bolts, as shown in the clay, was reproduced in the iron box. There was no possible question that the iron box was the identical one which had been long before buried in the cave. On the top of the box, too, was distinguishable despite the heavy coating of rust, in rude and irregularly formed characters, as if made by the strokes of a cold chisel, or some similar tool, the letters, 'W.K.', the initials of the veritable and eminent pirate Captain William Kidd.

Further inquiry developed the fact that Melechidescec Jacobs, the Brooklyn junk dealer, had purchased the box in a large dray load of scrap iron mostly made up of a cooking range, sash weights, gas, steam and water pipes, etc. taken from the wrecking firm of James & Co., and that James & Co. had taken such material from the family mansion occupied by the original John Jacob Astor at the time of his death, when tearing it down to make room for the new building. The indications thickened that the mysterious box contained the long lost and widely sought treasures of Capt. Kidd. One peculiarity of the box was that there had apparently been no way of opening it except by cutting it apart.

The top had been firmly rivetted in its place and this fact possibly indicated the reason of its purchase by Mr Astor at the moderate price of $5000, as the trader who found it had been unable to open it before his arrival in New York. As, however, we have no information of the contract between Mr Astor and Jacques Cartier, the amount named, $5000 may have been precisely the percentage agreed upon, which he received from the profits of his season's business in addition to a salary.

Mr Olmsted had an accurate copy made of all entries in the books of the Manhattan Bank as to the transactions of Mr Astor shown by such books from 1798 to 1802, and his English agent had similar copies made of all entries in the books of Roderick Streeter for the same period; also copies of any letters passing between the parties. The agent also looked up and reported everything available relative to the career of Capt. Kidd, the substance of which was as follows:

Capt. Kidd had won an enviable reputation in the English and American Merchant Marine as a brave and intelligent officer. For many years the English merchant vessels were preyed upon by pirates; numerous vessels had been captured and destroyed, and others robbed.

The depredations were largely along the coast of Madagascar and Mozambique, on the route of the English vessels in the India trade, and off the coast of South America, where the Spanish galleons bore great treasures from the Peruvian gold fields.

The depredations of the pirates became so great that the English merchants finally bought and equipped a staunch war vessel, placed the same under the command of Capt. Kidd, and sent him out expressly to chastize and destroy the pirates. As these pirates were known to have secured vast amounts of gold and gems, it was expected that Capt. Kidd might not only clear the infested seas of the piratical craft, but capture from them enough treasures to make the operation a profitable one.

After reaching the Coast of East Africa, news was received of the destruction by him of sundry piratical vessels containing much treasure, but the capture of this treasure seemed to excite his own cupidity, and he decided to himself engage in the occupation of being a malefactor. For some years thereafter he was literally the scourge of the seas.

He plundered alike other pirates and the merchant vessels of every nation. Finally, after a cruise along the Eastern coast of the United States, as far north as the port of Halifax, he, for some reason, decided to make a bold entry into the port of Boston, Mass., as an English merchant vessel, under the papers originally furnished him in England. Before entering Boston Harbor, he put ashore and concealed on Gardiners Island a considerable quantity of merchandise, consisting largely of bales of valuable silks and velvets, with a small amount of gold and silver and precious stones. These articles were afterward discovered and reclaimed by the owners of the vessel and sold for some £14,000, which was divided among them.

From the great number of vessels which he had destroyed and plundered, with their ascertained cargoes, it was known that the treasure thus discovered was but an insignificant fraction of what he had captured; it was known that gold and gems of vast values were somewhere concealed, and thence came the endless searches from Key West and Jekyl Island to Halifax for the treasure, which had thus far seemingly escaped human vision and utterly disappeared.

In fact, from the little care taken by Capt. Kidd as to the plunder hidden on Gardiner's Island, the owners of his ship concluded that to be merely a blind to divert their attention from the vastly greater wealth he had appropriated. A short time after his arrival in Boston he was arrested and sent to England, and at once put on trial for piracy. In two days he was tried, convicted and hanged. This illustrates the great progress in civilization since the benighted age, for now the most red-handed and popular murderers are allowed months for preparation and trial; are fêted; garlanded and made heroes of the day, and assigned with all priestly assurance to the mansions of the blest. His wife was not allowed to see him except for a half hour after the death sentence had been pronounced. They had a whispered conference, and at its close he was seen to hand her a card upon which he had written the figures 44106818. This card was taken from her by the guards and never restored, and every effort was made to induce her to tell the meaning of the figures, but she utterly refused, and even claimed not herself to know. The paper was preserved among the proceedings of the trial and a photographed copy secured by Mr Olmsted.

From the records of the trial, it appeared that Capt. Kidd was the only child of his parents; that he had been married for several years; that two children had been born to him, a daughter who died while yet a child and before the trial, and a son who survived both his father and mother.

It also appeared that his son ten years after his father's execution, enlisted as a private soldier in the English army and was killed in a battle near Stirling in 1715. The records of the English war office showed that the widow of this son applied for a pension under the then existing law; that her affidavit and marriage certificate showed her to have been married to the son of Capt. Kidd, and that no child had been born to them, and the usual pension was awarded to her and paid until her death in 1744. These facts settled the question as to any claims upon the treasure by descendants of Capt. Kidd.

The records of the trial also contained a report by experts upon the card given by Capt. Kidd to his wife, to the effect that they had applied to the figures upon it the usual tests for the reading of cipher writings, without avail, and that, if the figures ever had a meaning, it was undiscoverable. The same conclusion was reached by several people to whom Mr Olmsted showed the copy of the card.

In the summer of 1894, when Prof. David F. Todd, the Astronomer of Amherst College, was visiting the family of Mr Olmsted at Deer Isle, he one day amused himself by calculating the latitude and longitude of the house near the cave, and gave the result to Miss Marion Olmsted. As she was entering such results in her journal, she was struck by the fact that the figures for the latitude, 44 10′, were the same as the first four figures on the card, 4410, and that the other four figures, 6818, were almost the exact longitude west from Greenwich, which was 68 13′; a difference easily accounted for by a moderate variation in Capt. Kidd's chronometer. The latitude, taken by observation of the pole star, was absolutely correct. It appeared as though Capt. Kidd told his wife in this manner where to find the hidden treasure, but that, inasmuch as the government authorities had seized the card, she preferred silence toward those who had pursued her husband to his death, and the total loss to everyone of the treasure rather than, by a confession, to give it into the hands of his enemies. The very simplicity of the supposed cipher-writing had been its safeguard since all the experts had sought for some abstruse and occult meaning to the combination of the figures.

It appeared that in the year 1700, Lord and Lady Dunmore were returning to England from India, where the vessel upon which they had taken passage was fired upon and captured by Capt. Kidd. His first order was that every person on board should walk the plank into the sea, but several ladies who were passengers pleaded so earnestly for their lives that Kidd finally decided to plunder the cargo and passengers, and let the vessel proceed on her voyage.

The ladies were compelled, on peril of their lives, to surrender all their jewelry, and among the articles taken from Lady Dunmore, was a pair of superb pearl bracelets, the pearls being set in a somewhat peculiar fashion. Another pair, an exact duplicate of those possessed by Lady Dunmore, had been purchased by Lord Dunmore as a wedding gift to his sister, and the story of the two pairs of bracelets, and the loss of Lady Dunmore's pearls which were of great value, and of her pleading for her life to Capt. Kidd, is a matter of history as well as one of the cherished family traditions.

In 1801 Roderick Streeter wrote to Mr Astor that the then Lady Dunmore, in looking over some gems which he was offering her, had seen a pair of exquisite pearl bracelets which were a part of the Astor consignment and had at once recognized them as the identical pair taken by Kidd, nearly one hundred years before. She returned the following day with the family solicitor, bringing the duplicate bracelets; told and verified the story of the loss of one pair by Lady Dunmore; compared the two pairs, showing their almost perfect identity, showing certain private marks upon each, and demonstrating beyond question that the pearl bracelets offered by Mr Streeter were the identical ones seized by Capt. Kidd.

The solicitor demanded their surrender to Lady Dunmore, on the ground that, having been stolen, no property in them could pass even to an innocent purchaser. Mr Streeter then stated that he had asked for delay until he could communicate with the owner of the gems and asked for instructions from Mr Astor. Mr Astor replied, authorized the delivery of the bracelets to Lady Dunmore and asking Mr Streeter to assure her that the supposed owner was guiltless of wrong in the matter and was an entirely innocent holder.

He repeated the caution given also in sundry other letters, that to no one was the ownership of the gems sold by Mr Streeter to be revealed; they were to be sold as the property of Mr Streeter, acquired in the regular course of business. Lady Dunmore afterward sat to Sir Thomas Lawrence for her portrait and was painted wearing upon her arms the pearl bracelets thus curiously reclaimed and recovered. This portrait is considered one of the masterpieces of Lawrence, and is now in the collection of Mr Hall McCormick of Chicago.

By the discovery of the hole in the cave in Maine, after a lapse of nearly two hundred years, was thus curiously brought to light the apparent origin of the colossal Astor fortune. Prior to the acquisition of the Kidd treasures by the first American Astor, he was simply a modest trader, earning each year by frugality and thrift two or three hundred dollars above his living expenses, with a fair prospect of accumulating, by an industrious life, a fortune of twenty or thirty thousand dollars.

When he became possessed of the Kidd plunder, he handled it with the skill of a great general. He expanded his fur trade until it embraced the continent. The record of his checks given during the three years when he received the one million, three hundred thousand dollars shows that he expended over seven hundred thousand dollars of the amount in the purchase of real estate in the city of New York.

The entries of the various checks are recorded as 'Payment for the Wall Street property', 'The Bond Street Land' and the 'Broadway corner', etc., the description being sufficiently accurate, when verified by the comparison of the titles of record, to locate at this date every parcel of land bought, and all of which is still in the possession of the Astor family. Some twenty different tracts of land in what is now the very heart of the business and residence portion of New York were thus purchased, each one of which is now probably of more value than the price originally paid for the whole. In obtaining a knowledge of the various details already given, over two years had been spent by Mr Olmsted and his agents. The results seemingly reached may be summarized as follows:

1 Capt. Kidd had sailed the Maine Coast shortly before his arrest, and an iron box, marked with his initials, was afterward taken from the cave upon the land of Mr Olmsted, and this box afterward came into Mr Astor's possession.

2 Jacques Cartier had camped for many years, while employed by Mr Astor immediately adjoining the cave where the box was concealed, and his rapid increase in wealth and that of Mr Astor, were simultaneous.

3 Mr Astor's great wealth came from the sale, through Mr Streeter, of ancient Spanish and French gold, and of gems, some of which were proved to have been a part of the spoils of Capt. Kidd, which made it a reasonable presumption that all of such property was of the same character.

4 Captain Kidd was known to have captured and somewhere concealed gold and gems of vast value, and the card given to his wife just before his execution indicated by a plausible reading, the cave upon Mr Olmsted's land as the place of concealment.

5 The family of Capt. Kidd had long been extinct and no one could successfully contest with Mr Olmsted the ownership of the property concealed upon his land.

6 Having his evidence thus formulated, Mr Olmsted called upon the descendants of Mr Astor, accompanied by his attorney, Mr William M. Evarts, and demanded of them:

(a). a payment by them to him of the sum of $1,300,000, the amount received by Mr Streeter, with interest from the date of its receipt. The total amount, computed according to the laws of New York in force since 1796, was $5,112,234.30 and Mr Olmsted offered, on condition of immediate cash payment, to deduct the item of $34.30. This demand was refused.

(b). Mr Olmsted then demanded that the Astor family convey to him all the real estate in New York City purchased by their ancestor with the money received from Mr Streeter, with the accrued rents and profits from the date of its purchase, and this demand was likewise refused.

These refusals left to Mr Olmsted no alternative except to resort to the courts for the establishment of his rights, and an action was accordingly commenced.

The declaration filed by his attorneys, Joseph H. Choate, Stewart L. Woodford and Frederick W. Holls, set out in full the history of the claim from the beginning, and as has been detailed herein, and petitioned the court for alternative relief, (a) either that the descendants of John Jacob Astor pay to Mr Olmsted the sum of $1,300,000 with interest from the time of its receipt by Mr Astor,* or failing this (b) that Mr Astor be adjudged a trustee for the rightful owner of the money thus received, and that property purchased with such funds be ordered conveyed to Mr Olmsted.

To this declaration the Astor family, by their attorneys, Elihu Root and Edward Isham, denying all liability, upon the ground that the cause of action, if ever valid, was barred by the statute of limitations. To this answer the plaintiff demurred, alleging for grounds thereof that it appeared clearly from the pleadings that Mr Olmsted had been vigilant in the assertion of his claim, as soon as reasonable proof of its existence came to his knowledge, and, further, that the statute of limitations did not run as against a trust.

The demurrer was sustained by the Court on both grounds, the Court intimating, however, that when the case came to a hearing, the plaintiff must select and rest his case on one or the other form of relief demanded, and could not, in the same action, secure the alternative relief sought. After this decision, the defendants, filed a general denial of all the claims by Mr Olmsted.

This is the present status of the litigation, and it is expected that the case will be brought to final trial during the present year [1896].

From the dramatic character of the claim, from the eminent ability of counsel for each contestant, and from the large amount involved, it is needless to add that the trial will be watched with intense interest, and that it will stand as the 'Cause Célèbre' of our century.

[Later, when this bizarre story was circulated the following sentence was added which gave it, erroneously of course, the ring of true authenticity: 'The case was not tried but settled out of court for $5,000,000.']

---

* Making the total more than $5 million

Select bibliography

The first Astors were undemonstrative people. Although the Family Founder died a world-famous figure, not one of his sisters, brothers or children ever published a memoir about him or even passed on an anecdote that might have thrown light on his character. The first man to build up a picture of him was James Parton, a journalist sometimes described as 'the father of American biography' because of his many books about celebrated contemporaries. Although Parton was not personally acquainted with John Jacob and did not write his biography until nearly twenty years after Astor's death, he interviewed many people and scooped up all the current stories. No one can vouch for the accuracy of any of them but all books written about John Jacob bear the Parton stamp. Even the standard life of Astor, written by Kenneth Porter in 1931 and bristling with documents dealing with his life as a trader, is compelled to follow the Parton trail as far as his personality is concerned. Yet one has reservations, for Astor's rise in the world was due time and again to his ability to form warm friendships with men in key positions, and this prompts one to think that he had more wit and charm than is credited to him.

Astor's son and heir, William Backhouse Astor, was an even more shadowy figure, but thanks to the work done by Harvey O'Connell in his book on the Astors, published in 1940, the way has been pointed to a good deal of newspaper comment that otherwise might have been lost. This includes enquiries conducted by the City of New York into tenement housing; his relationship with the notorious Fernando Wood, Mayor of New York; and his attitude towards the Civil War. The house at Rokeby in upper New York – near Rhinebeck – where he lived with his wife (and which was built by his wife's father) is still standing. It no longer belongs to the Astors and is in sad disrepair with peeling paint and a dilapidated porch. Considering that it was occupied by a second generation Astor, still known as America's richest family, it is very modest; in England it would be described as a manor house.

Material on William Backhouse's two sons – John Jacob III and William Backhouse Jr – is more plentiful, for we have now reached the second half of the nineteenth century; John Jacob is one of the Prince of Wales'

hosts at the ball given at New York's Academy of Music and Mrs William Backhouse Jr is complaining that impossible people are being received into 'Society' over which she one day will rule as Queen. An invaluable book on this period is Lloyd Morris' *Incredible New York*.

Once we come to the sons of these two brothers – William's son, John Jacob IV, who went down in the *Titanic* and John Jacob's son, William Waldorf, who flounced off to England, there is a flood of material. I have listed the most interesting books but I would like to thank Mr Nigel Nicolson of England for allowing me to quote the letters written to his grandmother by William Waldorf; the US Navy Department for providing information on Vincent Astor's war service; and members of the Astor Foundation in New York for an account of their work. I would also like to thank the world's most impressive research library – the New York Public Library at Fifth Avenue and 42nd Street, originally founded by Astor money – for the sensationally quick and efficient service provided, and the British Museum newspaper library at Colindale which has no equal.

Virginia Cowles
L'Ancien Presbytère
Villeperdue
France

Astor, John Jacob *A Journey in Other Worlds: A Romance of the Future* D. Appleton & Co., New York 1894.

Astor, Michael *Tribal Feeling* John Murray, London 1963

Chittenden, Hiram M. *The American Fur Trade of the Far West*, 2 vols, The Press of the Pioneers Inc., New York 1935

Gallatin, Count, ed. *The Diary of James Gallatin, Secretary to Albert Gallatin, a Great Peace-Maker 1813–1827* Charles Scribner's Sons, New York 1916

Harrison, Mrs Burton *Recollections Grave and Gay* Charles Scribner's Sons, New York 1911

Harrison, Rosina *Rose, My Life in Service* Viking Press, New York 1975

Henry, Alexander *Travels and Adventures in Canada and the Indian Territory Between 1760 and 1776* ed. James Bain, Burt Franklin & Co., New York 1969

Hone, Philip *The Diary of Philip Hone 1828–1851* 2 vols, Dodd, Mead & Co., New York 1927

Irving, Washington *Astoria* G. P. Putnam's Sons, New York 1888

Kavaler, Lucy *The Astors: an American Legend* Dodd, Mead & Co., New York 1968

Lehr, Elizabeth D. *King Lehr and the Gilded Age with Extracts from the Locked Diary of Harry Lehr* J. P. Lippincott Co., Philadelphia 1939

Mann, Horace *Lectures on Various Subjects* Fowler & Wells, New York 1859

Marie, Queen of Rumania *The Story of My Life* Charles Scribner's Sons, New York 1934

McAllister, Ward *Society as I Have Found It* Cassell Publishing Co., New York 1890

Morris, Lloyd *Incredible New York* Random House, New York 1951

Myers, Gustavus *The History of the Great American Fortunes* Charles H. Kerr & Co., Chicago 1910

Nevins, Allan *American Social History as Recorded by British Travellers* Augustus M. Kelley Publications, New Jersey 1923

Obolensky, Serge *One Man in His Times* Astor-Honor, New York 1958

O'Connor, Harvey *The Astors* Alfred Knopf, New York 1941

Parton, James *Life of John Jacob Astor* American News Co., New York 1865

Porter, Kenneth *John Jacob Astor – Businessman* 2 vols, Harvard University Press, New York 1931

Riis, Jacob *The Battle with the Slum* The Macmillan Company, New York 1902

Smith, Matthew Hale *Sunshine and Shadow in New York* J. B. Burr & Co., Connecticut 1868

Sullivan, Mark *Our Times* 6 vols, Charles Scribner's Sons, New York 1926–35

Sykes, Christopher *Nancy, The Life of Lady Astor* William Collins Sons, 1972

Terrell, John U. *Furs by Astor* William Morrow & Co., New York 1973

Vanderbilt, Cornelius *Farewell to Fifth Avenue* Simon & Schuster 1925

Letters, Journals and Documents

Letters, Journals and Documents

Forum Magazine July 1931

Hansard 5 October 1938

Hogg's Weekly Instructor

Journal of Political Economy vol. XVI 'The Fortune of John Jacob Astor' by Anna Youngman, University of Chicago 1908

Letters of Henry Brevoort to Washington Irving Vol. II ed. George Hellman, G. P. Putnam's Sons, New York 1913

Letters of John Jacob to Washington Irving G. P. Putnam's Sons, New York 1916

Letters of Washington Irving to John Jacob Astor G. P. Putnam's Sons, New York 1915

Liberty January 1939

New York Packet 28 October 1788

New York Sun 18 March 1892

New York Times 31 August 1931, 27 October 1931

Report of the Metropolitan Board of Health 1866

Selections from the Correspondence of Theodore Roosevelt and Henry Cabot Lodge Charles Scribner's Sons, New York 1925

Sunday Pictorial 17 August 1931

The Tenement House Commission Report New York 1894

Town Topics April 1892, August 1892, February 1897

Index